AUGUSTINE AND LIBERAL EDUCATION

Augustine of Hippo (354-430 CE) — Bishop, theologian, philosopher, and rhetorician — has left a rich legacy for reflection upon relationships between Christianity and culture, between Christian catechises and liberal education, and between faith and reason. Contemporary scholars have turned from the universal to the particular; likewise educational institutions have begun to explore their roots, digging into their intellectual traditions for the resources for renewal of liberal education. The Enlightenment ideal of a universal rationality is no longer easily assumed, yet the modern university's ideal of "liberal education" seems to have been founded on just such a principle.

Augustine and Liberal Education sheds light on liberal education past and present, from an Augustinian point of view. Ranging from historical investigations of particular themes and issues in the thought of Saint Augustine, to reflections on the role of tradition and community and the challenges and opportunities facing universities in the next century, the contributors return to the sources of traditional reflection whilst exploring contemporary issues of education and "the good life." Essays on Augustinian inquiry in medieval and modern eras address critical questions on the role of rhetoric, reading, and authority in education, on the social context of learning, and on the relationship between liberal education and properly Christian catechesis. Contemporary questions on liberal education from philosophical, political, theological, and ethical perspectives are then explored in the essays which move from the past to the present.

This book offers a valuable contribution to the growing scholarship on Catholic universities and on Augustine of Hippo, engaging in "Augustinian inquiry" and pointing to possibilities for renewal in liberal education in the twenty-first century.

Kim Paffenroth and Kevin L. Hughes are Arthur J. Ennis Fellows, Humanities Program, Villanova University, USA.

Dedicated to Jack Doody,
teacher, scholar, innovator, and advocate of liberal education

Augustine and Liberal Education

Edited by
KIM PAFFENROTH and KEVIN L. HUGHES
Villanova University

Ashgate

Aldershot • Burlington USA • Singapore • Sydney

© Kim Paffenroth and Kevin L. Hughes 2000

Published by
Ashgate Publishing Ltd
Gower House
Croft Road
Aldershot
Hants GU11 3HR
England

Ashgate Publishing Company
131 Main Street
Burlington
Vermont 05401
USA

Ashgate website: http://www.ashgate.com

British Library Cataloguing in Publication Data
Augustine and liberal education
    1. Augustine, Saint, Bishop of Hippo - Influence
    2. Augustine, Saint, Bishop of Hippo - Views on education
    3. Education, Humanistic 4. Education, Higher - Philosophy
    I. Paffenroth, Kim II. Hughes, Kevin
    230'.071

Library of Congress Control Number: 00-132612

ISBN 0 7546 1334 8

Printed and bound in Great Britain by MPG Books Ltd, Bodmin, Cornwall

Contents

List of Contributors

Felix B. Asiedu did his undergraduate work at Swarthmore College and completed his doctoral studies at the University of Pennsylvania with a dissertation on Augustine's influence on Anselm of Canterbury. He currently teaches in the Core Humanities Program at Villanova University as an Arthur J. Ennis Postdoctoral Fellow in the Humanities.

Phillip Cary directs the philosophy program at Eastern College, St. Davids, PA, where he is also on the faculty of the Templeton Honors College. He has previously taught as an Ennis Fellow and subsequently a Barbieri Fellow in the Core Humanities Program at Villanova University. He has received both his graduate degrees from Yale (M.A., Philosophy; Ph.D., Philosophy and Religious Studies). His book, *Augustine's Invention of the Inner Self*, is forthcoming from Oxford University Press.

Mark J. Doorley earned a Masters in Divinity from the Washington Theological Union in 1988 and a Doctorate in Philosophy from Boston College in 1994. His book, *The Place of the Heart in Lonergan's Ethics* (Lanham, MD: University Press of America, 1996), examined the role of feelings in the ethical intentionality analysis of Lonergan. Mark has taught at Boston College, St. John's University in New York, and is currently a Visiting Assistant Professor in the Ethics Program at Villanova University.

Daniel Doyle, O.S.A., is an Augustinian priest and member of the Theology and Religious Studies Department at Villanova University, where he holds the rank of Assistant Professor. He graduated with a B.A. in Sociology from Villanova University in 1975; an M.S. in Psychology from Loyola College, Baltimore, MD, in 1978; and an M.A. in Sacramental Theology from the Washington Theological Union in 1986. He received his S.T.L. (1991) and S.T.D. (1996) in Patristic Theology from the Institutum Patristicum Augustinianum. His most recent publication was "Mary, Mother of God," in *Augustine Through the Ages, An Encyclopedia* (ed. Allan D. Fitzgerald, O.S.A.; Grand Rapids, MI: William B. Eerdman's). His present research projects focus on issues of ecclesiology in the North African Church, specifically the role of discipline in St. Augustine's preaching and the theology of the Roman primacy in St. Augustine's thought.

Marylu Hill received her Ph.D. in British literature from the University of Delaware in 1993, where she specialized in turn-of-the-century studies. She has been teaching since 1995 at Villanova University in the Core Humanities Program where she is an assistant professor. Her first book, *Mothering Modernity: Feminism, Modernism, and the Maternal Muse*, was published by Garland Press in 1998. Over the past two years she presented papers at various conferences, including the Modern Language Association and the Dickens Project conference, on the topics of Victorian photography, educational models for women in the nineteenth century, twentieth century readings of the Victorian age, and the use of spectacle in Victorian historical writing. Currently, she is working on a collection of essays on Victorian literature and photography, as well as a longer work on nineteenth century historicism and romance.

Kevin L. Hughes is an Arthur J. Ennis Postdoctoral Fellow in the Humanities at Villanova University. His research focuses upon ancient and medieval historical theology, and he has published articles on Augustine, medieval biblical interpretation, apocalypticism, and on the visionary theology of Hildegard of Bingen. He lives with his wife and daughter in St. Davids, PA.

John Immerwahr is Associate Vice President for Academic Affairs at Villanova University. He received his Ph.D. (1972) and M.A. (1969) in Philosophy from the University of Michigan, and his B.A. (1967) from Princeton University. Since 1973 he has taught Philosophy at Villanova University, where he won the Lindback Award for Distinguished Teaching in 1992. He has published numerous articles on Hume and other philosophical topics, as well as on teaching philosophy and public policy.

Richard M. Jacobs, O.S.A., is an Associate Professor of Education at Villanova University. He has authored two books, *The Vocation of the Catholic Educator* and *The Grammar of Catholic Schooling*, as well as numerous book chapters and journal articles focusing upon Catholic educational history, policy, and politics; the integration of communication theory, pedagogy, and educational administration as a means for the renewal of American public schooling; and the educational philosophy of St. Augustine. He currently serves as editor of the National Catholic Educational Association monograph series, Catholic Educational Leadership, and has served as guest editor for four issues of *The Journal of Management Systems*.

Thomas F. Martin, O.S.A., is Assistant Professor of Theology/Religious Studies at Villanova University. His particular area of study involves the thought and writings of Augustine of Hippo, in particular his biblical and spiritual thought. He has recently published articles in *Studia Patristica* and *The Downside Review*. He has lectured on the thought of Augustine in the United States, Italy, England, The Philippines, Peru, and Australia.

Andrew R. Murphy presently teaches as an Arthur J. Ennis Fellow at Villanova University. He received his Ph.D. in Political Science from the University of Wisconsin-Madison in 1996. His doctoral dissertation (currently under consideration for publication) examined the emergence of religious toleration as a central element of seventeenth-century Anglo-American political thought, and reflected on the continuing relevance of toleration for contemporary issues of diversity, multiculturalism, and identity politics. He has published articles in *The Review of Politics, The Journal of Politics, Polity*, and *Soundings*. He is currently working on two projects: an edited volume of the political writings of William Penn, and a comparative analysis of decline narratives in the ancient and modern world.

Kim Paffenroth currently teaches as an Arthur J. Ennis Fellow in the Core Humanities Program at Villanova University. He has also taught at the University of Notre Dame, Southwestern Michigan College, and Eastern College. He has received degrees in Theology from the University of Notre Dame (Ph.D.) and from Harvard Divinity School (M.T.S.); as an undergraduate he studied Liberal Arts at St. John's College, Annapolis. He has published extensively on the New Testament, including his book, *The Story of Jesus according to L* (Sheffield: Sheffield Academic Press, 1997). He has also published articles on Augustine, as well as translations of several of his works.

Debra Romanick Baldwin received her doctorate from the Committee on Social Thought at the University of Chicago. Her dissertation, "Conrad's Case Against Thinking," considered Conrad in light of the classical quarrel between the philosophers and the poets. In addition to subsequent studies on Conrad, her current research explores the relation between art and mental illness in nineteenth-century Russian literature. She began teaching ancient, medieval, and modern core texts at the University of Chicago's Center for Continuing Studies Basic Program for Adults, and now teaches in the Core Humanities Program at Villanova University.

Thomas W. Smith received his Ph.D. from the University of Notre Dame and is Assistant Professor of Political Philosophy in the Department of Political Science at Villanova University. He has published articles in ancient, medieval, and modern political thought and is currently working on a book about the pedagogy of desire in Aristotle's *Nicomachean Ethics*. He teaches ancient political philosophy and religion and politics.

Foreword

John Immerwahr, Kim Paffenroth, and Kevin Hughes

Whether we wish to describe our current culture as post-modern, late-modern, post-liberal, or something entirely new, it is clear that the Enlightenment ideal of a universal rationality is no longer easily assumed. And yet, the modern university's ideal of "liberal education" seems to have been founded on just such a principle. Academic disciplines as diverse as particle physics and Russian literature were once believed to be united by a commitment to rational objectivity in their approach to the topics, and particular histories and heritages were believed to produce only a bias to be avoided. But this is no longer the case. Thinkers like Alasdair MacIntyre have demonstrated that every "rationality" has a particular history and that the claim to "objectivity" serves as a thin veil over particular biases. Contemporary scholars have turned therefore from the universal to the particular. Likewise, educational institutions have begun to explore their roots, digging into their intellectual traditions for the resources for the renewal of liberal education. Of necessity, this task is a local project, as each institution comes to terms with its own particular heritage and history. But it is not a parochial process either; each local institution can offer the fruits of its labor to the broader higher education community. If liberal education has a future, it is in the collaborative work of many such particular traditions and modes of inquiry.

This volume therefore seeks to address both the particular and the universal. On the one hand, we are ultimately addressing questions as universal as how and why we should educate college students. But we are doing this by addressing quite specific issues raised by and about Augustine of Hippo, as he himself considered his vocation as teacher and the nature of learning, and as subsequent teachers and scholars have considered his life and the issues he raises. In this foreword, we will introduce these particulars, first by describing the genesis of this volume in the particular intellectual environment of Villanova University, and then by summarizing the analyses of Augustine given by the individual essays.

Villanova: A Renewed Commitment to Augustine and to Liberal Education

At one point in the *Confessions*, Augustine describes what we might, for want of another name, call an "Augustinian intellectual community":

> When I was with my friends, my mind was occupied with our talking and laughing, exchanging kindnesses, reading good books together, now joking, now being serious, disagreeing without animosity as one might disagree with one's own self (and finding that our rare disagreements seasoned our usual concord) teaching and learning from one another, sorely missing those who were gone and welcoming with joy those who came. These and such like signs coming from hearts that loved one another, through mouth and tongue and a thousand gracious gestures, were the kindling of a fire that melted our minds together and made the many of us one. (*Confessions* 4.8.13)

Typical of Augustine, the community he values so much is not a purely intellectual one. What he values is not just the serious intellectual exchange, but also the interpersonal community built on physical presence, love, and exchanges that lead to a melting fire.

This volume is a product of another Augustinian intellectual community, resembling in many ways the interchange that Augustine himself valued so intensely. In common with the authors of many scholarly books, the scholars whose essays are included in this volume bring impressive intellectual credentials. In additional, however, they are for the most part personal friends as well as intellectual colleagues. They are in regular, face-to-face dialogue, teaching and learning from each other around a wide variety of intellectual, pedagogic, and personal issues. Anyone who was walked by their common room will also attest to their love for one another and will have heard them "now joking, now being serious." These scholars make up an Augustinian intellectual community in another way as well. Although they represent a wide variety of philosophical and political positions, in one way or another, concern about the thought of Augustine of Hippo and a profound commitment to undergraduate liberal education are what has brought them together.

This unusual Augustinian intellectual community did not come about by accident. It is the deliberate creation of a remarkable teacher, thinker, and academic leader, John A. Doody, the Robert Birmingham Chair of Core Humanities and director of the Core Humanities Program at Villanova University. Doody was himself intellectually formed by his experiences as a a graduate student in the Philosophy Department at Notre Dame University in the late 1960s. At that time, he and a small group of fellow graduate students spontaneously formed into a remarkably rich intellectual community, inspired both by the philosophical rigor of the graduate program and also by the student ideology of the 1960s. While the content of their dialogue did not focus specifically on Augustine, in many ways the resulting community once again resembled the pattern described above by Augustine, a pattern that Doody would spend much of his subsequent career attempting to duplicate and expand in the other intellectual communities which he entered.

After leaving Notre Dame, Doody joined the Philosophy Department at Villanova University. Immediately he began to seek to create an intellectual community in his own philosophy classes. Almost all of the outstanding philosophy students who have graduated from Villanova since that time have been touched by Doody, and many still keep in close contact with him. But Doody was never the kind of teacher who was only interested in the intellectual elite. What excited him most was to bring all of his students into his intellectual world. Nothing would give Doody more pleasure than to recount a lecture or class discussion where the most unlikely students found themselves intellectually engaged, and where Doody by the choice of a question or example could create an intellectual spark even in the most unlikely interlocutor.

Doody's search for community was also a theme in his research. Increasingly his own reading focused on communitarian philosophies in Habermas, MacIntyre, and in a variety of other sources. To those who did not know him, his research could look like any other academic research project. But to those who knew him well, it was clear that in his research as well he was seeking a philosophical foundation for the type of community he was trying to create in his life.

By happy coincidence, Doody's own search found an increasingly fertile ground in his institution, Villanova University. Along with many other Catholic Universities in the United States, the last several decades at Villanova were a period of reflection and reexamination as the institution struggled to find a voice both vibrant in the contemporary world but also consistent with its faith-based missions. Villanova had traditionally been primarily a local and regional university, historically serving students from the diverse Catholic communities in the Philadelphia area. But in the late 1980s and 1990s, the university began to change rather dramatically, shifting from essentially a commuter school to a national and even international university, which served an increasingly talented and diverse undergraduate student body. This transformation both drove and was fueled by a re-examination of the University's mission, especially under the academic leadership of President Edmund J. Dobbin, O.S.A, and Dean of the College of Liberal Arts and Sciences, Kail Ellis, O.S.A.

Villanova had always seen itself as a primarily Catholic environment, but its Catholicism had traditionally been in some ways both unconscious and generic. If asked what made the school a Catholic University, many people might have answered, "It is a Catholic University because we have many Catholic faculty and students." There was much less energy given to a discussion of what the Catholic mission and heritage meant to its increasingly diverse population, and how Villanova's Catholic heritage would distinguish itself from other Catholic institutions.

Dobbin, Ellis, and other members of the community saw that the key to giving Villanova a distinct identity was to draw more heavily and more consciously on its Augustinian tradition. Villanova had been, of course, founded by Augustinian fathers in the 19th century, and members of the Augustinians had led the university as faculty, administrators, presidents, and members of the Board of Trustees. Rather than creating a new set of values, Dobbin, Ellis and others sought to make more explicit and relevant those values and traditions that had always been part of the university's history. In particular, they believed that a renewed commitment to three fundamental principles would provide the university's foundation and strength in the future: Augustinian values, a dialogue with post-modernism, and a focus on undergraduate teaching.

Augustinian Values. The university drew deeply on certain themes. One was the Augustinian notion of the "unity of heart and mind," which for the Villanovans came to mean that education at Villanova should not be conceived as purely intellectual, but should be rooted in values and the affective dimension. In addition to recovering its Augustinian heritage, the University began to stress much more actively the values of its patron, St. Thomas of Villanova, a 15th century Augustinian bishop famous for his devotion to the poor and marginalized of his own day. A second value was the "unity of knowledge." In the context of a modern university, the Augustinians wanted to stress a well rounded education that exposed students to many different disciplines and that, where possible, also stressed bridging the divisions between the disciplines. The final Augustinian value that the leadership stressed was that of community. The university, for example, began a series of steps designed to overcome the traditional divisions between faculty and staff, to try to make the university really live as a community. In the classroom that meant a shift to a more active style of learning, where students and faculty should interact together as learners.

Entering a Dialogue with Post-Modernism. Along with many other institutions (both Catholic and non-Catholic), Villanova's scholars — especially in its Philosophy and Theology departments — were attracted to continental philosophy, including existentialism, phenomenology, hermeneutics, and post-modernism. One of the boldest steps was the creation of a Ph.D. program in Philosophy, and the creation of its first two endowed chairs (one in Theology and one in Philosophy). With these steps, the University signaled that it wanted to continue to be part of the discussion of what post-modernism meant to contemporary Catholicism, Christianity, and indeed, all intellectual discourse. The revitalized Augustinian community was also revitalizing its connections to the larger intellectual community, with which it was eager to have a mutually productive dialogue.

Focus on Undergraduate Teaching. Throughout all of this, the mission of Villanova as an undergraduate teaching institution would be retained and strengthened. The signal from the top was clear, that the increased emphasis on scholarship, intellectual debate, and re-examination was intended to enhance the undergraduate teaching mission, not to detract from it.

Eventually and inevitably Villanova's administration and Jack Doody discovered that they were each pursuing the same vision. The administrators empowered Doody to broaden his vision further, and, at the same time, Doody pushed the administrators to enable him to extend his project. Doody was given the task of reshaping Villanova's Arts and Sciences Core. The centerpiece of the new Core was a course called the "Core Humanities Seminar." This was a two-semester course taken by all first year Arts and Sciences students at Villanova. Doody himself became the director of the program, and the course was designed to stress the Augustinian themes noted above: values, interdisciplinary thinking, and active and participatory learning. The course was conceived as a great books course, stressing ancient texts (including Augustine, of course) in the first semester, and, in the second semester, Augustinian themes as they were elaborated in modern texts.

Using his impressive rhetorical powers and his remarkable grasp of academic politics, Doody persuaded the various elements of the University that the Core Humanities Seminar would be an excellent first step in an outstanding undergraduate education. Although the course was initially intended only for Arts and Sciences Students, Doody gradually persuaded Villanova's professional schools (Engineering, Commerce and Finance, and Nursing) to build the program into their curriculums as well. What Doody did not always stress in his early presentations, however, was the fact that he really was not sure who would actually teach the seminars. While many of Villanova's full-time faculty were qualified to teach the seminar, the fact that the sections were deliberately kept to 15 or 16 students meant that Villanova needed many more qualified faculty members.

Doody's next step was to use the demand for the course as leverage to hire additional faculty to teach the course. Rather than relying on the existing departments to hire faculty to teach the seminars, Doody persuaded the University to create a new program, specifically charged with teaching the Core Humanities Seminars. To staff the growing program, Doody urged the creation of the Arthur J. Ennis Post-Doctoral Fellowship Program. (Arthur J. Ennis [1922-1994] was the first director of the Augustinian Historical Institute at Villanova University.) The plan was for these scholars to come to Villanova for a number of years, during which time they would teach Core Humanities, perfect their craft as teachers and establish themselves as scholars. Together with those existing Villanova faculty members who were teaching in the program, Doody soon had an extremely powerful teaching staff.

The program that resulted, however, was like no academic department that anyone had ever seen at Villanova before. A more typical academic department has faculty members spread through the ranks, with varying amounts of experience and exemplifying different stages of professional and personal evolution. The Core Humanities Program consisted almost entirely of recent Ph.D.s, from a variety of disciplines and schools. The main thing they had in common was an enthusiasm about undergraduate teaching and an ability to understand their own work within an Augustinian framework. Immediately they formed into a rather remarkable intellectual community of their own. The Core Humanities conference room became the site of endless academic discussions, debates, and arguments. The younger scholars also found and inspired colleagues and associates in other departments as well. The result was a rich cross-fertilization of ideas. They also pushed the institution in a number of ways. Wherever ideas were being discussed, the Core Humanities fellows were sure to be there.

The creation of the program was, in many ways, a fulfillment of Doody's dream in two ways. First, the young scholars themselves, with Doody as senior mentor and protector, recreated Doody's own ideal of an intellectual community. At the same time, their enthusiasm created a larger intellectual community among the hundreds of freshmen who worked with them in the seminars. One word that is frequently applied to Doody is "restless." Naturally enough, then, Doody was not satisfied with recruiting an outstanding faculty who would both teach the course and also provide intellectual stimulation for each other. His on going project is to widen the sense of Augustinian intellectual community among the students by working more closely with Villanova's offices of Student Life and Residence Life, in an effort to create what he calls "learning communities," where the Core Humanities Seminar program will increasingly become a more central focus of the living experience of Villanova's first year students.

Precisely as Doody hoped, bringing these younger scholars together did indeed create a vibrant intellectual community. Not surprisingly, the Core Humanities Faculty have challenged and pushed the broader institution in a number of ways. But one outcome of the community has been the creation of this volume. All of the authors are (or have been), in one way or another, involved in teaching the seminars, and most were recruited by Villanova specifically to teach the seminar. Several are also members of the Order of Saint Augustine, and work closely with the program from other departments. From the efforts of one man and one institution to make an Augustinian intellectual community a living and growing reality, members of that community now have come together to reflect on how the vision and theory of Augustine can be related to the present reality.

Augustine and Liberal Education

In recent years, universities of all types have worried and sometimes agonized over their missions and identities. The type of institution examining itself determines the kinds of questions they ask, and these can range from questions about denominational association, to questions about the exact clientele an institution is trying to reach, to the kinds of courses, programs, and degrees a school should offer. As myriad as these questions are, they all seem to revolve in different ways around a very fundamental question: What is undergraduate education all about? What are we trying to do, why are we doing it, and how should we do it?

As indicated in the previous section, Villanova has made this institutional soul-searching concrete in exploring its roots in the thought of St. Augustine of Hippo (354-430 CE). Bishop, theologian, philosopher, rhetorician, Augustine has left a rich legacy for reflection upon the relationships between Christianity and culture, between Christian catechesis and liberal education, between faith and reason. To further this goal, Villanova University has assembled an interdisciplinary community of scholars — full-time faculty, postdoctoral fellows, and part-time faculty — whose collaborative work in engaging in "Augustinian inquiry" with the entire student body points to the possibilities for renewal in liberal education in the 21st century. The essays gathered in this volume, from contributors both within Villanova and without, represent efforts to explore critically this conjunction between Augustinian inquiry and the renewal of liberal education.

Our first section presents three essays on Augustine's thoughts on education as he expresses them in his *Confessions*. Kim Paffenroth's essay examines the pear tree incident and relates it to Augustine's disgust at his own education, both how he was educated and how he has gone on to educate and corrupt others. Despite such negative evaluations on education, Augustine would nonetheless approve — indeed, long for — an education in which teachers and students could lose and rediscover themselves in their experience of the transcendent truth, and it is such an environment we should seek to create in our classrooms. Debra Romanick Baldwin's essay first traces the dynamics between fear and desire that characterize learning. She then goes on to compare Faustus and Ambrose as two models of teaching, whose contrasting and complementary styles ultimately show Augustine the human limitation and incompleteness that longs for the mystery of learning. Thomas Martin analyzes the *Confessions* as "spiritual exercises," showing us how Augustine both uses and transcends the models of learning that were common to many of the philosophical schools of antiquity.

The essays in Part II examine the idea of education in some of Augustine's other works. Phillip Cary does a remarkable job unpacking the Platonic elements of Augustine's thought, as well as putting Catholic and Protestant interpretations of Augustine into dialogue with one another. His conclusion is a humbling view of education as an expression of love, both of the subject matter and of the student, a love that recapitulates and fulfills the love of God and the love of neighbor. Daniel Doyle examines the theory and practice of Augustine's teaching as shown in his *Christian Instruction* and in his many sermons. The essay elaborates both the style and substance of Augustine's teaching, showing how he both uses and modifies classical rhetoric in his interpretation of Scripture. Kevin Hughes shows how Augustine's view of liberal education changed from one of enthusiastic appropriation to hostile rejection. His conclusion is a sobering reflection on the evils of self-love that permeate education (either in Augustine's time or ours), evils that can only be overcome by humility and a commitment to discipleship.

Part III examines the vexing issue of authority in Augustine's thought. For those of us who see Augustine as a champion of liberal (and liberating) education, his reliance on authority is problematic indeed. Richard Jacobs gives a sensitive interpretation of Augustine's *The Teacher*, showing how the goal of education for Augustine is to take students who assume the "truth of authority," and move them towards seeing the "authority of truth." Felix Asiedu offers us an extremely nuanced analysis of one of Augustine's lesser known works, *On the Advantage of Believing*, showing how exactly reason and authority interact to create knowledge and belief; of special concern to him is the issue of trust, of how one must earn (or regain) students' trust in order to teach. Mark Doorley elaborates for us the historical context and the epistemological basis of Augustine's idea of authority, showing how humility serves to limit and guide authority, thereby creating a uniquely Augustinian synthesis of the wisdom of authority that is applicable to any authoritarian situation, whether it is educational, political, or ecclesiastical. Andrew Murphy's essay shows how the same issues of authority and coercion that Augustine confronted in the Donatist controversy resurface in debates over religious toleration in seventeenth-century England, as both Augustine and the English Protestants support their positions with appeals to church unity, the (in)effectiveness of coercion, the objectivity of belief, and the violence of their opponents.

Finally, Part IV considers some of the implications of Augustine's thought for liberal education since his time. Marylu Hill shows how the practice of solitary reading — not lectures or discussions — is the cornerstone of liberal education, especially as typified in the practice of Ambrose and in the conversion of Augustine as described in the *Confessions*, and as later elaborated and challenged by thinkers such as John Henry Newman and John Ruskin. Her conclusion is both a challenge and an opportunity to reclaim this practice for our students, and especially to make it available to learners of non-traditional age, exactly the people who possess the wisdom and maturity necessary to confront difficult and challenging texts. Thomas Smith's essay explores the goals and motives for contemporary liberal education. His provocative conclusion is that the liberalism typified by such thinkers as Hobbes, Locke, and Rawls ultimately undermines liberal education, rendering it unattractive or even impossible. Paradoxically, although Christianity is often perceived as authoritarian and intolerant, its views of human life and purpose ultimately provide a more favorable setting for free inquiry and liberal education than liberalism can.

Taken as a whole, the volume represents our collective effort to come to terms with a particular tradition of inquiry in the light of contemporary challenges to the project of liberal education. Both by returning to the sources of traditional reflection and by keeping a critical eye on the present, we hope this collection contributes to the renewal of liberal education and a vital re-appropriation of Augustine's thought.

PART I
EDUCATION IN THE
CONFESSIONS

Chapter One

Bad Habits and Bad Company: Education and Evil in the *Confessions*

Kim Paffenroth

Introduction

As I have indicated formally and informally to my colleagues, readers, and students, many of my ideas for research and publication stem from my teaching of undergraduates, and this paper is no exception, as it comes directly from the questions raised in discussions with freshmen at the University of Notre Dame and at Villanova University. It therefore seems especially appropriate to include this essay here, in a collection intended to explore and elaborate the implications for modern education of the thought of Augustine, one of the greatest practitioners and theorists of pedagogy. It is also a perfect example of the benefits of learner based, active education, as I have learned more in my seminars than I could ever hope to in a lecture course.

In class discussions of the pear tree incident in Book 2 of Augustine's *Confessions*, students have in my experience consistently focused on the role of peer pressure in driving Augustine to commit the theft. And try as I might to steer them towards the *real* point of the story — to show the innate evil of humanity and to prove that Plato was wrong, that a person can and does commit evil actions knowing and loving them for their evil — the students always come back to the peer pressure: "Well, yes, he loved evil for its own sake and that makes him feel worse, but he wouldn't have done it if it weren't for his friends egging him on." I seldom mistake student intractability for insight, but this time they have the text on their side: "Yet alone, by myself, I would not have done it — such, I remember, was my state of mind at the time — alone I would never have done it."[1] Why does Augustine distract from his main point by bringing up the seemingly ancillary issue of peer pressure or bad influences from outside? This has led me to a more general consideration of the dynamics between good and evil, individuals and groups in the *Confessions*. The relation is especially important in the case of education, and I believe it has important implications for modern pedagogy.

Bad Company: The Pear Tree

Let us first look at the pear tree incident in Book 2, to see how the issue of peer pressure is raised. When Augustine first describes the theft, his companions are barely mentioned: "Late night — to which hour, according to our pestilential custom, we had kept up our street games — a group of very bad youngsters set out to shake down and rob this tree" (*Conf.* 2.4.9). The influence of Augustine's companions is clearly negative — they inculcate "pestilential custom[s]" in one another — but hardly crucial. Augustine does not say whose idea the theft was, and the companions' influence at first seems confined only to encouraging Augustine to stay out late; they do not seem to encourage him to steal. And when in the next paragraph Augustine turns to analyze the act, the companions disappear completely:

> Behold my heart, O Lord, behold my heart upon which you had mercy in the depths of the pit. Behold, now let my heart tell you what it looked for there, that I should be evil without purpose and that there should be no cause for my evil but evil itself. Foul was the evil, and I loved it. I loved to go down to death. I loved my fault, not that for which I did the fault, but I loved my fault itself. Base in soul was I, and I leaped down from your firm clasp even towards complete destruction, and I sought nothing from the shameful deed but shame itself! (*Conf.* 2.4.9)

From this description, a reader would surely not expect the subsequent statement that the companions were instrumental to Augustine's act of theft. In this description, they seem to be mere bystanders to the real drama, which is a confrontation between Augustine and evil.

That Augustine chose evil for its own sake in this case is clearly the central problem for him, but its exact implications for him are harder to elaborate. I have already characterized the point of the story as anti-Platonic, but this requires some nuance. On the one hand, Augustine later invokes Platonic ideas of the non-existence of evil as a solution to his problems with evil: "...evil is only the privation of a good, even to the point of complete nonentity.... Therefore, whatsoever things exist are good" (*Conf.* 3.7.12; 7.12.18).[2] But on the other hand, in his description of the pear tree incident, he insists that he knowingly chose evil for its own sake, and this would clearly seem to go against Platonic doctrine that all evil is chosen because some good is sought in it. From a Platonic point of view, evil actions are only misguided: "With regard to all these things, and others of like nature, sins are committed when, out of an immoderate liking for them, since they are the least goods, we desert the best and highest goods" (*Conf.* 2.5.10). While this may explain almost all sins, Augustine knows that if he can find one exception, then the system falls apart, and he thinks he has just such an exception with the pear tree. By insisting that he chose evil knowing it to be evil, Augustine has described it in a way that goes beyond a Platonic explanation. He insists that evil can be knowingly embraced with a kind of simultaneous attraction and revulsion that cannot be reduced to a mere mistake, but indicates a real and fundamental perversion in human beings.[3]

This points to the fundamental paradox of evil for Augustine: evil is at one and the same time non-existent, yet extremely powerful.[4] This paradox provided the basis of my Core Humanities course this spring, as it has been a powerful influence in literature dealing with evil: it is a measure of their greatness that authors like Milton, Dostoevsky, and Flannery O'Connor can simultaneously depict evil as utterly empty, yet terrifying in its power. For Augustine, this paradox arises in part from combining Platonic and Manichaean descriptions of evil, in order to create what he hopes is an adequate (if not always wholly satisfying) Christian account of evil. From the Platonic description of evil, Augustine takes the idea that evil is not a thing, a nothing, a lack, only a privation of the good, and has no separate existence on its own; and from the Manichaean description, he takes the idea that evil does exist, that it is actively and powerfully opposed to the good, and although it may not be as material as he once thought,[5] it is very real. But furthering the paradox is the fact that both the Platonic and Manichaean descriptions of evil are finally deficient for Augustine because neither adequately reckons with the power of evil, for both of them depict it as ultimately powerless and inconsequential. This is clearest for the Platonic view,[6] but it is equally so for the Manichaean: "I still thought that it was not ourselves who sin, but that some sort of different nature within us commits the sin. It gave joy to my pride to be above all guilt" (*Conf.* 5.10.18).[7] Any description of evil that regards it as not essentially part of the human person — either because it is only a mistake or because it is a substance wholly different and other from the human person — is inadequate and untrue for Augustine. If the Platonists are right, then all we need is education and guidance so as not to mistake evil for good, or lesser goods for greater ones; if the Manichees are right, then all we need is to divorce ourselves from the evil that has accidentally (and not essentially) become associated with us in our present incarnation. If either is correct, then we do not need the sacrifice of Christ or the grace of God, and "Christ died to no purpose" (Gal 2:21).

I take it then that the pear tree episode is the epitome of this paradox of evil. Augustine knowingly chooses nothingness instead of the infinity of God's goodness and love; he does not do this as a mistake, but with complete knowledge of what he is doing, even if he cannot say why he is doing it. (All of this, it must be understood, is from the point of view of Augustine's later telling of the story.) What can we now say about the part his companions play in this story that illustrates the paradoxical nature of evil? Their role has sometimes been taken as resolving the paradox. This could be done in one of two ways. Either the friendship is the lesser good that Augustine sought in the theft, and therefore the theft is understandable in Platonic terms: "Therefore, I also loved in it my association with the others with whom I did the deed" (*Conf.* 2.8.16).[8] Augustine did love "something," not "nothing"; even if that "something" is small and petty, it is not "nothing." But since the point of the story is to discredit (or at least move beyond) the Platonic description of evil, this interpretation clearly seems unacceptable. Augustine is equally adamant that he did love "nothing": "What fruit had I... from that theft in which I loved the theft itself and nothing else? For the theft itself was nothing" (*Conf.* 2.8.16). On the other hand, the companionship could resolve the paradox by being the final example of Augustine loving "nothing": "...my association with the others was itself nothing" (*Conf.* 2.8.16).[9] Although this seems closer to Augustine's thought, in that it does not reduce the scene to a Platonic explanation, the role of the friends seems again to be exaggerated. Augustine says he would not have committed the theft without his companions; he does not say that he committed it for the sake of their companionship. The companionship is at most a facilitation or enabling of his evil, not its goal or cause.

I think that the evil companionship is essentially another element of the paradox of evil, not a resolution to it, as indicated with Augustine's oxymoronic cry, "O friendship too unfriendly!" (*Conf.* 2.8.17). It is perhaps best seen as parallel to the pear tree story, not part of it. Loving the emptiness and uselessness of the theft is analogous to loving the emptiness and uselessness of his relationship with these friends, and neither admits of an explanation or reduction, except that both are powerful manifestations of evil. Empty, useless relationships are just as symptomatic of evil as empty, useless acts, and both are equally destructive. Both are strands of the confusing "knot" of sin that ends Book 2: "Who can untie this most twisted and intricate mass of knots? It is a filthy thing: I do not wish to think about it; I do not wish to look upon it" (*Conf.* 2.10.18).[10]

Although the "knot" imagery is prevalent at the end of Book 2, it is the imagery of "itching" that seems most relevant to Augustine's experience with his companions in theft. Augustine begins both Books 2 and 3 by indicating that his attachments to other people were the source of his problems: "What was there to bring me delight except to love and be loved?... I came to Carthage, where a caldron of shameful loves seethed and sounded me about on every side. I was not yet in love, but I was in love with love" (*Conf.* 2.2.2; 3.1.1). Augustine seems never to have been guilty of a deficiency of love, but rather always a surfeit. And these loves make Augustine "burn" and "itch": "Hence came my love for such sorrows... I was scratched lightly, as it were. As a result, as though from scratches made by fingernails, there followed a burning tumor and horrid pus and wasting away" (*Conf.* 3.2.4). The companionship of his fellow thieves is also described as "itching":

> If I had then merely liked the pears that I stole, and merely wished to eat them, I could have done so by myself, were doing that wrong deed enough to lead me to my pleasure. Nor would I have needed to arouse the itch of my desires by a rubbing together of guilty minds. But my pleasure lay not in the pears: it lay in the evil deed itself, which a group of us joined in sin to do. (*Conf.* 2.8.16)

Again, this quotation makes clear that Augustine did not find in the companionship the object of his love or pleasure. The choice of the "itching" imagery seems to fit Augustine's purposes particularly well here. An itch is not a cause of disease, but rather a symptom, just as the friends are not the cause of sin, but just another symptom. Likewise, scratching only makes something itch worse, just as the sinful friendship, the "rubbing together of guilty minds," only leads to more sinful behavior. Augustine's image brings out both the diseased nature of sin itself, as well as the compounding of it by the addictiveness of its symptoms.

Augustine did not commit the theft for the sake of this sinful friendship, but it is clear that this friendship exacerbated the pride, vanity, selfishness, and love of "deformed liberty" (*Conf.* 2.6.14), that are part of sin. While the group may not cause sin, it clearly leads to more sinfulness on Augustine's part. This seems to be part of an overall pattern in the *Confessions* of depicting group activities or human society in general as leading to greater evil and sin,[11] without removing the blame from the individual and placing it on the group. Indeed, the acquisition of language, of the ability to communicate and interact with other human beings, sounds hardly like a thing to be desired, but only marks the entrance "into the stormy society of human life" (*Conf.* 1.8.13), and is constantly misused by Augustine and those around him: "But if they would describe some of their lustful deeds in detail and good order with correct and well-placed words, did they not glory in the praise they got?... Thus youths who did not meditate on your law, or on your peace, but on foolish lies and court quarrels, would no longer pry from my mouth weapons for their madness" (*Conf.* 1.18.28; 9.2.2). Even childish play with others reinforces sin, by teaching pride and dishonesty: "I loved to win proud victories in our contests, and to have my ears tickled by false stories, so that they would itch all the more intensely for them" (*Conf.* 1.10.16; cf. 1.19.30). And for Augustine adults are, of course, only larger, more dangerous children, with more destructive and addictive pastimes, such as the baths (*Conf.* 2.3.6), theater (*Conf.* 3.2.2-4) and gladiatorial shows (*Conf.* 6.8.13). Practically every sin necessarily includes other people, at least as victims, but Augustine's examples seem to implicate them as co-conspirators and enablers: one might lie to oneself, or feel malice by oneself, but the temptation is greatly increased when surrounded by other sinners engaged in the same activity.

By way of contrast, it is worth considering the turning points in the *Confessions*, the points when Augustine or someone else is turned towards God, and noting that they are practically all solitary, or shared with just one other person, not a group.[12] The solitary reading of Cicero causes Augustine's first "conversion": "This book changed my affections. It turned my prayers to you, Lord, and caused me to have different purposes and desires. All my vain hopes forthwith became worthless to me, and with incredible ardor of heart I desired undying wisdom. I began to rise up, so that I might return to you" (*Conf.* 3.4.7). Augustine is later turned from astrology by his consultation with Firminus, followed by his solitary ruminating on the subject (*Conf.* 7.6.8-10). The vision(s) Augustine has at the end of Book 7 (*Conf.* 7.17.23-7.21.27) is the result of his solitary meditation on Scripture: "In a wondrous way all these things penetrated my very vitals, when I read the words of that least of your apostles, and meditated upon your works, and trembled at them" (*Conf.* 7.21.27). Victorinus is held back from converting because he is afraid of public opinion, "He was afraid of offending his friends" (*Conf.* 8.2.4), and he is also finally moved to convert through solitary reading, "Afterwards, through reading and longing, he drank in strength" (*Conf.* 8.2.4). Ponticianus' two friends are converted to the monastic life through the chance reading of the life of Antony while alone together: "He read on and was changed within himself, where your eyes could see" (*Conf.* 8.6.15). Augustine's own conversion is completely solitary, "That I might pour it all forth with its own proper sounds, I arose from Alypius' side — to be alone seemed more proper to this ordeal of weeping — and went farther apart, so that not even his presence would be a hindrance to me" (*Conf.* 8.12.28), and Alypius' follows with only Augustine present (*Conf.* 8.12.30). The reprimand that turns Monica from drinking is done when she is alone with a servant: "A maidservant, with whom she used to go down to the cellar, quarreled with her little mistress, the two being all alone, as it so happened... Wounded through and through by this taunt, she beheld her own foul state, and immediately condemned it and cast it off" (*Conf.* 9.8.18).[13] Finally, the climactic vision at Ostia is shared between Augustine and Monica alone: "We were alone... We transcended [our own minds], so that we attained to the region of abundance that never fails, in which you feed Israel forever upon the food of truth, and where life is that Wisdom by which all these things are made" (*Conf.* 9.10.23-24).[14] Augustine is strikingly consistent in portraying moments of conversion as solitary and intimate, not as communal.[15]

Let us summarize the dynamic between good and evil, individuals and groups in the *Confessions.* Throughout the book, the focus is clearly on the individual, Augustine, with implications for the reader, also an individual. Evil manifests itself in the individual through proud, selfish acts that are ironically and tragically self-destructive. These sinful individuals create or are born into groups and communities that foster and reinforce their sinfulness. On the other hand, God also intervenes in individuals' lives when they are alone through moments of revelation or conversion. Evil is so pervasive in human society, and so effectively uses human society to strengthen itself, that God acts decisively in people's lives most frequently when they are alone, not when they are in groups.

Bad Habits: Augustine's Experience of Education

Such a view of society and the pervasiveness of evil in groups is clearly evident in Augustine's description of education. In Augustine's experience, education is debasing in its goals, its practice, and its content. Its goals are only to advance one in an earthly career, to bring success, not wisdom, and it fosters as well as stems from human pride.[16] Augustine sees even his parents, as well meaning as they might have been, as contributing to this: "Their only care was that I should learn to make the finest orations and become a persuasive speaker" (*Conf.* 2.2.4). Augustine sees this in his own education, and later in his own profession as a teacher: "For the same period of nine years, from the nineteenth year of my age to the twenty-eighth, we were seduced and we seduced others, deceived and deceiving by various desires, both openly by the so-called liberal arts and secretly in the name of a false religion, proud in the one, superstitious in the other, and everywhere vain" (*Conf.* 4.1.1). He is indeed glad to stop teaching, so as not to corrupt anyone else further: "You set free my tongue, as you had already freed my heart from that profession" (*Conf.* 9.4.7). In its practice, education is just an ugly indulging in and exacerbating of vanity. Again, Augustine first sees this in his own teachers:

> For I played ball as a child; by such play I was kept from learning arts by which, as an adult, I would disport myself in a still more unseemly fashion. Did the very man who beat me act different from me? If he was outdone by a fellow teacher in some trifling discussion, he was more tormented by anger and envy than I was when beaten by my playmate in a ball game. (*Conf.* 1.9.15)[17]

He later finds himself behaving in the same way: "On the one hand, we pursued an empty fame and popularity even down to the applause of the playhouse, poetical competitions, and contests for garlands of grass, foolish plays on the stage, and unbridled lusts" (*Conf.* 4.1.1). And in its content, Augustine sees his education as empty and useless: "Nevertheless, O hellish flood, the sons of men are thrown into you with fees paid, so that they may learn these fables... I do not condemn the words, which are as it were choice and precious vessels, but that wine of error which through them was proffered to us by drunken teachers" (*Conf.* 1.16.26). Augustine was taught the wrong things, for the wrong reasons, in the wrong ways, and he learned his lessons so well that he carried on this debasing enterprise far into his adult life.[18]

There is one incident, however, in Augustine's classroom that he interprets positively, and that is the turning of Alypius away from his fascination with the circus:

> For on a certain day, as I sat in my usual place and my students were present with me, he came in, greeted me, sat down, and applied his mind to the subjects under discussion. By chance, there was a passage to be read lying in my hands. As I was explaining it, I thought that a comparison with the circus would be apropos... You know, O my God, that at that time I had no thought of curing Alypius of his disease. But he applied it to himself, and believed that I had said it only because of him. (*Conf.* 6.7.11)

Alypius never returns to the circus (*Conf.* 6.7.12). It is not only a rare instance of something positive coming from Augustine's teaching profession in the *Confessions*, but also the only "conversion" that takes place in a group (though it happens to an individual and not to the group itself). Alypius has indeed learned something, but it was not what Augustine intended, it was what God intended. Like the *tolle lege* scene, Augustine sees God at work in his classroom, using "chance" to move the hearer towards the truth contained in what is before him, even when that truth was overlooked and unintended by the teacher: "I had not rebuked him, but you who make use of all men, both the knowing and the unknowing... out of my mouth and tongue made coals of fire by which you cauterized a mind of such high promise and healed it."[19] The intention or even the presence of the teacher is irrelevant: only the students' submission to a higher power determines whether or not they will learn.

This is quite close to how Augustine described learning several years before in *The Teacher*, where the irrelevance of the teacher is also emphasized:

> For who is so foolishly curious that he would send his son to school in order to learn what the teacher thinks? But all those disciplines that teachers claim to teach, even those of virtue and wisdom, they explain with words. Then those who are called students consider within themselves whether what was said is true, each consulting that inner truth according to his own ability. Thus they learn.[20]

Students must acknowledge and submit themselves to the truth in order for learning to occur.[21] A teacher is there only as an occasion, not a condition.[22] For Augustine, learning, like conversion, is ultimately an inner, solitary act, an encounter between the learner and the truth. The occasion provided by the teacher may be a crucial one indeed, as it was for Alypius and Augustine, but the teacher must ultimately acknowledge his or her limited role, as well as acknowledging the primacy of the learner.

Augustine and Modern Pedagogy

Augustine saw education as he experienced and practiced it for much of his life as a powerful instrument of evil, yet another in a long list of group activities that only make people behave worse than they would have on their own. On the other hand, after his conversion, Augustine saw the positive role of learning, but saw the teacher as a very limited part of that activity. If for Augustine teachers are either evil or irrelevant, this would be a very daunting conclusion as we consider the implications of Augustine's ideas on evil and education for modern pedagogy. I believe that the implications are indeed humbling, but nonetheless ennobling and fundamental as we consider our vocation as teachers. Teachers must constantly remind themselves that their role is to assist their students in realizing *their own truth*. Let us focus first on the beginning of the italicized phrase. Neither we nor Augustine need to subscribe completely to a Platonic idea of recollection to see the implications of putting it this way, of emphasizing that the students' act of learning is *their own*. This thrusts to the forefront the idea just laid out, that the teacher is not the important person in the classroom. This is of course profoundly insulting to one's pride, but that is just the point. If we are to avoid the sinful pride that Augustine saw permeating the educational system of his time, we must constantly remind ourselves that we are not the stars of the educational show, only the students are. Students are not the "objects" of education, as though they were patients to be fixed by a doctor; nor are they "consumers" of education, a debasing mercantile metaphor that is finding its way into contemporary discussions of education, as though they were buying a commodity. Students are the substance, and learning is the goal of education. A simple way that I try to show this humble attitude in my classroom is by continuing the habit I learned at St. John's College, Annapolis, of calling students by their last names. It is a small gesture, but if I am calling them "Bobby" and "Jenny" while they are calling me "Dr. Paffenroth," isn't it not so subtly sending a message that I am the important person in the room, and that they are there "in order to learn what the teacher thinks" (*De magistro* 14.45)?

Further, emphasizing the students' role in learning shows that I cannot *give* real and transformative knowledge to my students. At best, such handing on of knowledge is training, not education; at worst, it is coercion or indoctrination. As Augustine saw, a real occurrence of learning happens when students see the truth of what is before them and make it their own. They own that truth, or more accurately, they now share it with the teacher, and the sum total of owned truth in the room has risen. Dante's description of how love increases the more it is shared expresses a similar situation:

> "How can each one of many who divide
> a single good have more of it, so shared,
> than if a few had kept it?" He replied:

> "Because within the habit of mankind
> you set your whole intent on earthly things,
> the true light falls as darkness on your mind.

> The infinite and inexpressible Grace
> which is in Heaven, gives itself to Love
> as a sunbeam gives itself to a bright surface.

> As much light as it finds there, it bestows;
> thus, as the blaze of Love is spread more widely,
> the greater the Eternal Glory grows.

> As mirror reflects mirror, so, above,
> the more there are who join their souls, the more
> Love learns perfection, and the more they love."[23]

Knowledge or love are spiritual gifts that increase with being shared, and it is such sharing and increasing that I try to facilitate and which gives me such joy in my classroom. I am most gratified as a teacher not when my students know something they did not know before, but when they use knowledge in a way that they did not before. A really good paper on Dostoevsky or Shakespeare — not a factually accurate one, but one that interacts with the text in order to get at the truth, one that shows that the text matters to the student and has made a difference in his or her life — still gives me a chill, and is my measure of whether I have accomplished something. (And lest one think such teaching is confined to the humanities, I would say I have gotten the same feeling when a student I was tutoring in geometry did a proof without my help.) The most cherished moments in my career thus far have been when I stood beside my students, David Champagne, Erica DePalo, and Kathryn Kramers when they were honored with Core Humanities Writing Awards. It is significant that Ms. DePalo's name is now permanently engraved on a plaque at Villanova, with no indication of her teacher's identity: her accomplishment is honored there, not mine, although I cherish hers more than any of my own accomplishments as an academic. As Augustine acknowledges in the case of one's own biological children, teaching may be one of the few times when vicariousness is not such a bad thing: it is at least an inevitable and happy part of the relationship, as one can say of one's student or one's child, "You are the only man of all men whom I would wish to surpass me in all things."[24]

Teachers should also remind themselves of the implications of the final word of the above description of teaching: we are there to help students get to the *truth*. Not only does this obviously exclude such grossly predatory acts as making sexual overtures to students, as well as such overtly selfish acts as neglecting one's teaching or using it as a platform for one's own opinions, but it should also make us pause over many other seemingly good or inoffensive motivations. I am in the classroom to serve and to further truth, not myself or my career, and also not my students' careers or earning power: again, these are the goals of training, not education. Nor am I there to make them feel good (or bad), nor to make them act in a certain way: these are the goals of persuasion, therapy, and advocacy, not education. All of these should be and often are the happy side effects of teaching, but if they enter into the teaching environment, if they become stated goals of teaching rather than collateral effects, then they ultimately undermine and debase education.

Education is most often a group activity, and as such it is subject to the temptations and challenges that infect and influence any group activity, as Augustine describes in the *Confessions*. Being in a group can exacerbate the drives of selfishness, vanity, and pride that are fundamental to sin. Such dynamics are clearly visible in the classroom when students and teachers "show off" for one another, but also more insidiously present when they pursue truth not for its own sake, but for the practical benefits it can bring to them, whether these are financial, emotional, or ethical. But I think Augustine would agree that if both students and teachers together pursue truth for its own sake, surrendering themselves in order to be receptive to the transcendent, objective truth, then education is one of the most selfless acts in one's life; but as one possesses and is transformed by this transcendent truth, education also becomes one of the greatest acts of self-realization and fulfillment.

Notes

1   *Conf.* 2.8.16 (trans. John K. Ryan; New York, et al: Doubleday, 1960). All subsequent references to the *Confessions* are from this translation.
2   On the Platonic elements to the pear tree story, see P. Rigby, *Original Sin in Augustine's* Confessions (Ottawa: University of Ottawa Press, 1987) 101-08.
3   Cf. Rigby, *Original Sin*, 103, "Augustine never abandoned the main tenets of the Platonic doctrine, but he does move beyond it."
4   Cf. G. R. Evans, *Augustine on Evil* (Cambridge, UK, et al: Cambridge University Press, 1982) 3: "If Augustine got pleasure from nothing but the theft itself in the pear-tree episode, then he got pleasure from nothing at all, for that was nothing. This remained the fundamental paradox of evil for him. *Deprivatio* is one thing — a mere absence; but *depravatio* is something altogether more fearsome in its positive potential for doing damage."
5   Cf. *Conf.* 5.10.20, "I postulated two masses opposed to one another, each of them infinite, but the evil one on a narrower scale, the good one larger." Cf. K. Paffenroth, "Paulsen on Augustine: An Incorporeal or Nonanthropomorphic God?" *Harvard Theological Review* 86 (1993) 233-35.
6   Cf. W. S. Babcock, "Sin and Punishment: The Early Augustine on Evil," in *Collectanea Augustiniana — Augustine: Presbyter Factus Sum* (eds. J. T. Lienhard, et al; New York, et al: Peter Lang, 1993) 235-48: 241, "The Platonic notion served the purpose of reducing evil to a parasite upon the good which, as a parasite, requires the good if it is to exist at all. But it does not account for the origin of evil; and, above all, it does not capture the active force of evil exerting itself in opposition to — even if wholly constrained by — the divine design."
7   On the Manichaean position and Augustine's reaction to it, see P. Brown, *Augustine of Hippo* (Berkeley: University of California Press, 1967) 46-48, 148-50; Evans, *Augustine on Evil*, 11-16.
8   This is the interpretation of J. J. O'Donnell, *Augustine: Confessions* (3 vols; Oxford: Clarendon Press, 1992) vol. 2, 141: "His principle, after all, is that nothing is nothing save evil, and that there is no thing-ness to evil that could attract even the wickedest of souls. To be sure, he settles for the slightest of attractions, the camaraderie of thieves — and amateur thieves at that. The principle is saved, at the price of his dignity."
9   Cf. Rigby, *Original Sin*, 107: "Book II ends with companionship as the motive for choosing to steal. But since the companionship is nothing, he is choosing nothing."
10   On the "knot" imagery, see Brown, *Augustine*, 275; Evans, *Augustine on Evil*, 4-5; Rigby, *Original Sin*, 107-08.
11   On this theme, cf. *de civ. Dei* 15.17; Brown, *Augustine*, 319-21; W. T. Smith, *Augustine: His Life and Thought* (Atlanta: John Knox Press, 1980) 142-44.
12   All of these events are listed as "conversions" by F. van Fleteren, "St. Augustine's Theory of Conversion," in *Collectanea Augustiniana — Augustine: "Second Founder of the Faith"* (eds. J. C. Schnaubelt and F. van Fleteren; New York et al: Peter Lang, 1990) 65-80. He lists "The presence of friends" as part of Augustine's "conversion" scenes (p. 69): I would concur, with the emphasis on the presence of one friend and not a crowd. The scenes are solitary or intimate, not communal.
13   On this scene, see K. Paffenroth, "Tears of Grief and Joy. *Confessions* Book 9: Chronological Sequence and Structure," *Augustinian Studies* 28 (1997) 141-54.

14 On the vision, see P. Henry, *La vision d'Ostie. Sa Place dans la vie et l'oeuvre de saint Augustin* (Paris: J. Vrin, 1938); Brown, *Augustine*, 128-31.

15 Though, of course, the conversion causes the person to rejoin the community, and causes the community to rejoice, as at Augustine's baptism (*Conf.* 9.6.14).

16 Cf. E. Kevane, *Augustine the Educator: A Study in the Fundamentals of Christian Formation* (Westminster, MD: Newman Press, 1964) 37: "Augustine holds the educational system partially responsible for the moral helplessness into which he fell and for his concomitant and resulting gradual alienation from God. Worst of all was the fateful fall into the common attitude of spiritual and intellectual pride with which the system was imbued."

17 For an examination of the negative effects that his own education later had on Augustine, see L. C. Ferrari, "The Boyhood Beatings of Augustine," in *The Hunger of the Heart: Reflections on the* Confessions *of Augustine* (eds. D. Capps and J. E. Dittes; West Lafayette, IN: Society for the Scientific Study of Religion, 1990) 55-67.

18 Cf. Kevane, *Augustine the Educator*, 39: "It is the very essence of the *Confessions* that Augustine embraced the system with his whole heart and soul, learned all its lessons, and made its pride his own."

19 On the "unintentional" as the "decisive value" of an action, see Nietzsche, *Beyond Good and Evil*, (trans. W. Kaufmann; New York: Random House, 1966) section 32 (p. 44). Although according to Nietzsche, Augustine "lacks in a truly offensive manner all nobility of gestures and desires" (*Beyond Good and Evil*, section 50), he could probably acknowledge that he did have a keen appreciation for the unintentional.

20 *De magistro* 14.45, my translation.

21 Cf. Kevane, *Augustine the Educator*, 291: "Underlying these positions is the bedrock of St. Augustine's metaphysical realism, which gives his teaching its objectivity in pedagogical matters. His concept of truth is objective, not subjective, coming down upon the teaching profession as a light which reveals an objective order of being, truth, and value. Both the human teacher and the human learner exist and function within this objective order and see their role in subordination to it."

22 On this discussion of teacher as occasion, see Kierkegaard, *Philosophical Fragments*, (eds. and trans. H. V. and E. H. Hong; Princeton, NJ: Princeton University Press, 1985) section I.B.b (pp. 14-18).

23 Dante, *Purgatorio* (trans. John Ciardi; New York: Mentor Books, 1957) canto 15, lines 61-75.

24 Augustine quoting Cicero in *Opus imperfectum contra Julianum* 6.22; it is quoted by Brown, *Augustine*, 135.

Chapter Two

Models of Teaching and Models of Learning in the *Confessions*

Debra Romanick Baldwin

Introduction

Perhaps what is most striking about the activity of teaching in the *Confessions* is its seeming superfluousness. After all, what Augustine comes to discover is that it is God and not he who is the teacher, and that he — professor of rhetoric, winner of declamation contests, writer of speeches to the Emperor — is in fact the student, accepting the grace of whatever wisdom is bestowed upon him. And everything, as it turns out, sifted through the retrospective filter of Augustine's memory, is part of the great lesson, which step by step, fumble by fumble, tear by tear, leads him finally to God. Even the very pain of his mistakes, the agony of his miserable state apart from God, the "rods of red-hot iron"[1] that chastize him in the midst of his pleasures, are means of God's teaching which by "sprinkling so much bitterness over that sweetness" (3.1.1) bring him back to that source which is his only true rest and sweetness. The bookish knowledge we might commonly associate with teaching is itself in no way necessary to faith — as we see in the example of Augustine's mother, pious and humble, but not learned. The intellect itself can even be an impediment to wisdom in that some sorts of knowledge — vain inquiries into the workings of creation without regard to the Creator of it — can distract human beings from their true good.

The *Confessions* itself ends with the problem of teaching, asking how one is to teach. The last lines ask, "How can men teach other men this wisdom? How can an angel teach an angel? How can an angel teach a man?" (13.38.53). The book closes with the reply that the answer is to be found in God: "This must be asked of you, sought in you, knocked for at you. So, so shall it be received, so shall it be found, so shall it be opened." At first, this answer seems to undermine the human activity of teaching altogether, suggesting that only God can be our teacher, and only after we ourselves have asked for it. But what, or who, makes us ask? By what intermediary means might we be opened up to our own needs? God's ultimate agency, far from subverting the human activity of teaching, underscores its importance and raises its stakes. The ending of the *Confessions* is directed at the teacher as well as at the learner, at a teacher who is a learner, who asks, seeks, and struggles to understand how best to affect others who seek understanding. And surely Augustine himself takes up this struggle. Teaching is central to his own activity — in his capacity as a bishop, as a polemicist, and as a writer of the *Confessions* themselves. But by posing teaching as a problem in his *Confessions*, he invites us also to enter into that struggle by considering where exactly the constructive activity of human teaching is to found.

Elements of Learning

In this book which bids us, again and again, to return to origins, it is worth returning to its beginning, to Book One, where Augustine first introduces the subject of teaching by describing how he himself was taught.[2] There he sets forth two different styles of teaching and two different mechanisms of learning: fear-inspiring compulsion and free curiosity or desire (1.14.23). Using threats and beatings, his teachers used his fear to compel him to learn his early lessons in reading and writing, and in learning Greek. The imposition of this discipline, established by his ancestors (1.9.14) and seemingly embedded in our condition as "sons of Adam" (1.9.14), Augustine claims was good for him (1.12.19), both because it forced him to learn what he would later make use of, and because he deserved this punishments — "so small a boy and so great a sinner" (1.12.19). Moreover, the pain of discipline was salutary as an antidote to corrupting pleasure. Strikingly, he compares the "master's cane" to the "martyr's trials" which "have the power to make a blend of healthful bitterness, calling us back to you from those deadly pleasures in the enjoyment of which we become separated from you" (1.14.23). Suffering itself calls us to the realm beyond it.

As a method of teaching, however, external compulsion is problematic. First, while Augustine describes its salutary effects, he emphasizes that those effects came about by God and *despite* the intentions of his teachers, who were themselves misguided about the ends of education: "[T]hey had no idea of how I was to use the education which they forced upon me except for satisfying the insatiable desires of that wealth which is poverty and that glory which is shame" (1.12.19). Moreover, despite any salutary effects of discipline, an external ordering which imposes rules can be harmful if exercised in the service of merely conventional laws, rules indifferent to "the eternal covenant of everlasting salvation" (1.18.28). Augustine gives the example of pronunciation rules which cause him and his teachers to be embarrassed at mispronouncing the word, *hominem*, while being proud of using that pronunciation to destroy a flesh-and-blood human being (1.18.29). But perhaps the most problematic element of external compulsion as a method of teaching is that it opposes itself to a student's will, instead of educating that very will. And "no one can act well against his will, even if what he does happens to be good" (1.12.19). Teaching is incomplete if it merely imposes information from without.

It is not surprising, then, when Augustine identifies a second mechanism of learning which does engage the will: the internal force of free curiosity. Indeed, comparing the two ways of learning, he says that the latter has more power (*maiorem habere vim* [1.14.23]). He gives the example of his nurses who, amidst "laughter and play and kindness," used his natural curiosity and desire to teach him how to speak his native tongue. In this passage, curiosity is linked importantly with the pleasure of giving an account of things:

> In this learning I was under no pressure of punishment, and people did not have to urge me on; my own heart urged me on to give birth to the thoughts which it had conceived, and I could not do this unless I learned some words; these I learned not from instructors but from people who talked to me and in whose hearing I too was about to give birth to what I was feeling. *It is clear enough from this* that free curiosity is a more powerful aid to learning." (1.14.23 [emphasis mine])

The example is a striking one to illustrate the force of curiosity because it is not clear where the curiosity itself lies. Is he curious to learn his nurses' language? Or is he curious to learn about the world, for which he needs language? Or is he rather curious to discover what he himself thinks about the world, to enter into the process of "giving birth" to ideas which speaking generates? The very indeterminacy of the example nevertheless serves to connect curiosity with two other elements. First, by contrasting it with fear and punishment, Augustine connects curiosity with pleasure, situating it in a realm of play which engages the heart. Secondly, that very pleasure is also linked to our ability to express ourselves in speech. The desire to know is linked to the desire to give an account. Longing is linked with generation — in the same way, perhaps, as erotic desire is connected with the desire to give birth.

Precisely because it seeks pleasure and satisfaction, curiosity is dangerous: it is erotic and undirected.[3] Although, as will be seen, it can lead to learning and will fuel Augustine's own desire to know God, so too it feeds his appetite for public shows and for those false tales which titillate desire (1.10.16). Augustine emphasizes the erotic nature of curiosity when he describes how his nurses first cultivated his curiosity to speak using "caressing language" (*blandimenta*) (1.14.23), quietly and gently anticipating the misdirected caresses much later that will divert him from what he truly seeks. The very indeterminacy of curiosity, its far-ranging hunger and ability to be channeled in various directions, Augustine describes as a "flux" (*fluxus*) (1.14.23). When directed at physical objects, this "lust to know" extends even to the morbid desire to look at a mangled corpse (10.35.54). This erotic indeterminacy makes curiosity at once a powerful and risky tool of teaching, one which — like discipline — must be channeled in the right direction.

Although it is not a necessary component of learning, curiosity — true to its erotic nature — is also connected with pleasure, pleasure both in language itself and in its claims of knowledge. Describing how he first learned to speak, Augustine says that he not only felt the longing to express himself, but also the pleasure in having done so. This pleasure, combined with the even further completeness which curiosity itself seeks, runs the risk of transforming curiosity into vanity. Curiosity "puts on the appearance of a zeal for knowledge, while you, in the highest degree, know everything" (2.7.13). Seeking to be God-like instead of God-seeking, "the proud ... deep and curious in their knowledge ... count the stars and the grains of sand" without asking who created them (5.3.4).

If curiosity and desire, on the one hand, and fear and compulsion, on the other, are both mechanisms by which one can learn, Augustine also sets them in a social context which constitutes a third principle: imitation. Curiosity and desire lead Augustine to imitate his nurses. Similarly, those who impose discipline are models in their own right, and Augustine accuses of hypocrisy the teachers who beat him for playing games while they themselves were engaged in their own no less trivial games. Such a teacher "[i]f he was defeated on some trifling point of argument by another schoolmaster ... was far more bitter and more tortured by envy than I was defeated in a game of ball by one of my playfellows" (1.9.15). Certainly not all sin is imitative, but imitation compounds sin, which leads Augustine to exclaim, "Considering the kind of men who were set up as models for me to imitate, it is no wonder that I was swept away into vanities and that I went out of your presence, my God" (1.18.28). This element of imitation underscores the deeply social context of teaching. By stressing it, Augustine subsumes pedagogy, what we say and how we teach, beneath ethics — who we are and how we act. For it is our example which works more deeply than our words. Accordingly, Augustine follows the players of adult games into a life of being "seduced and seducing, deceived and deceiving, the prey of various desires" (4.1.1) as he himself becomes a teacher of rhetoric.

These three elements — compulsion which works through pain and fear, free curiosity which seeks to satisfy desire, and imitation which accompanies both in their social context — are posed problematically in Book One, inviting us to consider how they are woven throughout the rest of the *Confessions*. We see these elements in his questing and desiring on so many levels, in the pains and disappointments which limit and chastize him, as well as in his relations with the many people with whom he comes into contact and indeed himself begins to teach. But it is in Book Five that Augustine returns explicitly to the question of teaching and teachers. This book marks a critical turning point in his intellectual and moral development as he turns away from the Manichaeans and towards Catholic Christianity, a turning point that is shown also in the structure of the book, which is dominated by the figures of two teachers. Its narrative begins in high anticipation of the coming of the Manichaean bishop, Faustus, and ends in surprise with the unanticipated illumination facilitated by the Catholic bishop, Ambrose. How, then, do these two teachers help us understand what, according to Augustine, constitutes productive teaching?

Two Models of Teaching

We have seen that for Augustine curiosity is connected with the desire to give an account of things through speech, which itself brings pleasure. Words themselves can take on a life of their own, their beauty imitating truth and offering some satisfaction of the desire which gave rise to them. It is this charm of beautiful speech claiming to be truth that first attracts Augustine to the Manichees. Manichaeanism was a quasi-Christian sect conveying an elaborate and poetic, seemingly dualistic, but ultimately materialist, pseudo-scientific cosmology. In Book Three, Augustine explains that he was attracted to the sect by its lofty language and its promises of truth, which he likens to birdlime, a sweet trap: "And they kept on saying: 'Truth, Truth'; they were forever dinning it in my ears, and the truth was not in them" (3.6.10). Yet their language was beautiful nonetheless, and describes it using a more complex image which separates more clearly the form and its content: glittering tableware containing unsubstantial food: "They in those dishes of theirs kept on putting before me glittering fantasies, and it would be better to love the actual sun, which is real to our sight at least, than those false fantasies which make use of the sight to deceive the mind" (3.6.10). Their teachings, this food, was not only unsubstantial, he says, but wholly illusory, and he likens it to the food one eats in dreams, as opposed to real food, the nourishment of true faith.

We might at first expect Faustus to relate to Ambrose in the same way that Manichaeanism itself relates to Catholic Christianity — namely, as deceptive form relates to truthful content. And Augustine does in fact build upon these two images in order to describe Faustus. Faustus is introduced as a trap, "a great snare of the devil" (5.3.3), after which the image quickly shifts to food and tableware: "What charmed people was the smoothness of his language ... [but] I was interested not so much in the dish and adornment of a fine style as in the substance of the knowledge which this celebrated Faustus was setting before me" (5.3.3). The metaphor is expanded and elaborated to describe Augustine's disappointment when Faustus arrives and fails to produce the hoped-for substance: "my thirst could not be relieved by expensive drinking vessels and a well-dressed waiter" (5.6.10). This smooth-talking Manichee, then, is a best-dressed server (*decentissimus ministrator*) of beautiful but empty words.

This description of Faustus develops the element of curiosity or desire on two levels, one precarious and one salutary. Faustus' smooth talking feeds the pleasure which curiosity takes in giving an account of things. His students' curiosity, seeking to give an account, mistakes a beautiful account for one that is truthful, thus leading them into dangerous illusion: "Their reason for thinking him wise and intelligent was simply that his way of speaking gave them pleasure" (5.6.10). It was this pleasure which first attracted Augustine to the Manichees. On the other hand, another, deeper level of his curiosity leads him beyond them. This is Augustine's curiosity *for* the truth — that hunger that makes him long hopefully for beautiful dishes and wait anxiously for the "waiter" who serves them — and it leads him beyond those things that cannot satisfy. The very desire that runs the risk of seeking illusion and resting in it, can also propel one beyond it. In this case, Augustine is fortunate enough to meet a replacement for the well-dressed waiter who serves empty platters, a servant of a different sort who serves the nourishment he seeks: he encounters Ambrose, the devout servant (*pium cultorem*) of God (15.13.23).

Ambrose offers real food: he "was healthily teaching salvation" (5.13.23), and doing so by means of an eloquence as impressive as that of Faustus. His "eloquence in those days gave abundantly to *Thy people the fatness of Thy wheat, the gladness of Thy oil and the sober intoxication of Thy wine*" (5.13.23). It is precisely that eloquence, not the ideas it contains, which first attracts Augustine, who seeks to test Ambrose's reputation as a fine speaker and to put it "on trial" (5.13.23): "I hung on his words, but I was not interested in what he was really saying and stood aside from this in contempt" (5.13.23). Only gradually does Augustine's attraction to the form lead him to appreciate the sustenance which it contains.

In particular, Ambrose provides Augustine with life-giving sustenance by liberating him from his painfully literal-minded reading of scripture. Whereas Faustus' speeches merely repeat "exactly the same things as the others are always saying, but ... much more elegantly" (5.6.10), Ambrose's words reanimate an issue that previously "had been a cause of death" (5.14.24) for Augustine. Before becoming a Manichee, he had rejected scripture because he thought its simple language was beneath him. Ambrose shows him that the simple words of scripture contain layers of meaning, that the humble language of the Bible is like a doorway "low and humble" (3.5.9), before which one must stoop and bring oneself low in order to apprehend the teachings within, "high and veiled in mysteries" (*velatam mysteriis*) (3.5.9). Taking passages from the Old Testament that Augustine had rejected, Ambrose explains them figuratively: "[H]e would draw aside the veil of mystery and explain in a spiritual sense the meanings of things which, if understood literally, appeared to be teaching what was wrong" (6.4.5). Thus while Faustus regurgitates his pre-rehearsed (5.6.11) Manichaean line whose demarcating materialism deadens, Ambrose reveals the living richness of the Bible, uncovering its multi-layered complexity in a figurative ascent that prepares Augustine to comprehend the idea of spiritual substance.

Juxtaposing the two teachers in this way, it is tempting to consider Faustus as a foil for Ambrose: Faustus as the model of a bad teacher offering form without content is set against Ambrose as the model of a good teacher offering truth. Yet Augustine's account is more complicated. To begin with, Faustus is a problematic model of a bad teacher. Augustine credits him for teaching him: "this Faustus, who to many people had been a real snare of death, now began, without willing it or knowing it, to unloosen the snare in which I had been caught" (5.7.13). Precisely the emptiness of Faustus' answers causes Augustine to seek the fullness of truth elsewhere, and the hold of Manichaeanism is loosened as a result. Like the teachers of Augustine's youth who punished him for the wrong reasons but whose punishment achieved a good end nonetheless, Faustus' teaching, whatever its intent, helps Augustine learn. More importantly, despite the metaphors with which he is introduced, Faustus' character is praised. Confronted with Augustine's difficult cosmological questions, "[h]e knew that he was ignorant of these things and was not ashamed to admit it" (5.7.12). Most strikingly, Augustine sets Faustus' limitation above his own desire at the time to learn scientific truths: "there is more beauty in the modesty of a mind that admits its faults than in the knowledge that I was seeking for" (5.7.12). High praise to bestow upon a "snare of the devil"!

Nor is Ambrose an unproblematic model of a good teacher. Although in Book Five he promises to be the guide who leads Augustine step by step to salvation, Book Six shows him stepping back from his students, a source of perplexity and seeming neglect. He is too busy for his students, and when they come in to hear him read aloud (as is customary), they find him always reading silently: "Often when we came to him ... we found him reading, always to himself and never otherwise; we would sit in silence for long time, not venturing to interrupt him in his intense concentration on his task, and then we would go away again" (6.3.3). Augustine and the other students try to fathom his reasons, guessing that Ambrose "wanted to be free from the disturbance of other people's business," or that he wanted to avoid having to explain to his students what he was reading, or that he was just saving his voice (6.3.3). Ambrose is — to say the least — hardly the model of an enthusiastic teacher eager to be at the heart of a learning community. His students, bewilderingly ignored as they sit silently around him waiting to be taught, are literally and figuratively peripheral to Ambrose's activity. Compare this image to that of Faustus, whose "own kind of enthusiasm, which was for literature" (3.7.13) causes him to begin a reading group with Augustine, attracting Augustine even after the latter's enthusiasm for Manichaeanism has waned (3.7.13). Their reading together is one of several places in the *Confessions* that reveal that Augustine, although condescending towards Faustus, was also very fond of him. Not only does he praise Faustus's character, as mentioned above, but in comparing him with Ambrose, Augustine notes that Ambrose's style was less entertaining and engaging (*minus tamen hilarescentis atque mulcentis*) than that of Faustus (5.13.23). Compared with this warm and intimate portrayal of Faustus, Augustine's Ambrose remains something of a cipher: "I could neither guess nor tell from my own experience what hope he had within him, what were his struggles against the temptations of his exalted position, what solace he found in adversity" (6.3.3). What, then, are we to make of the sympathy with which Augustine portrays Faustus alongside the peculiarity of his portrait of Ambrose?

Learning in Teaching

We have already seen that taken together, both teachers illustrate how powerful and central language can be in the activity of teaching. Both teachers impress Augustine with the eloquence through which they convey their ideas and move the hearts of their listeners. Their eloquence allows them to cultivate that element of pleasure reminiscent of Augustine's original teachers, the nurses who fostered his curiosity with pleasure amidst play and affection. That element of eloquence is also at the heart of Augustine's own activity in the *Confessions*, which is written in beautiful language full of poetic imagery. The very glittering dishes with which he describes the Manichaean teachings not only describe, but exemplify the power of poetic expression. In the same way, he uses vivid images of disease, torture, and imprisonment to shape how we view worldly pleasure, and images of freedom, bliss, and light to cultivate our desire for the knowledge of God. That poetic language can be used in the service of truth justifies why Augustine prefers seductive poetry to bad science: "For I can turn verses and poems into true nourishment" (3.6.11). In this way, Augustine, like Ambrose, seeks to convey the truth beautifully, deliciously.

At the same time, Augustine's more complex presentation of these two teachers underscores the idea that teaching is not merely about presenting truth persuasively or palatably. Teaching is not ultimately about repeating ideas or conveying information. However instrumental is Ambrose's eloquence in helping Augustine to reconsider the claims of Catholic Christianity, that eloquence itself does not immediately cause his conversion. Ambrose can open up Augustine to the depths of scripture, he can begin to move Augustine's heart, he can appeal to Augustine's reason, but he cannot simply illuminate him. One might say that Augustine's grasp of the truth which he seeks is not merely handed to him on a splendid platter. Rather, the pleasant eloquence of Book Five is followed by the tumultuous doubts and painful inner struggles of Books Six, Seven and Eight, in which Augustine turns inward and humbly discovers his own neediness. He discovers truth not from without, but from within.

By giving the unlikely figure of Faustus the sympathetic prominence that he is given in Book Five, Augustine destabilizes the straightforward authority of a teacher possessing truth. Faustus is a teacher who recognizes that he is also a student. He is willing to admit what he does not know. He is willing to read *with* Augustine, and not merely *for* him. In that willingness, he embraces teaching as a collaborative activity, prefiguring Augustine's own relationship with Alypius and Nebridius in Book Six. Originally a student of Augustine, Alypius becomes his friend and joins with him and Nebridius "in an ardent search for truth and wisdom" (6.10.17). Augustine describes their shared neediness and their mutual encouragement: "So there were together the mouths of three hungry people, sighing out their wants to one another, and waiting upon thee that Thou mightest give them their meat in due season" (6.10.17). By exemplifying the way in which, because of our fundamental incompleteness, learning and teaching can combine together in a collaborative activity, Faustus returns us to the human context of teaching. Admiring him, Augustine learns from his example. But that example is also problematic, for it is also the occasion for Augustine to indulge in a certain pride in his own intellectual superiority, evident in his description of how he chose to read with Faustus those books that Augustine "considered right for his kind of intelligence" (5.8.13).

While Faustus acknowledges his own limitation, it is Ambrose who evokes a sense of limitation in Augustine himself. Surely he does so first by the substance of his teaching, which liberates Augustine from his painfully literal-minded reading of scripture and opens him up to figurative levels of interpretation that he had never before considered. In consequence, Augustine's own sense of limitation takes the form of self-blame: "I began to blame that despairing attitude of mine which had led me to believe that the Law and the Prophets could not possibly stand up to hostile and mocking criticism" (5.14.24).

But perhaps the deeper sense of limitation which Ambrose is able to cultivate in Augustine comes not from his words, but from his silence. He instills in Augustine not only self-blame, but sheer perplexity. The passage in which Augustine describes Ambrose's silent reading is full of unanswered speculation as he tries to plumb the depth of the internal reflections of another. In fact, Ambrose, by his very example, by his very silence, turns Augustine inward, leading him to question himself. Ambrose exemplifies that internal turn by which Augustine will come to grasp the idea of spiritual substance. The turn is described in Book Seven: "I was admonished by all this to return to my own self, and, with you to guide me, I entered into the innermost part of myself" (7.10.16). It is precisely that inward turn which neither the compulsion of external discipline nor the pleasure of outward-looking curiosity can effect. Nor is it clear that Ambrose himself read silently in order to have this effect.

Indeed, perhaps what is most striking about Augustine's account of his teachers is the ever-present disjunctions between their activities and his own complex path of learning. For this reason, Augustine's juxtaposition of Faustus and Ambrose not only illustrates the several and separable strands of teaching that can lead to learning; it also underscores the very irony of teaching itself. We do not always know how and from whom we will discover truth. Augustine sought a truthful account from Faustus and did not find it; he sought mere eloquence from Ambrose and found a truthful account. However skillfully and truthfully a teacher might make use of the elements of learning, the process itself remains mysterious, its effects long-term and difficult to predict. The element of mystery and of incompleteness returns us again to the beginning and the ending of the *Confessions*, to the larger context in which teaching and learning both take place, and to the activity which seeks guidance for both: the humble prayer for the mysterious gift of God's presence and enlightenment.

Notes

1   *The Confessions of St. Augustine*, Rex Warner, tr. (New York: Penguin/Mentor, 1963) 350. All subsequent quotations from the *Confessions* are from this translation.
2   For a discussion of the return to origins in the *Confessions*, see Robert McMahon's elegant work, *Augustine's Prayerful Ascent: An Essay on the Literary Form of the Confessions* (Athens, GA: University of Georgia Press, 1989).

3   On the role of *curiositas* in Augustine's concept of sin, see N. J. Torchia, "St. Augustine's Triadic Interpretation of Iniquity in the *Confessiones*," in *Collectanea Augustiniana. Augustine: Second Founder of the Faith* (eds. J. C. Schnaubelt and F. Van Fleteren; New York, et al.: Peter Lang, 1990) 159-73.

Chapter Three

Augustine's *Confessions* as Pedagogy: Exercises in Transformation

Thomas F. Martin, O.S.A

Introduction

Pierre Hadot's seminal work *Philosophy as a Way of Life* challenges readers of the ancient philosophers to reconsider their approach to these assuredly distant texts. They are not, he argues, hypothetical presentations of abstract theories, but practical handbooks for performative self-transformation. This leads Hadot to a challenging redefinition of the very notion of ancient philosophy: "It is *philosophy itself* that the ancients thought of as a spiritual exercise."[1] The various elaborate explanations and often enigmatic maxims of ancient philosophical writings were not intended to be theoretical presentations of abstract theories, but practical descriptions of a distinct vision of reality which gave rise to and found expression in a particular *way of life*. The writings were deliberately pedagogical, leading to the absorption, internalization, and living of this distinct vision of reality. They formed part of a program and process which led to the transformation of the individual; as such, they were directed toward conversion.[2] One can see a verification of Hadot's assertions in Augustine's own "philosophical reading" of Cicero's *Hortensius* as he recounts early on in the *Confessions*. His encounter with this work enflamed him with the desire for Wisdom itself, not simply with wise theories or ideas:

> This book changed my way of feeling and the character of my prayers to you, O Lord, for under its influence my petitions and desires altered. All my hollow hopes suddenly seemed worthless, and with unbelievable intensity my heart burned with longing for the immortality that wisdom seemed to promise. I began to rise up, in order to return to you.[3]

This reading marked the beginning exercise of a conversion journey, the transformation of Augustine.

The intention of this essay is to draw upon Hadot's insights concerning ancient philosophy as suggestive of a distinctive and pedagogical way to read the *Confessions* of Augustine. There is much about education, educators, and being educated in this work. The Bishop of Hippo, I will argue, intended them in two ways: to function pedagogically as "spiritual exercises," and to provide a pedagogical model for such exercises. They were not simply nor solely meant to "uncover and reveal Augustine," undeniably one dimension of the work, but were just as importantly intended to "uncover and reveal" the very *lectores/auditores* of the *Confessions.*[4]

This century has seen a dizzying array of theories and reading keys, often contradictory and mutually exclusive, concerning the intent of the *Confessions.*[5] The bibliography and literature concerning just this one work of Augustine has virtually exceeded mastery by any single individual. This study will not propose to have uncovered the key for the work, though following the lead of Hadot, I will suggest that apart from the obvious apparent intentions of the narrative (right understandings of *catholica* and *scriptura* certainly stand out),[6] Augustine does have very specific designs upon his audience. These designs are concerned with his readers' transformation, not just Augustine's, and the *Confessions* provide, suggest, and even provoke *exercises* in this regard. Thus while the *Confessions* may initially appear to be all about Augustine, this itself is perhaps (ironically) a device to draw his audience in for a closer look at themselves.

In order to uncover this pedagogy of the *Confessions,* it will be necessary to begin with a brief consideration of Hadot's analysis of ancient philosophy, and how he envisions this discipline as "spiritual exercises." It will then be possible to place this notion against the narrative of the *Confessions* as a kind of reading grid. This, I will argue, reveals a *pedagogy,* carefully and subtly implanted within the very fabric of the narrative and its unfolding. In the process it will become clear that this pedagogy has desired outcomes which will need to be made explicit. The conclusion of this study will bring together the results of these explorations with a consideration of their implications for Augustine and education.

The Pedagogy of Ancient Philosophy

One must use an ancient and not a modern notion of philosophy in order to understand what these ancient philosophers intended to accomplish. Such is Hadot's contention.[7] Their "love of wisdom — philosophia," perhaps in contrast with many modern understandings of the philosophical pursuit, was concerned with attaining a "state of perfection of being and knowledge":

> . . . so each school would elaborate its rational depiction of this state of perfection in the person of the sage, and each will make an effort to portray him . . . In this transcendent norm established by reason, each school will express its own vision of the world, its own style of life, and its idea of the perfect man [*sic*].[8]

"Achievement" rather than mere "knowledge" was the guiding intention of the teachings of the ancient schools of philosophy. Their teaching was in the service of a vision of the world, a particular style of life consonant with living in such a world, and thus required the portrayal of some model suggestive of this achievement. The portrait of the philosopher that emerges from the text is intended to project a living embodiment of the philosophy: "the perfect human being." This model of perfection offers an horizon of attainment for the wisdom-seeker, and, Hadot argues, each philosophical school saw it necessary to provide the necessary "tools" to guide the seeker toward this horizon of perfection. These are the tools for *spiritual exercises*: "...every school practices exercises designed to ensure spiritual progress toward the ideal state of wisdom, exercises of reason that will be, for the soul, analogous to the athlete's training or to the application of a medical cure."[9]

One notes the multi-faceted models employed by Hadot to explain the program: academic, athletic, and medical, three dimensions of the classical *paideia* out of which and on behalf of which ancient philosophy flowed.[10] Academically, there is the pursuit of wisdom, with all of its cognitive implications. Athletically, there is the realization of a training program: workouts, drills, conditioning exercises — all comparable to what the athlete does in order to prepare himself for successful combat. Medically, there is therapy: remedial treatment and rehabilitation, mending and restoration, convalescence and recovery — this wide assortment of ancient "medical" treatments provided a rich vocabulary for another kind of cure. These three models also highlighted the need for both *receptivity* and *responsibility* on the part of anyone undertaking such exercises: there was nothing passive about this process. Each school accordingly drew upon various methods or tools, "exercises," designed to achieve the goal of the particular school: meditation, self-attentiveness, self-control drills, the use of maxims, etc.[11] The ancient philosopher had at hand a wide range of diverse practices that functioned as agents of learning, training, and healing.

It is important to note the holistic and comprehensive intentions operative here, and how these may strike the contemporary reader of the ancient texts as foreign. Hadot notes how moderns often accuse these philosophers of "bad writing," finding their works rambling, confusing, circuitous, repetitive. He suggests that the problem is perhaps with the reader, applying his or her "writing/reading standards" to these works, taking up these texts in pursuit of "pure theory." They were, in fact, thoroughly "oral" in their composition and intention. They were written in order to be *heard*. Oral transmission works within its own particular framework and imposes its own peculiar constraints:

> For the written works of this period remain closely tied to oral conduct. Often they were dictated to a scribe. And they were intended to be read aloud, either by a slave reading to his master or by the reader himself, since in antiquity reading customarily meant reading aloud, emphasizing the rhythm of the phrase and the sounds of the words, which the author himself had already experienced when he dictated his work. The ancients were extremely sensitive to these effects of sound. Few philosophers of the period we study resisted this magic of the spoken word, not even the Stoics, not even Plotinus. So if oral traditions before the practice of writing imposed rigorous constraints on expression and obliged one to use certain rhythmic, stereotypic, and traditional formulae conveying images and thoughts (independent, if one may say so, of the author's will),

this phenomenon is not foreign to written literature to the degree that it too must concern itself with rhythm and sound.[12]

When one adds to the obviously academic scope of these works their "training" and "therapeutic" intentions, their need for "pliability" becomes even more critical as does, perhaps equally, the problematic this creates for modern engagement with these ancient texts. Hadot highlights repeatedly the need for the contemporary reader to appreciate what is implied in the execution of this "oral model" where "systematic rigor" gives way to "idea association," where the actual *sound(s)* can be viewed as an integral part of the therapy.[13]

In this light, Hadot notes the intimate relationship that was intended to be developed between teacher and pupil,[14] a reminder that the "communication event" they envision is quite unlike the modern classroom or lecture hall or solitary reading of philosophical text. Perhaps, in this sense, the ancient and contemporary medical model of doctor and patient, one-to-one, face-to-face, remains a more helpful model for understanding the practice of ancient education:

> True education is always oral because only the spoken word makes dialogue possible, that is, it makes it possible for the disciple to discover the truth himself amid the interplay of questions and answers and also for the master to adapt his teaching to the needs of the disciples . . . what is inscribed in the soul by the spoken word is more real and lasting than letters on papyrus or parchment.[15]

Inscribing the soul, this was the intention of the dialogue. Hadot describes this method as *zetetic* — searching, with both a dialectical and rhetorical component, expressed in the form of both question/answer and continuous discourse. The "form" of these ancient texts serves specific dialectical and rhetorical aims and moves. This searching method and genre exhibit and demand the spontaneous. There is need for constant adaptation to the on-going demands created by the very nature of the method. Pliability and unpredictability are integral to such an approach — rather than a pre-set course and its rigorous unfolding.

In this process the philosopher as teacher/trainer/physician becomes, most importantly, "spiritual director," since it is ultimately the realm of the spirit that is at stake. Thus what moderns think of as philosophical treatises must be understood according to their ancient intention,

> . . . written not so much to inform the reader of a doctrinal content but to form him, to make him traverse a certain itinerary in the course of which he will make spiritual progress. This procedure is clear in the works of Plotinus and Augustine, in which all the detours, starts, stops, and digressions of the work are formative elements.[16]

With terms such as "spiritual progress" and "formation," the intention here is the "training of the soul." Hadot describes this training under the category of four necessary learnings that make up the core of the pedagogy of ancient philosophy:

learning to live, learning to dialogue, learning to die, and learning how to read. By way of these four learnings, *philosophia* becomes one's *way of life*. Hence, it will be important for understanding the pedagogy of the *Confessions* to consider briefly what Hadot wishes to be understood by these four "learnings."

Learning to Live

Essentially, philosophical learning is directed to "life," rather than simply "knowledge." Learning is intended to become "living," and so both "understanding" and implementing this "understanding" determine the make-up of the exercises involved in this kind of learning. The student must master this art of living, this taking up of a life-style, inevitably demanding a life conversion. It is here that training and therapy play their role, as a progressive, step-by-step regimen is undertaken, always a difficult and demanding itinerary requiring knowledge, understanding, insight, and asceticism. Hadot enumerates the varying components or dimensions of this particular "learning": *zetesis* (research), *skesis* (through investigation), *anagnosis* (reading), *akroasis* (listening), *prosoche* (attention), *enkrateia* (self-mastery), [*adiophonia*] (indifference).[17] These were incorporated into a four-fold process of attention, meditation, input, and various practical exercises that, taken together, made possible the attainment of a specific way of living that embodied the school of philosophy. This "educational product" that was a new "way of living" meant concretely that all aspects of living were now to be subsumed under, incorporated into, and shaped by a very determined and concrete sense of the appropriate shapes and contours of an ideal life-style: passions, personality, attitudes, sense of self, sense of being, relationships, material possessions, freedom, the will, moral behavior, a sense of the cosmos, happiness — all were made to accord with a vision of "an authentic state of life."[18] Perhaps surprisingly to some, Epicurus fully exemplifies this notion of philosophy as "therapeutics" (Hadot's term): "We must concern ourselves with the healing of our own lives" (*Gnomologium Vaticanum*, 64).[19] Here we see embodied the call to "learn to live."

Learning to Dialogue

In order to "learn to live," the philosopher turns to dialogue. The fact that dialogue is one of the chief routes for the attainment of wisdom highlights both the intensely personal and markedly communal nature of this journey. The dialogue demands of the student not just the obvious ability to be attentive to his/her partner in the dialogue, the philosopher-guide, it above all demands the "ability to converse with oneself."[20] Socrates remains the supreme exemplar of the demands made by this dialogical exercise: "...like an indefatigable horsefly, Socrates harassed his interlocutors with questions which put *themselves* into question, forcing them to pay attention to and take care of themselves."[21]

Hadot relocates the central concern of this dialogue away from "content" to the *heart* of the interlocutor. The dialogue begins "at home," with and within oneself, and its final concern transcends "*what* is being talked about" to arrive at "*who* is doing the talking."[22] Dialogue is ever dialectical as the interlocutor is constantly challenged to be steadfastly and conscientiously attentive to "maintaining the path." The rough, uneven, and seemingly unexpected makeup of this dialogical path is deliberate and intentional. Can one hold to the course? Distraction or inattention is to lose one's way. The dialectical and rhetorical obstacles posed by the teacher are tests to see if one can maintain the course: "All the circles, detours, endless divisions, digressions and subtleties which make the modern reader of Plato's *Dialogues* so uncomfortable are destined to make ancient readers and interlocutors *travel* a specific path."[23] The ever present challenge is not to go astray, not to lose the path. This, Hadot insists, is rough terrain, "combat, amicable but real,"[24] with neither partner unaware of the stakes and demands involved: "Dialogue is only possible if the interlocutor has a real *desire* to dialogue: that is, if he truly wants to discover the truth, desires the Good from the depths of his soul, and agrees to submit to the rational demands of the *Logos*."[25] True dialogue demands an almost obstinate devotion to the exercise of dialogue itself. Yet, despite this emphasis upon the actual exercise of dialogue,[26] on a deeper level there remains an awareness that underlying this holding to the path is a dedication and commitment to the pursuit of truth and goodness. One is not just learning to dialogue, one is learning to live: "for reasonable people, the measure of listening to such discussions is the whole of life" (Plato, *Republic*, 450b).[27]

Learning to Die

"[H]e who remains faithful to the Logos risks losing his life."[28] Learning to live is inseparable for the ancients from learning to die, as Hadot notes the importance in all ancient philosophy of learning the task of how to face death. Socrates, more than any other philosopher, is the embodiment of this central role played by "training for death" in the philosophic life.[29] This learning could take on a variety of diverse forms, depending upon the school: for the Epicurean, thought of finitude conferred infinite value on the present moment;[30] for the Platonists, this same concern became constant effort to turn away from the individual and subjective to that which is universal and objective.[31] In every case, this learning means facing *timor mortis*, leading to a "contempt for death" as a hallmark of the attainment of a philosophical nature.[32] Hadot notes, in this regard, how all the schools converge upon common themes concerning death: "the insignificance of human affairs, contempt for death, and the universal vision....[33] 'Hence such a man,' affirms Plato, 'will not suppose death to be terrible.'"[34] Marcus Aurelius cites this same text of Plato in his own stoic *Meditations* (7.35).

It is in the Neoplatonic tradition of Plotinus and Porhyry that this "learning to die" reached a certain explicit focus, if not culmination point. For them spiritual exercises were meant to train one for the kind of vision necessary to transcend all that is mortal and material. Hadot quotes the *Ennead*:

> If one wants to know the nature of a thing, one must examine it in its pure state, since every addition to a thing is an obstacle to the knowledge of that thing. When you examine it, then remove from it everything that is not itself; better still *remove all your stains from yourself and examine yourself*, and you will have faith in your immortality.[35]

Here is a method for "learning to die": *examine* and *remove*. This concerns both the object regarded and the one regarding. The goal in this case is the attainment of faith in immortality, as knowledge and experience converge in the *experience* of one's own purification that at last leads to true *understanding*. In this Neoplatonic instance, the final goal of "learning to die" is nothing less than "annihilation," the loss of one's own individuality.[36] All that remains at the end of this path is the One. According to this particular scheme of learning to die, the final outcome is the elimination of the learner! "He is no longer himself, nor does he belong to himself, but he is one with the One, as the center of one circle coincides with the center of another."[37]

Learning to Read

These learnings — to live, to dialogue, to die — hinged upon a final important learning that made the previous three possible. Embodied within the works of the ancient philosophers was the necessary teaching that would make possible true living, vigilant dialoguing, and noble dying: the necessary components of the perfect way of life. Yet, since one had to take up texts in order to learn this, it became equally vital that one learned *how* to read them. With what intention, with what scope, with what rule of interpretation?

> Our claim has been, then, that philosophy in antiquity was a spiritual exercise. As for philosophical theories: they were either placed explicitly in the service of spiritual practice, as was the case in Stoicism and Epicureanism, or else they were taken as the objects of intellectual exercises, that is, of a practice of the contemplative life which, in the last analysis, was itself nothing other than a spiritual exercise. It is impossible to understand the philosophical theories of antiquity without taking into account this concrete perspective, since this is what gives them their true meaning.[38]

Learning to read meant going beyond texts and their seemingly grand theories and elaborate explanations, the obvious "dogmatic edifices" contained therein. One had to be able to "read" beyond this theory, to find there an "existential attitude" that was not only to be attained but most importantly maintained:[39] ". . . the written work is a reflection of pedagogical, psychagogic, and methodological preoccupations."[40] Hadot cannot repeat enough the "concrete" rather than "theoretical" context for even the seemingly most abstract works of Aristotle, where the intention is "concrete situations created by specific academic debates." These must be met by a training where students are to learn, not a "system," but "the technique of using correct methods in logic, the natural sciences, and ethics."[41] Instead of reading out of these works a "system," what is to be sought is "a method for training people to live and look at the world in a new way."[42] To do this, "the soul must turn inward upon itself."[43] Reading leads to spiritual exercises.

This is not our reading, but the "reading aloud" of the ancient world. Power was at work here, as actual words were actually spoken and thereby released their power upon the hearer. These spoken words, deliberately placed at the service of the dialogical model explored above, provided the dialogue with impetus and energy. "We have forgotten how to read,"[44] Hadot insists, highlighting the need to rediscover the formative power of the ancient model. It is the kind of reading that allows for the text to continue to speak, even when text has been left behind. It involves learning "how to pause, liberate ourselves from our worries, return into ourselves, and leave aside our search for subtlety and originality, in order to meditate calmly, ruminate, *and let the texts speak to us.*[45]

What Hadot is proposing here is an "exegetical concern." Augustine describes a similar process of reading in his *Confessions*:

> So I resolved to make some study of the Sacred Scriptures and find what kind of books they were. But what I came upon was something not grasped by the proud, not revealed either to children, something utterly humble in the hearing but sublime in the doing, and shrouded deep in mystery. And I was not of the nature to enter into it or bend my neck to follow it. When I first read those Scriptures, I did not feel in the least what I have just said; they seemed to me unworthy to be compared with the majesty of Cicero. My conceit was repelled by their simplicity, and I had not the mind to penetrate into their depths. They were indeed of a nature to grow in Your little ones. But I could not bear to be a little one; I was only swollen with pride, but to myself I seemed a very big man.[46]

Learning to read is, in the final analysis, a question of interpretation, of hermeneutics, the learning of a disciplined reading that imposes certain "hermeneutical restraints" upon the reader.

The *Confessions* as Spiritual Exercises

Even a merely casual acquaintance with Augustine's *Confessions* could prompt immediate connections with Hadot's portrayal of ancient philosophy as spiritual exercises, guided by the four learnings just considered.[47] Much of Augustine's story is a "learning to read," as shown by his stormy reading history of the Old Testament, Manichaean texts, Cicero, Paul, the Platonists. His story is also an impassioned, almost desperate "learning to live," embodied in the turmoils and journeys of love, happiness, eloquence, friendship, success. Along the way, he learns about death during his plight over the death of his friend, prompting the mourning of human mortality, countered by his narrative of Monica's death, viewed now in the hope and promise of eternal life. And all of this is deliberately placed into the framework of a rich and multi-dimensional dialogue: with God, with self, with audience — opponents, the curious, his own brethren and friends, even future readers. Indeed, on a variety of levels, Augustine's *Confessions* seem to confirm and re-affirm Hadot's insights about ancient philosophy as spiritual exercises. On the other hand, a close reading also suggests that the *Confessions* attempt a profound subversion or perhaps radical relocating of the "classical" model explored by Hadot. To the question of the *Confessions* as "spiritual exercises" we will now turn, seeking to uncover their own unique pedagogy.

A Question of Audience

Augustine's own remarks in his *Retractations* are brief, and yet they are an important indicator of his own perception of the work:

> The thirteen books of my *Confessions* praise (*laudant*) the just and good God for my evil deeds and my good deeds (*de malis et de bonis meis*), and they rouse up towards Him (*in eum excitant*) the human intellect and affections (*humanum intellectum et affectum*) — that, at least, is what happens to me — it happened to me when I wrote them, they do the same when they are [now] read. What others feel (*sentiant*) concerning those things, they themselves will see; yet I know that they greatly pleased and still please (*placuisse et placere*) many of the brethren (*multis tamen fratribus*). The first to the tenth books are written about myself (*de me*); the remaining three, about sacred scripture (*de Scripturis sanctis*); what is written in them from '*in the beginning God made heaven and earth*' until the sabbath rest (*usque ad sabbati requiem*).[48]

This is Augustine's late in life estimation of his *Confessions*. He clearly highlights in this description their "effect": *excitare* and *placere*.[49] They rouse up and please their "reader" (*cum leguntur*).[50] Augustine does not note what the reader has learned about Augustine, or about his understanding of Scripture, or even about his praises of God, what might be called the *information* of the narrative. Rather, he privileges what happens *to* the reader — and that reader even includes Augustine.

This concern for the "reader" rather than the "author" makes itself evident at key points in the course of the narrative of the *Confessions*.[51] While it is obvious that specific "theological-pastoral" concerns drive the narrative — anti-Manichaean,[52] anti-Donatist,[53] anti-Pagan[54] — it is equally apparent that Augustine has another audience in mind. In Book Two, he interrupts the narrative briefly but poignantly to remind his audience and perhaps even himself why he is recounting certain events: "And why [do I recount these things]? So that whoever reads them may reflect with me on the depths from which we must cry to you. What finds a readier hearing with you than a heart that confesses to you, a life lived from faith?"[55] This "call" functions as a kind of course realignment for the narrative. The reader is directed away from Augustine and towards a deeper and shared knowledge about the self. It is a call to go within, to one's own heart and the life of faith welling up there. In the same Book, he once again deflects the attention of the reader when talking about his own *mala et nefaria opera*:[56]

> Is there anyone who can take stock of his own weakness and still dare to credit his chastity and innocence to his own efforts? And could such a person think to love you less, on the pretext that he has had smaller need of your mercy, that mercy with which you forgive the sins of those who turn back to you? If there is anyone whom you have called, who by responding to your summons has avoided those sins which he finds me remembering and confessing in my own life as he reads this, let him not mock me; for I have been healed by the same doctor who has granted him the grace not to fall ill, or at least to fall ill less seriously. Let such a person therefore love you just as much, or even more, on seeing that the same physician who rescued me from sinful diseases of such gravity has kept him immune.[57]

Augustine addresses his readers: to seek to know my deeds and yet not realize the need to recognize and acknowledge the grace of your own healing and strength is ingratitude. And as the narrative proceeds, this attention to his readers only intensifies. In Book Nine, his touching account of Monica and her death turns him to his "eavesdropping" listeners:[58]

> Inspire others, my Lord, my God, inspire your servants who are my brethren, your children who are my masters, whom I now serve with heart and voice and pen, that as many of them as read this may remember Monica, your servant, at your altar, along with Patricius, sometime her husband. From their flesh you brought me into this life, though how I do not know. Let them remember with loving devotion these two who were my parents in this transitory light, but also were my brethren under you, our Father, within our mother the Catholic Church, and my fellow citizens in the eternal Jerusalem, for which your people sighs with longing throughout its pilgrimage, from its setting out to its return. So may the last request she made of me be granted to her more abundantly by the prayers of many, evoked by my confessions, than by my prayers alone.[59]

Here the readers, identified as Augustine's own fellow servants, brothers and sisters, God's sons and daughters, are implored to pray for his parents—the narrative of Monica and Patricius is intended to inspire others and thus evoke their own prayerful remembrances to be joined with the prayer of Augustine.

It is in Book Ten of the *Confessions* that the audience is brought to center stage perhaps more prominently than anywhere else in the narrative:

> What point is there for me in other people hearing my confessions? Are they likely to heal my infirmities? A curious lot they are, eager to prey into the lives of others, but

tardy when it comes to correcting their own. Why should they seek to hear from me what I am, when they are reluctant to hear from you what they are?[60]

At this point Augustine briefly turns to the "truth" question: how does his reader know that what Augustine says is true? He will answer this question by an invitation to love: "they will believe me if love has opened their ears."[61] And this affirmation is preceded by a principle that once again suggests the real intentions behind this narrative: "Is to hear from you about oneself anything other than to come to know oneself?[62] Augustine offers this maxim in the form of a question to his readers in the form of a challenge: turn your intention and attention towards your own listening. In the end, it is not Augustine they need to listen to, not Augustine about Augustine, but rather God about oneself:

> When the confession of my past evil deeds is read and listened to[63] — those evil deeds which you have forgiven and covered over to make me glad in yourself, transforming my soul by faith and your sacrament — that recital arouses the hearer's heart, forbidding it to slump into despair and say, "I can't." Let it rather keep watch for your loving mercy and your gentle grace, through which every weak soul that knows its own weakness grows strong. It is cheering to good people to hear about the past evil deeds of those who are now freed from them: cheering not because the deeds were evil but because they existed once but exist no more.[64]

Augustine reminds perhaps even himself that this very confessing continues to be an "exercise" for him. Its very execution still serves to transform *non possum* into *vigilantia*. And this exercise prompts him to turn again to the love of his "audience" as the guarantee of this dialogue: "the love which is within them by which they are good tells them that I do not lie in my confessing, and this charity in them believes me."[65] There is clearly more than a standard author-reader relationship at work here. It is this shared *caritas* that enables Augustine to call the reader/hearer *animus fraternus* and invite them to their own prayerful *respiratio* and *suspiratio* on behalf of Augustine: "Let them sigh with relief (*respirent*) over [my good deeds] and with grief (*suspirent*) over [my bad deeds] and let both hymns and laments ascend into your presence from the hearts of my brethren which are your censers."[66]

Augustine, however, is not yet done with his audience. He turns to them for one final time at this point in his narrative before returning to his own *confessio*:

> So then, when I confess not what I have been but what I am now, this is the fruit to be reaped from my confessions; I confess not only before you in secret exultation tinged with fear and secret sorrow infused with hope, but also in the ears of believing men and women, the companions of my joy and sharers in my mortality, me fellow citizens still on pilgrimage with me, those who have gone before and those who will follow, and all who bear me company in my life. They are your servants and my brethren, but you have willed them to be your children and my masters, and you have ordered me to serve them if I wish to live with you and share your life. This command of yours would mean little to me if it were only spoken, and not first carried out in deed as well. So I do likewise,

and I do it in deeds and in words. I do it under your outstretched wings and would do it in grave peril, were it not that under those wings my soul is surrendered to you and to you my weakness known. I am a little child, but my Father lives for ever and in him I have found a guardian suited to me . . . To such people, then, the people you command me to serve, I will disclose myself not as I have been but as I am now, as I am still, though I do not judge myself. In this way, then, let me be heard.[67]

If these are intended to be *The Confessions of St. Augustine*, Augustine, in a surprising way, manifests a deep concern that they also become the *"Confessions of My Readers."* This is done most gently here as he reminds his readers of a shared pilgrimage, a shared *confessio*, a shared obligation to both word and deed. This incorporation of the reader into the narrative suggests the pedagogy of the *Confessions*: this is also the story of his companions in joy and sharers in mortality.

Clearly, at the time of their writing he has already become a controversial figure and there is certainly an "apologetic" dimension to all of his. However, when all these comments are taken together, they suggest that while this is indeed an *exercitatio Augustini*, it is equally intended to be an *exercitatio lectorum et auditorum*:[68] "Why should they seek to hear from me what I am, when they are reluctant to hear from you what they are?"[69] If this is so, then Hadot's analysis of ancient philosophy's spiritual exercises suggests further lines of exploration regarding how these same exercises might unfold in the course of the narrative of the *Confessions*. Can one find there exercises for learning to live, learning to dialogue, learning to die, and learning to read?

Learnings: to Live, to Dialogue, to Die, to Read

Exercitatio is to be found throughout the narrative of the *Confessions*: the *exercises* of his youth that were to lead to both knowledge and eloquence;[70] Monica's encounter with the Carthaginian bishop "well-trained" in scripture;[71] his encounter at last with the "well-practiced," but disappointingly shallow Faustus;[72] the "stretching" that the reading of scripture demands;[73] Augustine's need for "preparedness" in order to read Isaiah;[74] the apophatic "exercise" of considering one's inner trinity of being, knowing, and willing.[75] These are all cases where Augustine explicitly uses the term *exercitatio* and its cognates in the course of the narrative. They are merely suggestive, however, of a more subtle and complex *exercitatio* offered by Augustine through both the form and content of the narrative. Here one can find actual learning, potential practice models, and real exercises, all interwoven deftly into the very fabric of this narrative. Hadot calls attention to the demanding moves made by ancient texts, daunting to the modern reader, but purposefully intended to "force" the ancient reader/hearer to move with and within these dynamics. The narrative in its zigzagging and winding turnabouts, in its seemingly erratic and capricious moves was, argues Hadot, deliberate and intentional. One must read it as an attempt to break down resistance and awaken attention, not of course as an end in itself, but rather in order to render the "exerciser" ready and fit, not for the text, but for the living implied and exemplified by the text.

Hadot's "taxonomy" of ancient learnings is not meant to suggest that its four-fold delineation provides a neat and rigorous framework for approaching ancient writings. Their unsystematic nature (for the modern) belies that fact. These intentions, as part of their effectiveness, were interwoven subtly, artfully, even enigmatically into the fabric and progression of the discourse of the narrative:

> In philosophical works such as these, thought cannot be expressed according to the pure, absolute necessity of a systematic order. Rather, it must take into account the level of the interlocutor, and the concrete tempo of the *logos* in which it is expressed. It is the economy proper to a given written logos which conditions its thought content . . .[76]

Hadot can speak about the *tempo* and *economy* of ancient texts. Here he is speaking about Plato's writings, but they suggestively provide insight and clues regarding the *tempo* and *economy* of Augustine's narrative text. As has been seen, the narrative functions not only on Augustine's behalf, but equally on his audience's behalf, seeking to turn them back upon themselves, prompting possible first steps of a transformative journey, one that Augustine himself models, theorizes upon, and clearly strives to precipitate.

It may be suggested that this functions on two levels for Augustine's audience. On the one hand, and following Hadot's model, the themes of living, dialoguing, dying, and reading permeate the entire narrative. Christ as Life, a Psalm-driven dialogue, sin as death, a humble reading posture before the Scriptural word: those who take up Augustine's *Confessions* cannot put them down unaware of what *they* must learn about living, dialoguing, dying, and reading. Yet these learnings as proposed by Augustine are, in themselves, never abstract nor theoretical. They are incorporated into and even modeled by Augustine's own description of a real and living journey, from death into life, thereby suggesting to his audience a framework for the consideration of their own journey(s); the very process embodies a call to their own real conversion. Augustine is not providing interesting reading about someone else, but, in fact, about the self of the reader. This call takes the form of an invitation to eavesdrop upon a real dialogue — Augustine's own multi-layered exchange — only to discover that this dialogue is about oneself, and that at that very moment of insight another dialogue ought to begin. Obviously, the *Confessions* offer lessons in reading — from Virgil's *Aeneid*, to Cicero's *Hortensius*, to Manichaean texts, to philosophical works, and at last to the Word of God, the Scriptures. The final three books and their exegetical explorations embody how this kind of reading nourishes life, unfolds into dialogue, and provides hope against death. Indeed, one could develop at great length the profound content within these four learnings that permeate the narrative from first to last line, the final product being an intricate weaving together of form, method, and content.[77] Every sentence, paragraph, and page assaults the reader with description, analysis, and questioning invitation — to live truly, to dialogue honestly, to die trustingly, and to read correctly. They are unfolded amidst a relentless return to themes of interiority, truth, the *catholica*, beauty, and goodness. Above all there is Augustine's embrace by Christ and of Christ: *Verbum, Filius, Virtus, Sapientia, Veritas*,[78] the true *Magister bonus*.[79] Christ, *Via, Veritas, Vita* is surely the *magister* of these *Confessions*:

> Accordingly I looked for a way to gain the strength I needed to enjoy you, but I did not find it until I embraced the mediator between God and humankind, the man Christ Jesus, who also is God supreme over all things and blessed for ever. Not yet had I embraced him, though he called out, proclaiming, "I am the Way and Truth and the Life," nor had I know him as the food which, though I was not yet strong enough to eat it, he had mingled with our flesh; for the Word became flesh so that your Wisdom, through whom you created all things, might become for us the milk adapted to our infancy. Not yet was I humble enough to grasp the humble Jesus as my God, nor did I know what his weakness had to teach. Your Word, the eternal Truth who towers above the higher spheres of your creation, raises up to himself those creatures who bow before him; but in these lower regions he has built himself a humble dwelling from our clay, and used it to cast down from their pretentious selves those who do not bow before him, and make a bridge to bring them to himself. He heals their swollen pride and nourishes their love, that they may not wander even further away through self-confidence, but rather weaken as they see before their feet the Godhead grown weak by sharing our garments of skin, and wearily fling themselves down upon him, so that he may arise and lift them up.[80]

Augustine is "exercising" his readers *into* Christ, the Christ of the *fides catholica*,[81] a learning rooted in *doctrina catholica, pia, sana, sobria, rationalis*.[82] Christ is indeed both the *via* and *patria* of these Confessions.[83]

The learnings in the *Confessions* unfold within an explicit pedagogy that is based on Christ and the scriptures. But it is also carried out on a methodological level by the very construction and direction of the narrative, where Augustine continually entices and draws his reader into the narrative. In this sense Augustine's endeavors are thoroughly rhetorical and persuasive.[84] This has been suggested already in considering Augustine's strategic appeals to his audience, where he insists that the only appropriate disposition for reception of his narrative is *caritas*, a clear indication that there must be a more than "academic" interest when taking up this text. Yet by the very way he unfolds the narrative, Augustine powerfully yet subtly lures his reader into these exercises. It is striking how he makes himself vulnerable by the incredibly frank yet remarkably discreet self-revelation. No Christian bishop had ever been so "public" about the depths out of which he was brought to conversion. But in this very revelation, Augustine succeeds in cutting off the commonplace escape routes of excuse and put-off. Claims to have sunk too low are exposed and shattered by Augustine's own graced ascent to new heights. This frankness and honesty is also clearly intended to establish an intimate rapport between Augustine and his reader-student, thereby making possible the surprising transpositions that occur throughout the narrative. Those who come to Augustine as "students" have models like Alypius, who ceases to be student and becomes *frater cordis*,[85] or Nebridius, who becomes *dulcis amicus meus*.[86] To become a student of Augustine, what in so many ways the narrative invites, can have unexpected learning outcomes.[87]

Yet perhaps the most intriguing tool for these exercises is to be found within the very fabric of Augustine's self-narrative. The power of the language and images, the intensity of the movement, the passion of its candor, the intricacy of its recurring interwoven themes, the profound depth of self-revelation, the constant heightening of the stakes involved: none of this, it may be argued, is mere display or arbitrary disclosure. "*Percussisti cor meum verbo tuo, et amavi te*,"[88] Augustine tells his Lord. But the reader's heart is under the same assault from Augustine's words: "*Augustine, percussisti cor meum verbo tuo* — Augustine, you have shattered my heart with your word." Here one understands why Augustine has asked that *caritas* be the receptacle for his words.

One example of how he does this is to be found in the very deliberate ways in which he concludes each book and prepares his "students" for the book to follow. The final lines of each of the thirteen books, when placed together, both sum up the entire journey of Augustine and invite the "student" to undertake the journey of transformation. A sampling of these conclusions will suffice to make this apparent, and will take us to the conclusion of these explorations.

Book One

> In a living creature such as this everything is wonderful and worthy of praise, but all these things are gifts from my God. I did not endow myself with them, but they are good, and together they make me what I am. He who made me is good, and he is my good too; rejoicing, I thank him for all those good gifts which made me what I was, even as a boy. In this lay my sin, that not in him was I seeking pleasures, distinctions and truth, but in myself and the rest of his creatures, and so I fell headlong into pains, confusions and errors. But I give thanks to you, my sweetness, my honor, my confidence; to you, my God, I give thanks for your gifts. Do you preserve them for me. So will you preserve me too, and what you have given me will grow and reach perfection, and I will be with you; because this too is your gift to me — that I exist.[89]

Augustine's *confessio* does sum up the movement and drama of Book One, his early years. Yet they now are restated here in a universal way so that no reader would be unable to insert their own "ego" into the narrative: *non mihi ego dedi haec, ut sim tu dedisti mihi*. Is there any serious reader of Augustine here, who in speaking these words aloud would not realize that he or she is speaking not only Augustine's "*I*"? Suddenly the narrative has become one's own. Any even implicit "yes" to Augustine's recapitulation merges almost imperceptibly into one's own "yes": *non mihi ego dedi haec, ut sim tu dedisti mihi*. Here it is no longer exposition, but maxim, a gnomic restatement that can easily penetrate the heart and provide focus for the mind of the reader.

Book Two

> Who can unravel this most snarled, knotty tangle? It is disgusting, and I do not want (*nolo*) to look at it or see it. O justice and innocence, fair and lovely, it is on you that I want (*volo*) to gaze with eyes that see purely and find satiety in never being sated. With you is rest and tranquil life. Whoever enters into you enters the joy of his Lord; there he will fear nothing and find his own supreme good in God who is supreme goodness. I slid away from you and wandered away, my God; far from your steadfastness I strayed in adolescence, and I became to myself a land of famine.[90]

Questions asked by Augustine are always dangerous — intended always to disturb whatever audience is before him! When asked aloud by the reader, the discourse once again shifts in the direction of the one asking. Further, the tug of the *nolo/volo* rehearses a theme that will persist throughout the narrative. But asked in the first person, it once again turns back upon the reader. The pervasiveness of the first person singular throughout the narrative, when read aloud, cannot help but reverberate back upon the one speaking. All of this suggests clearly that Augustine does indeed have intentions upon his reader.

Book Four

> O Lord our God, grant us to trust in your overshadowing wings: protect us (*nos*) beneath them and bear us (*nos*) up. You will carry us (*tu portabis, tu portabis* [twice repeated]) as little children, and even to our grey-headed age you will carry us still (*tu portabis*). When you are our strong security, that is strength indeed, but when our security is in ourselves, that is but weakness. Our good abides ever in your keeping, but in diverting our steps from you we have grown perverse. Let us turn back to you at last, Lord, that we be not overturned. Unspoilt, our good abides with you, for you are yourself our good. We need not fear to find no home again because we (*nos*) have fallen away from it; while we (*nobis*) are absent our home falls to ruins, for our home is your eternity.[91]

As often throughout the narrative, Augustine has imperceptibly slipped from the *ego* to the *nos* — a narrative not of the *I* but of the *we*. In these moves, the reader has been abruptly drawn into the narrative, the change of person transposing it from being "Augustine's story" to becoming my story, our story, a story carried forward by God (*tu portabis* is thrice repeated). The language is all about both movement and stability, as seemingly contradictory notions unite: *firmitas* and *revertamur*. The reader feels the tension.

Book Thirteen

One final excerpt is perhaps helpful since it comes from the final Book of the work, a conclusion to the trilogy of Books 11, 12, and 13, where Augustine has left behind the text of his own life for a consideration of the text of Genesis. There is, however, the very same drawing in of the reader into the narrative's dialogue and, once this step has been taken, can the reader resist the self-implications?

> We, therefore, see these things you have made, because they exist, but for you it is different: they exist because you see them. Moreover when we see that they exist, we see it outside ourselves, but when we see that they are good, we see it by inner vision, whereas you see them as created in no other place than where you saw them as non-existent things you willed to create. Once our heart had conceived by your Spirit we made a fresh start and began to act well, though at an earlier stage we had been impelled to wrongdoing and abandoned you; but you, O God undivided and good, have never ceased to act well. Some of our works are indeed good, thanks to your Gift, but they will not last for ever, and when they are done we hope that we shall rest in your immense holiness. But you, the supreme Good, need no other good and are eternally at rest, because you yourself are your rest. What human can empower another human to understand these things? What angel can grant understanding to another angel? What angel to a human? Let us rather ask of you, seek in you, knock at your door. Only so will we receive, only so find, and only so will the door be opened to us.[92]

These concluding lines of the *Confessions* both sum up the whole, and for one final time invite the reader to enter into the exercises that have been unfolding since the opening lines of the work. Surely there is a deliberate echoing of the opening *fecisti nos ad te* and the *cor nostrum inquietum est* that introduce the work, along with the deliberate highlighting of *nos* and *tu*, *requies* and *movere*, *foris* and *intus*, *male* and *bene*: all the persistent themes and concerns of the *Confessions* are summarized and reaffirmed here. It may surely be argued that all of these terms and concepts, precisely because they are so ardently charged, are deliberately placed both to provoke the heart of the reader one more time, as well as to teach, inform, and call those hearts to enter upon the only sure path that leads to life. The poetry and dynamism of the prose does not suggest a passive reader, but one willing to be inflamed by the passion of the text, and so at last to undertake a journey deferred, or, if already undertaken, to give oneself even more wholeheartedly to it. There is, as has been seen throughout these explorations, little sense that Augustine is simply telling his story, or, in the final three books, offering exegetical advice. The intensity of the discourse operates on the level of the heart. And the entire work ends on a final note of *exercitatio* that suggests unfinished business: *petere, quaerere, pulsare*. The Matthean call (Matt 7:8) to ask, to seek, to knock certainly concludes the *Confessions*, but in a way that suggests a beginning: the *exercitatio* continues, as asking, seeking, and knocking now become a "way of life."[93] But this unfinished task remains a far cry from the young student of the earliest books of the *Confessions*, whose learning and longing was ever met with despair and frustration.

This ending is filled with hope, longing, and promise: "so will the door be opened to us."

The "Learnings" of the *Confessions*

In his *Confessions*, Augustine both comfortably operates within and yet provocatively subverts the traditions of the philosophical schools, the models of ancient philosophical learning explored and articulated by Pierre Hadot. Augustine demonstrates that he is fully conversant with and masterfully adept at the methods and tools, learnings and exercises that were the hallmark of ancient philosophy as a "way of life."[94] On the surface there are marked similarities with the dialogues of Plato, the admonitions of the Stoics, the mystical ascents of Plotinus. In this sense, the narrative of the *Confessions* shows itself driven forward by the same passionate pursuit for life-giving wisdom. The work is not the exposition of dazzling ideas and speculative constructs, but of a quest for fullness of life, a quest that in itself seeks to be life-giving, a searching not satisfied with any reality less than Life itself: "*Deus meus vita mea,*[95] *ut discerem te*"[96]: God is the purpose and goal of these learning exercises. Every page of the *Confessions* both explores, exemplifies, and explains this kind of learning for life, supported by and converging with its auxiliary learnings in the art of dialogue,[97] of dying,[98] and of reading.[99] Augustine even provides the antithesis and antitype of true learning in his dark portrayal of the Manichaean pedagogy, the cruelty of the schools of his childhood, and the hypocrisy of the *aulas* of lies and arrogance that marked the political world of Milan.[100] Augustine teaches how not to teach and learns how not to learn.

However, his most radical assault upon the ancient schools is directed specifically towards their exercises in self-transformation. It is precisely in his own attempts at self-transformation that Augustine experienced the most abject insufficiency and deepest disappointment. Augustine portrays himself as the consummate failure in self-transformation, someone who seemingly had every opportunity and fortuitous turn of events possible: brilliance, eloquence, friends, powerful patrons. They take him to the top: Imperial Rhetor. But Augustine turns everything around. What he achieves is hypocrisy, selfishness, slavery to habits, insecurity, and unhappiness. His own "failure" can be seen as a living denunciation of these traditions of "self-mastery" (*enkrateia*).[101] The ancient schools did indeed offer spiritual exercises intended for "self-improvement" and "self-transformation." They did indeed promise a pedagogy that would produce the "perfect human." Hadot notes the flowering of this tradition of self-mastery in Augustine's own day with the ascendancy of the Plotinian model:

> If you do not yet see your own beauty, do as the sculptor does with a statue which must become beautiful: he removes one part, scrapes another, makes one area smooth, and cleans the other, until he causes the beautiful face in the statue to appear. In the same way, you too must remove everything that is superfluous, straighten that which is

crooked and purify all this is dark until you make it brilliant. Never stop sculpting your own statue, until the divine splendor of virtue shines in you . . .[102]

The learning paradox of the *Confessions* is that its *exercitationes* are all designed to turn the "student" away from traditional models of spiritual exercises. In a way it is a call to put aside any "self-transformative," "self-sculpting" models. Augustine persuades, argues, and demonstrates in favor of surrender and self-submission to the *magisterium*, and discipline and regime of the *"bonus et solus magister"*[103] and his *"schola pectoris."*[104] It was precisely this model that Pelagius rejected, as Augustine recounts late in life in the *De dono peserverantiae*.[105] While Pelagius saw it as the self-abdication of the student, Augustine never ceased insisting that it was the only path of salvation for the student: *"non ego vita mea sim: male vixi ex me, mors mihi fui: in te revivesco."*[106] The pedagogy of the *Confessions* with all of its attendant spiritual exercises is not for the sake of self-transformation in any classical sense of the term. Instead, it demands the surrender of the self to the One alone who can heal and transform: "Without you, what am I to myself but a guide to my own downfall — *quid enim sum ego mihi sine te nisi dux in praeceps."*[107]

Conclusion

Pierre Hadot's study of the pedagogy of ancient philosophy provides much insight into Augustine's own pedagogical efforts all too briefly explored in the course of this essay. The warm reception of Hadot's call to recover ancient philosophy's concern for spiritual exercises ought, in the same light, enhance the potential value of the *Confessions* in this regard.[108] Hadot's admonition that "we have forgotten how to read,"[109] would equally apply to works like Augustine's. Of course, the world of Late Antiquity is not the Modern or Post-Modern world. Yet Augustine would certainly insist that the pursuit of Wisdom, Truth, and Life ought still to inflame and excite human hearts. He certainly proposes a radically theocentric and Christocentric model that would dismay many in today's academy (but perhaps no more or less than in Augustine's own day). He did not then (nor perhaps would he today) apologize for a learning model that emphasizes interiority, disciplined dialogue, reading aloud and together, the widest possible learning horizon, love between student and teacher (experienced in the love of God, of course!), the deepest commitment to the pursuit of truth, and all the *exercitationes* necessary to awaken, test, train, deepen, and yes, even strain the student. Such is the pedagogy of the *Confessions*. For Augustine, these exercises were ever grounded in a redemptive model of learning, with Matt 7:7 as the "slogan" of this school: they were exercises in asking, seeking, and knocking before Wisdom's door, thereby allowing the classroom of one's heart to become temple, study, observation post, bridal chamber, as well as place of promise and hope that even this learning process will be overtaken by the sure knowledge of encounter. In this sense, the *Confessions* do indeed offer a comprehensive "handbook of exercises" for today, where curriculum, method, and their operative demonstration turn all into fellow students before a single Master who cannot but succeed: "I love you, Lord, with no doubtful mind but with absolute certainty. You pierced my heart with your word, and I fell in love with you."[110] Perhaps these final words of Augustine suggest that, beyond the model proposed by Hadot, there was, in fact, another "learning" for the Bishop of Hippo which encompassed and transcended all other learnings: learning to love. The *philosophia* that Augustine learned was, even more than a "way of life," a "way of love." Here, finally, is the framework, content, and challenge of all "Augustinian learning."

Notes

1   Pierre Hadot, *Philosophy as a Way of Life: Spiritual Exercises from Socrates to Foucault,* (ed. with an introduction by Arnold I. Davidson; trans. Michael Chase; Oxford: Blackwell, 1995) 126, emphasis in the original. While Hadot's analysis has been positively received, at least some suggest that not all philosophy in the ancient world was directed towards the "conversion" implied by the notion of spiritual exercises and did engage in "pure theory." See the review by François Renaud, *Journal of the History of Philosophy* 35 (1997) 639.

2   See the generally receptive reviews of Hadot's work, Renaud, *Journal of the History of Philosophy* 35 (1997) 637-640; Lloyd P. Gerson, *The Philosophical Quarterly* 47, no. 188 (July, 1997) 417-420. For a critique of what is called his "existential" model, see Maria Antonaccio, "Contemporary Forms of *Askesis* and the Return of Spiritual Exercises," *The Annual of the Society of Christian Ethics* 18 (1998) 69-92, a critique based upon what she sees as the "antitheorist" assumptions of Hadot: ". . . the universalism of his approach to *askesis* is in the end undercut by his antitheorist assumption that these practices are prior to and separable from their conceptual or metaphysical background" (p. 81). Certainly Augustine, as will be seen, would not and could not separate the "existential" from the "conceptual."

3   *Ille vero liber mutavit affectum meum et ad te ipsum, Domine, mutavit preces meas, et vota ac desideria mea fecit alia. Viluit mihi repente omnis vana spes et immortalitatem sapientiae concupiscebam aestu cordis incredibili et surgere coeperam, ut ad te redirem* (*Conf.* 3.4.7). The English text of the *Confessions* throughout this study will be taken from *The Confessions*, introduction, translation and notes Maria Boulding, O.S.B., The Works of Saint Augustine, A Translation for the 21st Century, I/1, ed. John E. Rotelle, O.S.A. (Hyde Park, NY: New City Press, 1997).

4   The question of the intended audience of the *Confessions* continues to be debated and is obviously a critical dimension in understanding the scope and purpose of the work. I will address the specific question of audience below. For now it is important to ask whether Augustine intended this work to be *read* or *heard*: should one consider this work, at least in its origins, as primarily *text* or *discourse*? The answer ought to have distinct implications for approaching the work. Augustine's own remarks, explored in the course of this essay, will suggest both, since reading was normally done aloud. (Augustine records his surprise at Ambrose's silent reading, *Conf.* 6.3.3.) Thus even

when Augustine refers to his "readers," he is aware that they are "hearing" his work. A "hermeneutic for hearing" is perhaps not, as might seem obvious, the same as a hermeneutic for what is presently understood as "reading a text." Language, narrative and argument operate differently in oral discourse — and not only was the work intended to be read out loud, for more than likely such reading would normally take place in a group setting. Contemporary *readers* of the *Confessions* who are desirous of exploring Augustine's original intentions for the work should, I will argue, think in terms of *hearing* the work. See Walter J. Ong, *Orality and Literacy: The Technologizing of the Word* (New York: Routledge, 1982).

5   In his Introduction to the *Confessions*, Trapè analyzes an array of often contradictory theories concerning the unity and purpose of the work: Agostino Trapè, "Introduzione," in *Sant'Agostino, Le Confessioni* (trans. and notes, Carlo Carena; 3 ed.; Nuova Biblioteca Agostiniana I (Rome: Città Nuova Editrice, 1991) xix-xxii.

6   E.g. *Conf.* 7.7.11.

7   See Hadot, *Philosophy as a Way of Life*, 53.

8   Hadot, *Philosophy as a Way of Life*, 57. The English translation of Hadot's work consistently uses "man" for human being. I will not alter this language, trying to be faithful to the translator's intention, and presume that it is to be taken inclusively.

9   Hadot, *Philosophy as a Way of Life*, 59.

10   Peter Brown provides an engaging introduction into this *paideia* in his *Power and Persuasion in Late Antiquity: Towards a Christian Empire* (Madison, WI: The University of Wisconsin Press, 1992).

11   See Brown, *Power and Persuasion*, 59-61.

12   Brown, *Power and Persuasion*, 62. If the "medicine" was, at least to some extent, embedded in the very sound, this certainly creates "translation" problems. The maxim *"traduttore traditore"* takes on a more toxic character in this world of orality: see Pedro Laín-Entralgo, *The Therapy of the Word in Classical Antiquity* (ed. and trans. L.J. Rather and John M. Sharp; New Haven: Yale University Press, 1970). For this reason it will be important to note the character of Augustine's original Latin text which will be provided in the notes. This discourse was intended to be received as a specific form of oral/aural "medicine."

13   Hadot, *Philosophy as a Way of Life*, 62.

14   This is quite apparent in Augustine's early "philosophical" dialogues, as he takes over a traditional model learned from Cicero and other classical masters.

15   Hadot, *Philosophy as a Way of Life*, 62.

16   Hadot, *Philosophy as a Way of Life*, 64.

17   Hadot, *Philosophy as a Way of Life*, 82-89.

18   Hadot, *Philosophy as a Way of Life*, 83.

19   Hadot, *Philosophy as a Way of Life*, 87, see 114, n.59.

20   Hadot, *Philosophy as a Way of Life*, 91.

21   Hadot, *Philosophy as a Way of Life*, 89.

22   Hadot, *Philosophy as a Way of Life*, 89.

23   Hadot, *Philosophy as a Way of Life*, 92, emphasis added.

24   Hadot, *Philosophy as a Way of Life*, 91.

25   Hadot, *Philosophy as a Way of Life*, 93.

26   See Hadot, *Philosophy as a Way of Life*, 92: "What counts is not the *solution* of a particular problem, but the *road* traveled to reach it" (emphasis added).

27   Hadot, *Philosophy as a Way of Life*, see 119, n.100.
28   Hadot, *Philosophy as a Way of Life*, 93.
29   Hadot, *Philosophy as a Way of Life*, 95.
30   Hadot, *Philosophy as a Way of Life*, 95.
31   Hadot, *Philosophy as a Way of Life*, 96.
32   Hadot, *Philosophy as a Way of Life*, 97.
33   Hadot, *Philosophy as a Way of Life*, 95.
34   *Republic* 486a; see Hadot, *Philosophy as a Way of Life*, 97 and 121, n.127.
35   Plotinus, *Ennead* 1, 5, 7, 10, 28-32, emphasis Hadot's; see Hadot, *Philosophy as a Way of Life*, 100, 122 n.144.
36   Hadot, *Philosophy as a Way of Life*, 101.
37   Plotinus, *Ennead*, 6,9,10,14-17; see Hadot, *Philosophy as a Way of Life*, 122, n.152.
38   Hadot, *Philosophy as a Way of Life*, 104.
39   Hadot, *Philosophy as a Way of Life*, 104.
40   Hadot, *Philosophy as a Way of Life*, 105.
41   Hadot, *Philosophy as a Way of Life*, 105.
42   Hadot, *Philosophy as a Way of Life*, 107. Precisely in this context Hadot refers to Augustine's *De Trinitate*, in particular his consideration of images of the Trinity within: "Augustine is not trying to present a systematic theory of trinitarian analogies. Rather, by making the soul turn inward upon itself, he wants to make it *experience* the fact that it is an image of the Trinity" (Hadot, *Philosophy as a Way of Life*, 107).
43   Hadot, *Philosophy as a Way of Life*, 107.
44   Hadot, *Philosophy as a Way of Life*, 109.
45   Hadot, *Philosophy as a Way of Life*, 109.
46   *Conf.* 3.5.9.
47   Commentators consistently note the revolutionary nature of the *Confessions*. No ancient author, no early Christian bishop, no "Father of the Church" had ever done before what Augustine did in terms of religious self-disclosure.
48   *Retr.* 2.6.1.
49   One cannot help but note the "rhetorical" import of this statement. In *De doctrina christiana* he notes the three-fold task of rhetoric: "*docere ut instruat, delectare ut teneat, flectere ut vincat*," (*De doct.chr.* 4.12.27, 13.29).
50   Once again it must be remembered that this "reader" is not the modern reader. It is, as I have argued above, very likely an *audible* and *shared* reading.
51   Here one must note the important studies of Brian Stock, *Augustine the Reader: Meditation, Self-Knowledge, and the Ethics of Interpretation* (Cambridge, MA: The Belknap Press of Harvard University Press, 1996); as well as that of Harry Gamble, *Books and Readers in the Early Church: A History of Early Christian Texts* (New Haven: Yale University Press, 1995).
52   With their prominent role in the *Confessions*, it is obvious that the Manichaeans are certainly a main concern. Augustine directly tackles many of their doctrines and practices and dismantles and discredits them. Indirectly, much is also going on: the text of the *Confessions* is a veritable weaving of scriptural texts into a single tapestry, most noticeably the *Psalms*. The work ends with *Genesis*. The Manichaeans. rejected the Old Testament as the work of a lesser God, not the God of Jesus Christ. Every time Augustine employs the Old Testament he is arguing against the Manichaeans, most notably and explicitly in *Conf.* 9.4.8.

53   Anti-Donatist intentions are implied whenever Augustine emphasizes the *Catholica*: *Conf.* 6.4.5; 7.5.7; 7.7.11; 7.19.25. The Donatists posited a "pure church" and here Augustine presents a model of post-baptismal struggle. In 13.23.34 we find the *corpus permixtum*! Do we find *apologia* in, e.g. 10.3.3-4, preceded by 10.2.2 (the truth of what he is saying is known to God)? The Donatists liked to draw upon Augustine's checkered history and suggest that he was still a Manichaean.

54   Esp. *Conf.* 7.11.27.

55   "*Et ut quid hoc? Ut videlicet ego et quisquis haec legit cogitemus, de quam profundo clamandum sit ad te. Et quid propius auribus tuis, si cor confitens et vita ex fide est*" (*Conf.* 2.3.5).

56   *Conf.* 2.7.15.

57   "*Quis est hominum, qui suam cogitans infirmitatem audet viribus suis tribuere castitatem atque innocentiam suam, ut minus amet te, quasi minus ei necessaria fuerit misericordia tua, qua domas peccat conversis ad te? Qui enim vocatus a te secutus est vocem tuam et vitavit ea, quae me de me ipso recordantem et fatentem legit, non me derideat ab eo medico aegrum sanari, a quo sibi praestitum est, ut non aegrotaret, vel potius ut minus aegrotaret, et ideo te tantumdem, immo vero amplius diligat, quia per quem me videt tantis peccatorum meorum languoribus exui, per eum se videt tantis preccatorum languoribus non implicari*" (*Conf.* 2.7.15).

58   Augustine addresses them as he prays to God, and they "overhear" their own names as he calls upon God's name.

59   "*Et inspira, Domine meus, Deus meus, inspira servis tuis, fratribus meis, filiis tuis, dominis meis, quibus et corde et voce et litteris servio, ut quotquot haec legerint, meminerint ad altare tuam Monicae, famulae tuae, cum Patricio, quondam eius coniuge, per quorum carnem introduxisti, me in hac vita quemadmodum nescio. Meminerent cum affectu ipo parentum meorum in hac luce transitoria ut fratrum meorum sub te patre in matre catholica et civium meorum in aeterna Hierusalem, cui suspirat peregrination populi tui ab exitu usque ad reditum, ut quod a me illa poposcit extremum uberius ei praestetur in multorum orationibus per confessiones, quam per orationes meas*" (*Conf.* 9.13.37).

60   "*Quid mihi ergo est cum hominibus, ut audiant confessiones meas, quasi ipsi sanaturi sint 'omnes languores meos'* (*Ps.* 102.3). *Curiosum genus ad cogonscendam vitam alienam, desidiosum ad corrigendam suam. Quid a me quaerant audire qui sim, qui nolunt a te audire qui sint.*" (*Conf.* 10.3.3).

61   "*...sed credunt mihi, quorum mihi aures caritas aperit*" (*Conf.* 10.3.3).

62   "*...quis est enim a te audire de se nisi cognoscere se?*" (*Conf.* 10.3.3).

63   A clear reminder of the oral/aural context of this "reading."

64   "*Nam confessiones praeteritorum malorum meorum, quae remisisti et texisti, ut beares me in te, mutans animam meam fide et sacramento tuo, cum leguntur et audiuntur, excitant cor, ne dormiat in desperatione et dicat: "Non possum," sed evigilet in amore misericordiae tuae et dulcedine gratiae tuae, qua potens est omnis infirmus, qui sibi per ipsm fit conscius infirmitatis suae. Et delecta bonos audire praeterita mala eorum, quia iam carent eis, nec ideo delectat, quia mala sunt, sed quia fuerunt et non sunt*" (*Conf.* 10.3.4).

65   "*...dicit enim eis caritas, qua boni sunt, non mentiri me de me confitentem, et ipsa in eis credit mihi*" (*Conf.* 10.3.4).

66   *Conf.* 10.4.5.

67 *"Hic est fructus confessionum mearum, non qualis fuerim, sed qualis sim, ut hoc confitear non coram te secreta exsultatione "cum tremore" et secreto maerore cum spe, sed etiam in auribus credentium filiorum hominum, sociorum gaudii mei et consortium mortalitatis meae, et comitum vitae meae. Hi sunt servi tui, fratres mei, quos filious tuos esse voluisti, dominos meos, quibus iussisti ut serviam, si volo tecum de te vivere. Et hoc mihi Verbum tuum parum erat si loquendo praeciperet, nisi et faciendo praeiret. Et ego id ago factis et dictis, id ago sub alis tuis nimis cum ingenti periculo, nisi quia sub alis tuis tibi subdita est pater meus et idoneus est mihi tutor meus . . . Indicabo ergo talibus, qualibus iubes ut serviam, non quis fuerim, sed quis iam sim et quis adhuc sim; 'sed neque me ipsum diiudico'* (1 Cor.4:3). *Sic itaque audiar"* (*Conf.* 10.4.6).

68 Regarding Augustine and the Patristic tradition of *exercitatio* see *"Exercitatio"* in *History of Theology, I, The Patristic Period* (eds. Angelo Di Berardino and Basil Studer; trans. Matthew J.O'Connell; Collegeville: The Liturgical Press, 1996) 7-8; Lewis Ayres, "The Christological Context of Augustine's *De trinitate* XIII: Toward Relocating Books VII-XV," *Augustinian Studies* 29 (1998) 111-39, esp. 113-18; Frederick van Fleteren, "Ascent of the Soul," in *Augustine through the Ages: An Encyclopedia* (General Editor, Allan D. Fitzgerald, O.S.A.; Grand Rapids, Michigan: William B. Eerdmans Publishing Company, 1999) 63-67.

69 *Conf.* 10.3.3.

70 *Conf.* 1.17.27.

71 *Conf.* 3.12.21.

72 *"...cotidiana sermocinandi exercitatio"* (*Conf.* 5.6.11).

73 *Conf.* 6.5.8.

74 *Conf.* 9.5.13.

75 *Conf.* 13.11.12.

76 Hadot, *Philosophy as a Way of Life*, 105. To this it may be added that the apparent obscurity of ancient texts was often viewed as a specific invitation to "strain" and "stretch" oneself in order to go more deeply into the text.

77 One critique of Hadot's thesis is that he exaggerates the notion of *exercitatio* at the expense of *doctrina*. Augustine's narrative shows how both can be intimately complementary: see Antonaccio, "Contemporary Forms of *Askesis* and the Return of Spiritual Exercises,"esp. 76-78.

78 See *Conf.* 11.9.11.

79 *"...bonus et solus magister,"* *Conf.* 11.8.10; see also 9.9.21; 10.31.46; 12.18.27; etc.

80 *"Et quaerebam viam comparandi roboris, quod esset idoneum ad fruendum te, nec inveniebam, donec amplecterer "mediatorem Dei et hominum, hominem Christum Iesum, qui est super omnia Deus benedictus in saecula"* (1 Tm. 1:5), *vocantem, et dicentem: "Ego sum via, veritas et vita" (Jn.* 14:7), *et cibum, cui capiendo invalidus eram, miscentem carnii, quoniam "verbum caro factum est" (Jn.* 1:14), *ut infantiae nostrae lactesceret sapientia tua, per quam creasti omnia. Non enim tenebam Deum meum Iesum humilis humilem, nec cuius veritas, superioribus creaturae tuae partibus supereminens subditos erigit ad se ipsam, in inferioribus autem, aedificavit sibi humilem domum de limo nostro per quam subdendos deprimeret a se ipsis et ad se traiceret, sanans tumorem et nutriens amorem, ne fiducia sui progrederentur longius, sed potius infirmarentur videntes ante pedes suos infirmam divinitatem ex participatione tunicae pelliciae nostrae et lassi prosternerentur in eam, illa autem surgens levaret eos"* Conf. 7.18.24.

81   *Conf.* 7.19.25.
82   See *Conf.* 5.5.9; 6.4.5, 5.7; 7.19.25; 12.22.31; 13.25.38.
83   This is not the place to explore the centrality of Christ in the thought of Augustine. It is
      my intention to argue elsewhere for the Christocentric intentions that provide unity to
      the seemingly unwieldy thought of Augustine.
84   There continues to be great interest in Augustine the rhetor, a topic that cannot be
      explored here.
85   *Conf.* 9.4.7: "*frater cordis mei.*" This is precisely the journey of Alypius, who began as
      "student" but became "heart brother" and "friend."
86   *Conf.* 9.3.6.
87   See esp. *Conf.* 6.7.11ff., where the narrative shifts to Alypius' "learnings."
88   *Conf.* 10.6.8.
89   " . . . *Quid in tali animante non mirabile atque laudabile? At ista omnia Dei mei dona
      sunt, non mihi ego dedi haec: et bona sunt et haec omnia ego. Bonus ergo est qui fecit
      me, et ipse est bonum meum et illi exsulto bonis omnibus, quibus etiam puer eram. Hoc
      enim peccabam, quod non ipso, sed in creaturis eius, me atque ceteris, voluptates,
      sublimitates, veritates quaerebam, atque ita irruebam in dolores, confusiones, errores.
      Gratias tibi, dulcedo mea et honor meus et ficudia mea. Deus meus, gratias tibi de donis
      tuis; sed tu mihi ea serva. Ita enim servabis me, et eugebuntur et perficiuntur quae
      dedisti mihi, et ero ipse tecum, quia et ut sim tu dedisti mihi*" (*Conf.* 1.20.31).
90   "*Quis exaperit istam tortuossimam et implicatissimam nodositatem? Foeda est; nolo in
      eam intendere, nolo eam videre. Te volo, iustitia et innocentia, pulchra et decora
      honestis luminibus et insatiabili satietate. Quies est apud te valde et vita
      imperturbabilis. Qui intrat in te, intrat "in gaudium domini sui" (Mt. 25:21) et non
      timebit et habebit se optime in optimo. Defluxi abs te ego et erravi, Deus meus, nimis
      devius ab statilitate tua in adulescentia et factum sum mihi regio egestatis*" (*Conf.*
      2.10.18).
91   "*O Domine Deus noster, in "velamento alarum tuarum" speremus, et "protege" nos et
      porta nos* (cf. *Ps.* 62.8). *Tu portabis, tu portabis et parvulos et "usque ad canos"* (*Is.*
      46.4) *tu portabis, quoniam firmitas nostra quando tu es, tunc est firmitas, cum autem
      nostra est, infirmitas est. Vivit apud te semper bonum nostrum, et quia inde aversi
      sumus, perversi sumus. Revertamur iam, Domine, ut non evertamur, quia vivit apud te
      sine ullo defectu bonum nostrum, quod tu ipse es, et non timemus, ne non sit quo
      redeamus, quia nos inde ruimus; nobis autem absentibus non ruit domus nostra,
      aeternitas tua*" (*Conf.* 4.16.31).
92   "*Nos itaque ista quae fecisti videmus, quia sunt, tu autem quia vides ea, sunt. Et nos
      foris videmus quia sunt, et intus quia bona sunt: tu autem ibi vidisti facta, ubi vidisti
      facienda. Et nos alio tempore moti sumus ad bene faciendum, posteaquam concepit de
      spirituo cor nostrum; priore autem tempore ad male faciendum movebamur deserentes
      te: tu vero. Deus une bone, nunquam cessasti benefacere. Et sunt quaedam bona opera
      nostra ex munere quidem tuo, sed non sempiterna: post illa nos requieturos in tua
      grandi sanctificatione speramus. Tu autem, bonum nullo indigens bono, semper quietus
      es, quoniam tua quies tu ipse es. Et hoc intellegere quis hominum dabit homini? Quis
      angelus angelo? Quis angelus homini? A te petatur, in te quaeratur, ad te pulsetur: sic,
      sic accipietur, sic invenietur, sic aperietur* (see *Mt.* 7:7-8)" (*Conf.* 13.38.53).

93   The importance of the Matthean theme for Augustine cannot be overemphasized. One final dimension of these "exercises" is to be found in the final three books of the work, an aspect of the *Confessions* that has stymied and puzzled commentators finding them to be "out of line" with the first ten books. However, from the start the *Confessions* have been concerned about "reading."

94   This is seen in his persistent attention to *sapientia* and its identification as *vita*. At the same time he presents a complete description that makes clear the comprehensiveness of this *philosophia*: the *Confessions* has its metaphysics, theodicy, epistemology, cosmology, ethics, dialectics, and even rhetoric. See Henri-Irénée. *Saint Augustin et La Fin de la Culture Antique* (Paris: E. De Boccard, Éditeur, 1938, 1949) for a thorough exploration of Augustine's understanding of and approach to this "*studium sapientiae*."

95   See e.g. *Conf.* 1.1, 13, 17; 3.6; 4.12; 7.1; 10.6, 17, 28.

96   *Conf.* 10.26.37.

97   With God as *the* dialogue partner: "*tu me alloquere, tu mihi sermocinare*" (*Conf.* 12.10.10). It is precisely because God speaks to the heart of Augustine that he himself can authentically speak to others: "*ideo loquor*" (*Conf.* 10.1.1; cf. 11.22.25); "*ergo ut verum loquar, de tuo loquor*," over and against "*qui loquitur mendacium, de suo loquitur*" (*Conf.* 13.25.38; cf. 12.25.34).

98   Augustine mobilizes all his rhetorical forces and talents to exhort, move, and persuade in this regard: "*moriar, ne moriar*" (*Conf.* 1.5.5); "*in istam dico vitam mortalem an mortem vitalem*" (*Conf.* 1.6.7); "*obsudueram stridore catenae mortalitatis meae*" (*Conf.* 2.2.2); "*et occidis nos [Domine], ne moriamur abs te*" (*Conf.* 2.2.4); "*o putredo, o monstrum vitae et mortis profunditas*" (*Conf.* 2.6.14); "*mirabar enim ceteros mortales vivere, quia ille, quem quasi non moriturum dilexeram, mortuus erat, et me magis, quia ille alter eram, vivere illo mortuo mirabar*" (*Conf.* 4.6.11); "*vita morientium mors viventium*" (*Conf.* 4.9.14); "*beatam vitam quaeritis in regione mortis: non est illic*" (*Conf.* 4.12.18); "*haesitans mori morti et vitae vivere*" (*Conf.* 8.11.25); etc. The death/life antithesis is exploited to its fullest possible conceptual and rhetorical limits here.

99   Augustine reads Virgil, Aristotle, Cicero, the Manichaean tomes, the Academicians, and the Platonists; he tries to read the scriptures, but tosses them aside. Yet by the end of the work, *all* he reads is Scripture.

100 "*Quam ego miser eram et quomodo egisti, ut sentirem miseriam meam die illo, quo, cum pararem recitare imperatori laudes, quibus plura mentirer, et mentienti faveretur ab scientibus . . .*" (*Conf.* 6.6.9).

101 In this regard, see the analysis of *enkrateia* by Stanley K. Stowers, *A Rereading of Romans: Justice, Jews, and Gentiles* (New Haven: Yale University Press, 1994) esp. 44-46, 58-74. Despite modern exegetical disassociation from Augustine's reading of *Romans*, Stower's study of Paul and the notion of *enkrateia* suggests that at least on some levels Augustine did read Paul correctly. See also Hadot, *Philosophy as a Way of Life*, 59, 86, 135.

102 Hadot, *Philosophy as a Way of Life*, 100.

103 *Conf.* 11.8.10.

104 *Conf.* 9.9.21.

105 *Pers.* 53.

106 *Conf.* 12.10.10.

107 *Conf.* 4.1.1.

108 In this regard see the perceptive comments of David Tracy in his "Tradition of Spiritual Practice and the Practice of Theology," *Theology Today* 55 (1998) 235-41. Drawing upon Hadot's work he notes the "crisis of form" in contemporary theological education, a concern that perhaps could be extended beyond the classrooms of theology.

109 Hadot, *Philosophy as a Way of Life*, 109.

110 *"Non dubia, sed certa conscientia, Domine, amo te. Percussisti cor meum verbo tuo, et amavi te" (Conf.* 10.6.8).

PART II
EDUCATION IN AUGUSTINE'S OTHER WORKS

Chapter Four

Study as Love: Augustinian Vision and Catholic Education

Phillip Cary

Introduction

As a Protestant contributing to the self-understanding of a Roman Catholic University, I was struck by the tendency of Catholics and Protestants to suspect one another of authoritarianism, though for different reasons. Protestants have historically accused Catholics of adding extraneous authorities to the scriptural Word of God,[1] while Catholics often see in the Protestant doctrine of "Scripture alone" a kind of epistemological authoritarianism, which places all hope of knowledge in the authority of Scriptural revelation and none in the power of human reason. In this essay my interest is to identify that feature of Roman Catholic thought, not present in Protestantism, which makes this Catholic suspicion possible, and to explore its problems and pedagogical implications. That feature, I suggest, is a specifically Augustinian conception of *reason* which has largely dropped out of Protestant thought, and which has moreover in recent centuries become problematic (and therefore highly interesting) in Roman Catholic thought. This conception originates in Augustine's distinctive version of Christian Platonism, which is deeply indebted to the philosophy of education depicted in Plato's Allegory of the Cave. My interest in it stems from the fact that it illuminates my own practice as a teacher of the humanities, even though (in concert with both Protestant and Catholic theology) I cannot accept the robustly Platonist epistemology which Augustine sees as its foundation.

The Catholic commitment to *faith and reason* as "the two wings by which the human spirit rises to the contemplation of truth"[2] means that Catholic theology necessarily has implications for pedagogy and theories of education. The Protestant insistence on *faith alone*, on the other hand, is narrowly theological in its commitments and thus leaves open many questions about the role of reason in other areas of human life. For Protestantism reason is not to be relied on for saving knowledge of God, but that hardly means it has no role in education. It is just that Protestant theology *per se* has little to say about that role, in contrast to Catholic theology, which (quite plainly in the teaching of John Paul II) does have implications for the nature and practice of education. Hence there is nothing inconsistent about Protestants learning a thing or two from Catholic theories of education. Nor are Protestants much different from Catholics in finding problems with the Platonist foundations that Augustine originally tried to place under this account of reason. Hence the inquiry I am entering into here is one in which Protestant and Catholic may share. In tracing the origin, problems and pedagogical possibilities of this particular feature of Catholic thought, I am hoping to continue my contributions to the self-understanding of a Catholic university, and thus make some return for a multitude of favors Protestants like myself have received from Catholics, most prominent of which is John Paul II's exposition of a living Augustinianism for the 3rd millennium.

Reason and Authority

I have perhaps already said enough positive things about religious authorities to be suspected of authoritarianism, so that is the first issue to address. To begin with, the concept of authority I am concerned with is Augustinian, which means it is pedagogical rather than political. In Augustine's usage authority (*auctoritas*) belongs to teachers, not to kings. Political rulers are not said to have authority, but rather power or sovereignty (*potestas* or *imperium*). The root sense of Augustine's usage of the term "authority" is that in which a grammarian, for example, speaks with authority on matters of grammar.[3] In just this sense, Augustine believes, the teachers of the Church have authority: what they teach about Christ should be believed, as grammar students should believe the teaching of the grammarian. Hence for Augustine and the medieval tradition after him the authority of the Church is the authority of its teachers, the bishops and their predecessors the apostles and prophets (whose teaching is found in the Scriptures) and ultimately the authority of Christ himself, that teacher whose name is Truth.[4] In the middle ages this basic pedagogical sense of the word was extended to embrace the texts which contain the teachings — hence the "authorities" to which medieval writers so frequently appeal. But the great expansion of usage by which political power came to be called by the name "authority" seems not to have occurred until the Enlightenment, perhaps as the result of the critique of authority which was at the epistemological heart of that epochal movement of Western culture.

For the Enlightenment, authority is suspect because it is not reason — or, more precisely, because it means submitting to the reason of another rather than developing one's own.[5] In this suspicion it was adopting an Augustinian contrast and re-valuing it. For it was Augustine who taught the West to think in terms of the contrast between authority and reason, which is closely linked to his epochal contrast between faith and understanding.[6] In Augustinian thought up to the Reformation, faith is always belief in what some authority teaches,[7] while understanding is the exercise of reason by which the mind sees the truth for itself. The two terms are not merely contrasted but dynamically related, as the pedagogical function of authority is precisely to help one come to understand the truth by one's own reason.[8] The dynamic can be illustrated by the process that occurs in a math class: students typically begin by accepting formulas and theses on the authority of their teacher (e.g. copying down the Pythagorean formula and memorizing it) believing that these words and symbols are correct even though they do not at first see how. But of course the good teacher's goal is not for students to regurgitate the formula on demand but rather to understand for themselves what it means, or to "see it" with the eye of their own mind as Augustine would say. Thus faith comes first (we begin by believing what we are taught) but the end is understanding (seeing for ourselves). This pedagogical function of authority is what Augustine has in mind when he insists that "unless you believe, you shall not understand."[9] Our goal is to see God with our own mind's eye, but the road to that destination is long; we have a lot to learn and many obstacles to overcome both within and without, and we must begin by believing what the Church teaches about Christ. In terms of the authority/reason contrast, this means that "authority is first in time, but reason is first in reality."[10] That is to say: reason is primary, because understanding is what all education is about, but faith in what we are taught is the starting point of the journey.

This basic pedagogical view of authority is presupposed by Immanuel Kant in his classic essay, "What is Enlightenment?" Kant defines enlightenment in terms of the transition from the status of a minor under tutelage of a teacher to the status of an adult who thinks for himself — a transition, in Augustinian terms, from authority to reason. Thus in one sense Kant's definition of Enlightenment simply states what every Augustinian believes is the goal of education. But in making enlightenment a cultural program rather than just a pedagogical goal, Kant contributed to the political extension of the meaning of "authority." Kant's social critique implies that there are cultural powers that oppose enlightenment, behaving like bad teachers who want their students to memorize formulas rather than understand them — institutions which oppress the citizen by trying to keep him in a state of tutelage like a minor, incapable of thinking for himself. Hence from the standpoint of the Enlightenment as a social program, "authority" comes to designate that which blocks or supplants understanding rather than a pedagogical aid to it — and thus the word acquires the negative connotation which is endemic to modern usage but absent from Augustinian and medieval usage.

Not just the word, but the thing itself is under suspicion. In America (whose culture is in so many ways the child of the Enlightenment) the dictum that "no one can tell me what to believe" is presented as the expression of something like an inalienable right. One can imagine the trouble this must cause an institution which assigns its clergy the duty of teaching people what to believe. Indeed one need not imagine, but only go to church and see. While the Roman Catholic magisterium continues to hold the line on this point (despite widespread disaffection within the ranks of American Catholics), mainline Protestantism in America in the past century has to a large extent given up the assignment — its clergy typically avoid teaching people what to believe, because this would be offensive to their congregation, and mainline Protestant clergy are justly famed for their inoffensiveness. (This, I take it, is why a distinctively Protestant theology now exists in America only in the orbit of the evangelical churches.)[11] The difference is related to the distinctive feature of Roman Catholic thought that so interests me. For the classic Protestant insistence on "faith alone" implies, when seen in its Augustinian context, a profound dependence on *authority alone*.[12] Protestants must believe what they are taught on the authority of Scripture or they believe nothing much at all, and in a culture which inculcates suspicion of all religious authority (including that of the Bible) this means the dissolution of Protestantism.

My interest is in the shape of the Catholic alternative to the Protestant dependance on "authority alone." But first allow me to explicate this description of Protestantism, which American Protestants are apt to find offensive and American Catholics damning — both as a result of shared Enlightenment assumptions, I would argue. To put the point briefly and in its most favorable light: Protestant theology is dependent on authority alone because it conceives of God as a person. For persons have the authority to speak for themselves — to give themselves to be known by saying who they are. Trying to get around this authority by ignoring what other persons have to say for themselves means disrespect for their personhood and thus precludes knowing them as persons.[13] Therefore knowing other persons is quite different from understanding mathematics: believing what another person has to say is an ultimate form of knowledge in the one case but not the other. Hence the Protestant insistence that we know God by believing what the Word of God teaches — by faith alone, based on the authority of Scripture alone — assumes a quite different epistemology than the Platonist pedagogy underlying Augustine's account of reason and understanding.[14] The knowledge of God is based on hearing what God has to say for himself, not seeing him with the mind's eye in a vision of eternal Truth. It is that concept of vision (and its implications for pedagogy and ethics) which has dropped out of Protestant thought, and which I am interested in understanding in this essay.

The Un-Catholic Augustine

Augustine believes that to understand is to see the truth, and that Truth is God.[15] Hence eternal life, which is happiness,[16] consists in that fullness of understanding which the later Augustinian tradition calls "beatific vision," that seeing of God which makes us eternally happy. What the soul most deeply wants is to see God: that is why "our hearts are restless until they find rest in Thee."[17] Our restlessness is a function of our distance from God, which is a function of how far we are from seeing him, which is in turn a result of sin, our failure to love God with all our hearts. Hence education and ethics are concerned with the same fundamental problem, our failure to love Truth, which is our failure to love God. This failure is the central problem of Augustine's soul, which drives the narrative of the *Confessions*.

If the mind is an eye whose nature is to see Truth, this is because Plato's Allegory of the Cave is fundamentally correct about who we are. The Allegory is about education, Plato tells us,[18] and the moral of the story is the primacy of reason over authority. The Sophist teachers who propose to put knowledge into their students' heads do not know what they are doing, for the power of knowledge is already in us, and those who want to attain real knowledge must learn to see for themselves.[19] The metaphorical apparatus which Plato uses to make this point reappears in Augustine's epistemology: understanding as seeing (the metaphor of intellectual *vision*),[20] the turn or conversion from darkness to light,[21] the ascent from sensible things to intelligible things,[22] the First Principle as the shining Sun, the dazzlement of the mind's eye when it first tries to contemplate that Sun,[23] the gradual training of the mind's eye to look first at shadows and reflections and then at illuminated Forms and finally at the Sun, the source of light itself,[24] which Plato calls the Good and which Augustine in addition calls Truth and God.[25] A further piece of the picture is added when Plato in another dialogue describes the motive of this ascent as love,[26] a point which Augustine eagerly accepts and interprets in light of the Biblical command of charity, to love God with one's whole heart, soul, mind and strength.[27]

One crucial difference between Augustine's epistemology and the Allegory of the Cave is that Augustine locates the illuminated Forms or Platonic Ideas *within* the Sun. For Augustine argues that Platonic Forms or Ideas, being eternal and unchanging, can be located nowhere else but in God, who is the only eternal, essentially unchangeable substance.[28] Hence Augustine can speak of Platonic Forms as Ideas in the divine Mind (following Plotinus) or, more characteristically, of God as "the unchangeable Truth which contains all that is unchangeably true."[29] Since all that is *in* God *is* God,[30] this means that every time we see an unchanging truth we see God. Our minds thus constantly catch glimpses of God without realizing it. Whenever we make judgements by an unchanging standard of truth we enjoy the light of Truth itself, not in the fullness and clarity of beatific vision, but in a fragmentary and transitory anticipation of it, "seeing through a glass darkly."[31] To see why Augustine might think this, imagine yourself in a math class, having the insight which moves you from believing in authority to understanding for yourself. One moment you are poring over a formula and scratching your head, mumbling, "I don't get it," and the next moment you look up and say, "Aha! now I see it!" This is a moment of pure intellectual joy, quite unlike the joys of the flesh, it is clean and clear and unencumbered by things of this earth. Now imagine — if you can — that this moment could last forever, embracing not merely one mathematical truth, but the whole of mathematical Truth together with all the unchanging truths which give form to this changing world, all caught up and united in one comprehensive, simple Truth. That is beatific vision.

Augustine is surely wrong about this, and neither Catholics nor Protestants can accept his Platonism in quite this full-blooded form. In Catholic terms, the problem is that Augustine assumes beatific vision is the natural fulfillment of the human intellect.[32] Unless we bring extraneous complications to our interpretation of Augustine, we are faced with the fact that in his conception of reason, the function of reason is to see truth, and Truth is God. Most Catholic Augustine scholars, motivated I think by an honorable filial piety,[33] are committed to denying that Augustine holds this view, and therefore they must bring extraneous complications to their interpretation of Augustine in order to make his thought safe for Catholicism. But this also makes it less interesting, less challenging and powerful than it actually is. As with many other great figures of the Christian past, the unacceptable Augustine is the more powerful Augustine, the one from whom we have the most to learn.

My challenge to those who want to make Augustine a good Catholic on this score is to find any place where he blames the mind's failure to understand God on its natural limitations rather than on some sinful defect in human nature. The distance separating Augustine from God in the *Confessions*, for instance, is always portrayed as resulting from disordered love.[34] For Augustine only sin separates us from God.[35] Therefore, once our soul is restored to its natural health, no longer weakened and corrupted by sin, it will do what it was made for: it will understand and enjoy God. Of course the restoration of human nature is impossible without grace, which is like medicine for the diseased eye of our mind, strengthening it to endure the brilliant splendor of God's glory. But Augustine's account of nature and grace omits the Thomistic keynote of a supernatural elevation of the soul necessary to transcend its inherent natural limitations.[36]

The reason for this omission is clear when we realize that Augustine's Platonism leaves no room for what Thomas calls "intelligible species." For Augustine, as I have argued, the intelligible things seen by the human intellect are unchanging Forms existing in God's Mind and thus identical with God's essence. For Thomas, on the other hand, there are such things as created forms, intelligible and unchanging yet "embodied" (as Aristotle taught) in changing material. These "intelligible species" — unchanging forms which are not God — are the natural object of the human intellect.[37] Having no place for such things in his Platonist ontology, Augustine has no object for the mind's eye to see but God. It is as if to say, everything we see is Light. When the light shines in our eyes we may learn much about other things (the things God has created, using the Forms in his mind as a kind of blueprint), but all real understanding of those things comes from seeing the light that made them, as all understanding of the properties of a triangle drawn on a chalk board is really understanding of unchanging and intelligible truths which are not made of chalk and will never be erased.

Even the Catholic scholars who wish to rescue Augustine from such an interpretation admit that this is the most straightforward reading of his many references to God as the light of the mind.[38] Hence the feature of Catholic thought I am concerned with in this essay — the Augustinian conception of reason which provides an alternative to Protestant dependence on "authority alone" — is itself a problematic feature of the Catholic tradition. The project of reviving it has run aground in various ways, from the 19th century "ontologists"[39] to De Lubac's attempt in the middle of the 20th century to find an alternative to the "extrinsicism" of the neo-Thomist concept of the supernatural (the view that the supernatural order of grace has very little to do with the natural experience of human life).[40] The ultimate settlement of this painfully contested issue in 20th century Catholic theology has been basically the following. On the one hand, the vision of God is not natural to the human mind but a supernatural gift. On the other hand, the *desire* for this vision is intrinsic to the human mind, a graced aspect of our very being from the beginning.[41] It is this second point that has received most extensive development in Roman Catholic theology since Vatican II, and it has recently been incorporated into the magisterial teaching of the Roman Church in an emphatic and unmistakable way by John Paul II.[42]

If I am correct in my (drastically abbreviated) summary of this history,[43] then Catholic educators are faced with an interesting problem. On the one hand, they are instructed in no uncertain terms to view the desire to see divine Truth as the central thread of education.[44] On the other hand, the most natural philosophical foundation for this view, which is Augustine's Platonist concept of reason as the human mind's natural capacity to see divine Truth, is off limits. Hence the Catholic alternative to Protestant "authoritarianism," as I have described it, is deeply problematic to Catholics themselves, yet they are instructed, by the highest authority, to work out this conception of reason and relate it to their practice of education.[45] The pope has, in effect, presented Catholic educators with a difficult and perhaps very fruitful problem, which he plainly hopes will be an open field for patient and joyful research.[46] Framed in terms of Augustine scholarship, the problem is: how can we use Augustine's pedagogical insights about the centrality of the love of truth without accepting his Platonist epistemological foundations? It is a good problem for Protestants too — one of John Paul's many gifts to the whole Christian world.

The reason for thinking this problem might be fruitful can be brought out by contrast with the dominant form of educational theory in America today, which I shall call "the discourse of the educationists." By this I mean the kind of theorizing and advice which comes to us college teachers from graduate programs granting degrees in a subject called "higher education." My experience with this discourse is entirely practical rather than theoretical, for I have no stomach to read the stuff. But surely no one involved in discussions of curriculum or strategic planning in an American university or college can be unfamiliar with it. It is basically a sociological discourse supplemented by cognitive psychology. In the tradition of American sociology, it is deeply conformist: analyses of contemporary American society are used to ground policy recommendations about how to adjust to social realities rather than change them. Hence college teachers are instructed about the mindset of Generation X or their net-using successors and admonished about how to meet their needs — all in the interest, of course, of meeting larger social needs.

The discourse proceeds with no reference to the life of the mind or the love of truth, much less to any moral defects which might impede them. In short, it operates in ignorance of the central concerns of Western philosophy of education from Plato to Augustine and on to John Paul II.

The center of these central concerns is love of truth, which makes the connection between education and human happiness. In the classical philosophic view of education represented by Augustine, liberal education (the learning appropriate to a free person rather than a slave) forms human character by strengthening it with the virtues necessary for the pursuit of truth, which is the pursuit of happiness. Thus any pedagogy not based on the students' innate love of truth is not liberal education but training for servants — nowadays we call it "job training." In one of the predictable ironies of human life, job training is not suitable preparation for a good job. Employers recognize this in practice, as they typically seek out graduates of elite universities, which do not provide much in the way of job training. Most companies typically offer their own on-the-job training, and are looking for something else from the universities, something quite different from what careerist undergraduates look for. These undergraduates and the educationists who wish to meet their needs insist on "practical" job preparation, while the employers want smart and capable people who are good at problem-solving and thinking for themselves. It's enough to convince a philosopher that the business world really is in closer touch with reality than the educational world.

Augustine's philosophy of education and its classical cousins should not be confused with any variant of the discourse of the educationists such as "values education." The latter assumes a dichotomy between fact and value that is wholly alien to classical thought, which knew only of truth, not "fact."[47] Truth is not value-neutral, but the highest value, the Good of the Intellect, to lose which is ultimate misery.[48] Indeed it is too pale to say Truth is valuable: it is lovely, beautiful, delightful. As Cicero puts it, in phrasing that is more Augustinian than Augustine, "there is nothing sweeter to the human mind than the light of truth."[49] This is what the discourse of the educationists cannot say. It can defend the value of education, but it persistently misses the point, as in a recent essay contest that invited undergraduates to answer the question, "Is knowledge useful?" Speaking strictly from the point of view of classical philosophy, it is not, except incidentally. Knowledge, like wisdom and truth, belongs in the realm of the beautiful and the happy rather than the useful, for it is an end in itself rather than a means — something we seek for its own sweet sake rather than to use in getting something else. That it is also useful is no accident, but beside the point. Like happiness, it might be useful for getting jobs (wouldn't most employers rather have happy employees?), but only a fool would seek it for that reason.[50]

Ethical Implications: Study as Love

In his treatise *On the Trinity*, Augustine treats study as a form of love, the desire to learn what one does not yet know.[51] He illustrates this by a long analysis of the central activity of the humanities — interpretation, the search for the meaning of words. Interpretation, especially of the Scriptures, is a central topic of his influential treatise *On Christian Doctrine* (written about the same time as the *Confessions)*, but he developed the foundations of his theory of interpretation more than a decade before, in the context of his early proposal for a program of education in the liberal arts.[52] The basic idea is that the inquiring mind desires to pass from (sensible) words to (intelligible) things, and this desire is nothing other than the love of truth. This is why the mind loves problems of interpretation (e.g. obscure passages in the Scriptures), for in moving from problem to solution — from initial puzzlement to final insight — the love of truth is put to work, exercised and strengthened in the most delightful way.[53] This is Augustine's theoretical conviction, and we can see it in practice in countless sermons and exegeses, where his mind is attracted to the cruxes and puzzles rather than to the obvious passages.[54] He wrestles difficult texts with a kind of joy and abandon, like an experienced mathematician who knows that if she just turns this one formula over in her mind long enough, a world of insight is bound to open up to view.

Teaching too is love, though of a different kind.[55] While study is love of truth, and therefore falls under the first and greatest commandment ("You shall love the Lord your God..."), teaching demands love of another human being, and therefore falls under the second great commandment ("Love your neighbor as yourself"). To put teaching and learning in the category of love is, for Augustine, to put it in the realm of ethics — for Augustinian ethics is, famously, an ethics of love, based on an exegesis of these two commandments. This means that the guiding principles of Augustinian pedagogy are no different from the guiding principles of Augustinian ethics. Here I would dwell on three such principles or rather virtues: purity, humility, and charity. These concern the right ordering of love regarding (respectively) external things, ourselves, and God. A contemporary educational practice grounded in the cultivation of these virtues is problematic in theory and would be highly controversial if institutionalized, which of course is why I am particularly interested in them.

Purity

In his most dualistic moments, Plato identifies purity as the basis of the moral virtues.[56] Purity means separating the soul from the body — cleansing it from the taint of the body, as Augustine once put it.[57] The pure soul is practicing for death, when the soul will be wholly separated from the body and thus have the opportunity to go to a better world, the realm of Platonic Forms where it belongs.[58] This means it has no desire for the things of this earth, and thus no motive for intemperance, cowardice or injustice.

No one believes this dualist style of moralism anymore, and no Augustine scholar wants to stress the degree to which Augustine shares it.[59] Hence a serious look at both the problems and possibilities of Augustinian purity must acknowledge the extent to which, for Augustine, turning to God does mean turning away from the body. This is perhaps clearest at the beginning of *Confessions*, book 7, where Augustine is explaining why, before his encounter with Platonist philosophy, he did not understand the nature of God. Having no notion of intelligible being, his mind ranged over sensible beings, and he tried to make images of God out of them. He desperately wished to escape his phantasms, the sensory images in his mind, but as he could imagine no alternative to them, they kept returning to the eye of his mind like a cloud of gnats one tries to wave away from one's face.[60] Judging by *Confessions* 7, the "turning [*conversio*] to the phantasms," which for Aristotle and Aquinas is a necessary stage in all human knowledge,[61] is for Augustine a consequence of human fallenness, for it leads away from God and immerses us instead in sensible things. Platonism teaches Augustine to turn away from such external matters and turn toward the human mind itself, which is the true image of God.[62] There he finds a power of judgment which allows him to ascend above sensible images, for it judges them by a higher standard, the light of unchanging Truth.[63]

Let us set aside our prejudices against dualism for a moment and examine this connection between critical judgment and purity. Of all the cultures in the history of the world, surely we in America at the onset of the third millennium have the most reason to be critical of sensible images. A vast and sophisticated technology of manipulation floods our minds with them every day. The problem with sensible images, as any Platonist will tell you, stems from their power to engage our affections — to excite both pain and pleasure, and therefore instill both fear and desire. This of course is why advertisers put so much money into producing them. They can teach us to desire, and therefore to buy. Such teaching has no need for truth: we hear the upbeat music, see the young bodies on the screen dancing and playing volleyball on the beach, and cannot forget the words, "The Pepsi generation! Drink it in! Drink it in!" The commercial makes no claims to truth, and thus runs no risk of false advertising. It simply presents a memorable image linking Pepsi, youthful beauty, and a good time. And of course it is made more memorable by incessant repetition. Thus name recognition is created and sustained and linked with images of pleasure, so that we are more likely to buy Pepsi the next time we have a chance. The whole process is designed to work without ever triggering anything like critical judgment or the pursuit of truth. The last thing the advertisers want us to do is start asking questions like "*Should* I buy a Pepsi?" or "*Is it true* that Pepsi is the best thing to drink now?" And so it goes with our political campaigns, our religious institutions and our education, all of which aim increasingly to please the consumer rather than to raise awkward questions about what is really true.

Sensible images are fun, but critical judgment is hard work. It is also often boring, especially when encountered in the discourse of others. Watching a Pepsi commercial goes down much easier than reading a critical analysis of it. Our students are quick to contrast "being analytical" with "being emotional," and they know which one they like. By and large, they have little firsthand experience with the search for truth, without which critical analysis has no point. Thus boredom may be a sign that a media-fed mind has been temporarily released from the power of images and now does not know what to do with itself. For instance, serious political analysis, in comparison to political commercials, is boring. One engages in it either because one wants to find out the truth about some aspect of contemporary politics, or because one is assigned to do it in school. The real educational value of the latter lies in the possibility that it might slip over into the former — as when a beginning piano student, trudging through her finger-exercises, suddenly begins to make music.

In a fallen world truth may be an acquired taste, as Mozart is for someone raised on contemporary pop: you don't know what you're missing until you've acquired the skill to enjoy it. Education means acquiring the skill to enjoy truth, which is why it demands a certain degree of purity — of separation from the swirl of sensible images designed to attract our attention and desire. The practice of this purity is a discipline, an *ascesis* of turning away from pleasure, which depends on gestures as simple as turning off the TV in order to do one's homework. I have not yet convinced my son of the importance of this particular gesture, though I am working on it, and I am willing to impose it upon him. Yet the aim of the discipline is not renunciation but freedom, as when a prisoner reads law books in his cell, escaping from the noise and allure of the TV sets which are placed nearly everywhere in US prisons. The Platonist virtue of purity is above all the reclaiming and mastery of one's own attention, freeing it to love truth rather than appearances. An ethic of purity in higher education would emphasize the value of students learning to be quiet and alone — the way one is when immersed in a good book, rather than engaged by the latest in innovative multimedia technology.

What Plato is wrong about is the extent to which truth is present in the sensible world.[64] Such is the brunt of Aristotle's criticism, which is directed fundamentally against the separation between Form and matter in Plato's doctrine of Forms,[65] a separation which in turn motivates the separation of soul and body that Plato calls purity. Aristotle's insistence on a turn to the phantasms is grounded in Plato's own awareness that we begin — temporally, at least — with appearances.[66] Augustine registers that same awareness when he ascends through the powers of the soul by exercising critical judgment *upon the deliverances of the senses*.[67] The question is this: how much of the truth of the resulting judgment is dependent on the truth of the images themselves? Here is a long discussion, one of the great exercises of critical judgment in the history of Western philosophy. I only have time to remark that to think critically about the dualistic ethic of purity is itself an exercise of that purity which Plato wished to inculcate. In his criticism of Plato's theory of Forms, Aristotle was not simply recommending a return to the captivity of the cave, a mere uncritical immersion in sensible images. And the fact that Plato backed off from the radical dualism of his middle dialogues to advocate a more "mixed" and "impure" approach to life in his later dialogues[68] may well reflect his response to the critical judgments of his brilliant young student Aristotle.[69] Hence we are in good company if we pursue a less radical version of the virtue of purity, not based on a rejection of bodily things *per se*.

Humility

Christianity has its own reasons for backing off from radical dualism, of course. Most notable is the doctrine that the Word of God himself chose to become flesh — and did not thereby become impure, but rather purified human nature. This has epistemological implications, because it means that the saving truth about God is not something one could have figured out for oneself by the use of one's own reason. The universal and eternal Truth became bound up in a most unanticipated way with historical particulars: an individual human life, born of a Jewish woman and ending on a Roman cross, and then, if one can believe it, raised from the dead on the third day. Thus, for a Christian, the pedagogical priority of authority to reason takes a very particular form: one must believe the apostles' teaching about Christ if one is ever to understand God ("unless you believe, you shall not understand"). This requires humility, as can be seen from the crisis it caused in Augustine's own education.

In the third book of *Confessions*, Augustine describes himself in his student days reading Cicero and then the Bible. The one set him on fire with love of Wisdom, but the other bored him.[70] It was partly a matter of words, the one so eloquent, lofty and moving, the other so awkward and low in its diction, especially in the Old Latin translation Augustine knew. He found himself unable to stoop low enough to go through the door of this lowly text. The point that interests me here is that Augustine finds faith to be something lower than reason, not the source of higher and more glorious insights. Faith requires humility because it means submitting to a lowly authority, a text which any classically-trained rhetorician (or modern Biblical critic) can see at a glance is not well-made.

But the contrast goes deeper than that. The text he liked so much better contained not just Cicero's pretty words, but Aristotle's thought. Cicero's *Hortensius* was modeled on Aristotle's *Protrepticus*,[71] written while Aristotle was still a student in Plato's Academy, in criticism of the rhetorically-based education of the rival school of Isocrates.[72] Aristotle was defending a strictly philosophical and dialectical approach to education, arguing that seeking knowledge for its own sake is not only more noble, but more conducive to happiness than seeking knowledge only for its usefulness. Augustine was thus reading a Latin paraphrase of a great philosophical tract against careerist education, based on a powerful account of the mind's ultimate capacities and desires. This was his introduction to the classic philosophical notion of reason that we have been examining throughout this essay.

It showed him a glimpse of where happiness lay, but it was not sufficient to take him there, for the humility of faith is required before the beatitude of understanding.

It was the humility of faith, Augustine concludes, that the pagan Platonists did not know. In their intellectual pride, they thought of themselves as "the few" who were beyond the need of tutelage by external authority, unlike the "many" who were best led by authority (including the authority of pagan civic religion).[73] They had seen for themselves, and therefore had no need to become like little children learning their first lessons. Anyone can see that children need to be humble under the authority of their schoolmasters, Augustine assumes, but Christianity makes humility a permanent feature of this mortal life — so long as we are still *in via*, on the way to our heavenly home, but not yet arrived.

Humility, therefore, is the virtue that corresponds with authority as purity corresponds with reason. It is a virtue Augustine associates especially with the Incarnation as the remedy for the impurity of our mind's eye,[74] and the Church (Christ's body) as a place of convalescence for all of us, the "many" whose eyes are too weak to see God clearly. Humility is the virtue of *Confessions* 8 as purity is the virtue of *Confessions* 7. For what Augustine learns from the Platonist experience of insight in Book Seven is not only that God is there to be seen with the mind's eye apart from things of the senses, but that his own eyes are not ready to see, too impure, too dazzled by the brightness of the intelligible Sun.[75] Hence if he is ever to catch more than a glimpse of the eternal Light, he must humble himself under the yoke of Christ, and join the "many" who are purified by faith, being of one body with the multitude of unlearned Christians who live by the authority of the Church.[76] Thus the conversion scene of *Confessions* 8 finally brings him down low enough to pass through the lowly door that had stymied him in *Confessions* 3.

Humility is one of the most offensive of Christian virtues to talk about, because in its epistemic or pedagogical sense it requires us to be *docile* — which literally means "teachable," but now of course is a term of abuse. Humility is the virtue of children, of minors — the kind of people who are not ready for Enlightenment and therefore should submit docilely to authority. Yet of such is the kingdom of heaven, on an Augustinian reckoning. Humility is also the common ground upon which Protestant and Catholic hash out their differences. According to Augustine, there is a dynamic leading from authority to reason, by way of humility. In his early writings he calls it *purification by faith*,[77] but later he prefers the Pauline phrase *justification by faith*.[78] The famous dispute between Catholics and Protestants concerns the Protestant insistence on attaching the qualifier *alone* to the later formulation. Do we remain like children believing our teacher's words? Or is there a love which leads us beyond the words to the eternal things they signify?

It is characteristic of Luther to say that he never gets beyond the most childish lessons. He confesses (clearly meaning to set an example for his readers) that he is always going back to his catechism,[79] that most un-Platonic, un-Socratic form of education, where one memorizes answers rather than pursues questions. The catechism is also the original form of mass education in Europe, suitable not for the few who have the leisure for a liberal education, but for the many who need to be told what to think about controverted matters of faith. Like the formulas "faith alone" and "scripture alone," the Protestant catechism is designed to indicate a minimum of what is necessary for salvation, not the whole range of what an inquiring mind might want to know. But on Luther's reckoning we ought to be in no hurry to proceed beyond these humble words, but rather come back to them again and again, repeating them, taking them to heart, singing them like the lyrics of a favorite song that comfort us on a dark night, for Luther is convinced it is enough to hear God's word without seeing Him.

But what are we to do about the desire to see, with all its potential for pride and error, but also its hope of ultimate understanding? Here I think Kierkegaard helps us out by the way he contrasts the teaching of Socrates and of Christ.[80] For according to Platonism (as we have already noticed in the Allegory of the Cave), the capacity to know the truth lies within, and therefore the teacher is "inessential" — merely a midwife to assist at the birth of someone else's thoughts, as Socrates describes himself.[81] But for Christianity the teacher is essential, because the Truth we want to know is our Teacher himself, Christ, who is the Eternal found in time. And that leads to a different understanding of the relation between humility and truth. For in addition to the difference between the teachers, there is a difference in the claims made by their stories.

Both Socrates and Christ would have us begin with humility, a self-critical or repentant moment when we recognize we are in the wrong. And both Platonism and Christianity have a story to tell about how one proceeds from that point to get beyond error and ignorance. When Socrates' difficult questions drive young Meno to epistemic humility and the recognition of his own ignorance, he is disheartened, ready to give up hope of ever finding the truth. But Socrates tries to set him back on the path of inquiry by telling him a story about the soul's ability to recollect things it learned in a previous and better life.[82] This Platonic myth, like the Allegory of the Cave, is not meant to be believed as literal or historical truth; rather it encourages Meno in the hope that the knowledge he now realizes he does not have, may yet be found within his own mind. Christianity too tells an encouraging story to those it humbles, but asks them to take it more literally — as the history of a living man rather than a myth of the soul. Requiring of us the humility to submit our reason to the external authority of this Gospel, this story about Christ, it also offers us hope — for the story is about how the Truth of God came to earth and dwelt among us.[83] The project of Augustinian reason (that power of the human mind whose desire is called study) is to interpret this story, moving from our initial faith in it to an ever deeper understanding of the truth to which it points — a truth which is, in the end, nothing other than the universal Truth which gives being and intelligibility to all truths.[84] It is a movement we can only hope to complete by entering eternal life. Protestant dependence on faith alone, on the other hand, means clinging for dear life to the Gospel story, believing that this is enough, for in clinging to the Gospel of Christ we cling to Christ himself,[85] who is eternal life in person, Truth in the flesh.

Perhaps these two approaches are not ultimately incompatible. But that is another discussion, and a long one.

Charity

"Charity" (*caritas*) in Augustine means rightly-ordered love and all its works, not simply alms-giving. Thus charity is the name for any act by which we willingly obey the twofold command of love for God and neighbor. It is the heart of all the virtues, the essence of Christian ethics, and by and large we are uncomfortable with it. For according to Scripture, Jesus gave clear priority to love of God, which he called "the first and great commandment,"[86] and most of us (along with most of our Catholic students) find it hard to understand why the Christian God should want love for himself to come first. Doesn't the Church teach us to be unselfish, and shouldn't God set the example?

It is only in modernity that "unselfishness" has come to replace the traditional Christian understanding of charity, which seems to its critics far too self-centered or acquisitive.[87] Augustine, on the contrary, assumes that we always try to get what we love, which is why love is the fundamental motivating force in the universe.[88] To love God is to desire union with God, and the reward for such love is to get what you desire. But since God already has perfect union with God, he has nothing further to get. He dwells in complete and eternal happiness, and therefore the only possible motivation for his commanding us to do anything is *our* happiness.[89] Thus love of God comes first not for God's sake but for ours — for in God lies our true happiness. Love of neighbor comes second because it makes no sense apart from an understanding of what makes our neighbor happy. To love our neighbors means to help them find happiness, which means to help them love God.

The pedagogical implication of this is that teachers should care for their studies first and their students second. How else shall they teach the most fundamental thing, which is love of truth? Since teachers teach by example, their most important obligation is to study, to love truth for its own sake, so that their students may learn to do likewise.[90] To this extent every good teacher is a scholar first and a teacher second. This does not mean she must be a "productive" researcher in the careerist sense, but it does mean that teaching will always to some extent pull her away from her first love. And this is where "unselfishness" enters the picture. For the love of truth, being a form of charity, is a gift of God — and God gives gifts not simply for the good of the recipient, but for the good she may do for others. Hence (to put the point in medieval terms) *the contemplative life* is closest to our ultimate goal as human beings, but few people get to live it, for those who are good at it are needed in *the active life*: they must go back and help others who are not so far along the road to truth. This can be illustrated from the teaching career of Augustine.

The most immediate outward effect of Augustine's conversion is that he quit his teaching job in order to devote himself full-time to the scholarly study of philosophy.[91] The crisis leading up to his conversion was in large part driven by his need to have free time for serious thinking and scholarship.[92] (Free time — Latin *otium* — is the equivalent of Greek *schole*, whence our word *scholarship*.) Having found the moral courage to give up his rising expectations — his hopes that his academic career would open out onto a profitable marriage and a post in the government[93] — Augustine was finally ready to give himself entirely to the pursuit of real and lasting happiness through philosophy, the love of wisdom.[94]

But the life he converted for was not the life he eventually got. After a few years spent writing philosophical dialogues and the occasional polemic against the Manichaeans, his usefulness to the Church was recognized and he was ordained priest against his will.[95] Submitting his will to the will of the church, he henceforth put his talents and his restless pursuit of truth to work in the service of his neighbors in the church. He became a different kind of teacher — a bishop, a preacher of sermons to the illiterate and a writer of treatises and polemics for an audience of churchmen around the Mediterranean. And quite contrary to his original plans, he became the most important teacher in Western Christendom.

No wonder he complained so frequently of overwork.[96] Teaching is hard, because love of neighbor is hard. It is like Dorothy Day's favorite quote from Dostoevsky: love in practice is a harsh and dreadful thing compared to love in dreams.[97] Instructing the ignorant (which is one of the spiritual works of mercy, and hence an act of charity)[98] is hard work, especially when, as in our culture, the ignorant have previously been instructed to feel entitled to their ignorance (the dictum "no one can tell me what to believe" is most frequently uttered by those who have no interest in learning to think for themselves). The work is harsh and dreadful, for the soul feeds on beauty (nothing is more beautiful than truth),[99] and ignorance is ugly and disheartening, like a paper written by a student who has never learned to write well and would rather be watching TV. It is an act of generosity and charity to read such a mess carefully and try to see what insight might lie behind the cliches and thoughtlessness, and it is a yet deeper charity to bear with the militant ignorance of students who think such writing ought to be good enough.

It is like this. The mind loves clarity, as the eye loves to see a sharply-focused photograph rather than a blurry one. Trying to understand the expressions of an ignorant mind is like looking at a blurry photograph: some areas are so confused that there is nothing really to see, but in others the dim outlines of a thought can be perceived, if one is willing to look hard enough and risk getting a headache. The will to look hard for patterns and insight in the blurriness is love. It is love of truth put in the service of love of neighbor — indeed love of the truth in the mind of one's neighbor rather than in oneself.

The wonderful thing is that it is so often rewarded. There are of course those students who come to us with minds already alive and growing, and they are easy to teach. But there are others who seem to have forgotten the taste of truth, content with the images they have been fed since childhood. The wonder of teaching, its unaccountable gift, is that sometimes something a teacher says or does helps set such a person in motion towards truth, thinking for herself.

This then is the difficult situation of the Christian teacher, caught between superior and inferior knowledge, the authority of Christian teaching on the one hand and the clamoring needs of students on the other, required to submit humbly to the first and attend charitably to the second. Or so it appears when we are tired and dispirited. But of course, the task is to perceive more clearly than this: to see the comfort and truth in the authority of Christian teaching as well as the loveliness taking shape in our students' minds when, submitting to our authority, they go through their finger-exercises practicing the music of truth.

Notes

1   Since "Scripture alone" is a much-controverted catchword, let me be clear on what I understand by it. I take its basic meaning to be that nothing should be taught as necessary to salvation which is not found or implied in Scripture; cf. e.g. the 39 articles of the Church of England, article 6 (in Leith, p. 267). On this understanding, there is no inconsistency in attributing authority to pastors, creeds and catechisms (as I shall proceed to do below) so long as such authority is understood to be derived from Scripture alone.

2   John Paul II, *Fides et Ratio*, preamble.

3   For the authority of the grammarian (in explicit contrast to the leading of reason), cf. *On Music* 2.1.1. Notice likewise that Augustine's early works frequently mention the authority of pagan philosophers, e.g. *Against the Academics* 1.3.7, 1.9.24, 2.10.24, 2.13.30, 3.7.14, and 3.18.41.

4   John 14:6, a very important passage for Augustine.

5   Cf. Kant, "What is Enlightenment?"

6   For the authority/reason pairing and its relation to the faith/understanding pairing, cf. *On Order* 2.9.26ff, *The Usefulness of Belief* (sometimes translated "On the Profit of Believing") 1.2 and 17.34, and *On True Religion* 24.45-25.47.

7   E.g. according to Aquinas' definition of faith, "the intellect of the believer is convinced by divine authority, so as to assent to what it does not see," *Summa Theologica* II-II, 4.1.

8   This is a general point about all pedagogy, not just in matters of religion: "the order of nature is such that *whenever we learn something* authority precedes reason," *On the Morals of the Catholic Church* §3. Education thus moves from faith to understanding, as "all those things which to begin with we simply believed, following authority alone, we come to understand" (*On True Religion* 8.14).

9   This quotation from Isaiah 7:9 (LXX) is the motto of Augustine's epistemology; cf. *On Free Choice* 2:2.6, *On the Teacher* 11.37, *On Faith and the Creed* 1.1 (cf. 10:25) and *On the Trinity* 15:2.2.

10   An elegant formulation, meant to be memorable: *Tempora auctoritas, re autem ratio prior est*. Augustine proceeds to explain: *Aliud est enim, quod in agendo anteponitur, aliud quod pluris in appetendo aestimatur* ("For what comes first in our actions is not what is valued most in our desires").

11   This is not to say there is no theology at all in the orbit of the mainline churches.
         But that which has deepest roots in the Reformation traditions is also that which
         is most intensively engaged in ecumenical dialogue with Roman Catholic theology,
         resulting in a new kind of theology which its advocates label neither Protestant nor
         Roman Catholic but "evangelical catholic" theology (as in the subtitle of the
         flagship journal of the movement, *Pro Ecclesia: a Journal of Catholic and
         Evangelical Theology*).

12   The phrase appears several times in Augustine, always referring to an intellectually
         immature form of life (*On Order* 2.9.26, *On the Usefulness of Belief* 16.34, and *On
         True Religion* 8.14).

13   For details of this argument cf. Cary, "Believing the Word." For a similar Catholic
         account of interpersonal knowledge based on belief in the other's word, cf. John
         Paul II, *Fides et Ratio*, section 32.

14   In my view it is a fundamentally Biblical epistemology, in which the "heart" — in
         Hebrew the organ of reason and understanding — is connected more often with
         hearing than with seeing. Cf. Wolff, pp. 40-44 and 74-79. The contrast between
         this Biblical epistemology of hearing and the Platonist epistemology of vision is
         summed up in what I am told is a German proverb: the eyes believe themselves, but
         the ears believe other people.

15   When Augustine says Truth (*veritas* rather than *verum*) he means God, and in
         everything I proceed to say about Augustine it must be borne in mind that "Truth"
         and "God" are two names for the same thing. Augustine is hardly alone in this
         identification (cf. Aquinas, *Summa Theologica* I, 16.5, and John Paul II, *Veritatis
         Splendor*, section 83). The primary Biblical support for this identification is John
         14:6, when Christ says, "I am the Way, the Truth and the Life."

16   *Beata vita*, a key term in Augustine's early writings, is Cicero's translation of
         eudaimonia, the Greek philosophers' term for happiness. Augustine argues that a
         happy or blessed life is necessarily an eternal life in *City of God* 11.11 and 14.25
         (cf. the preface of book 7: *vitam beatam, quae non nisi aeternam est*, a claim based
         on the immediately preceding argument of 6.12). Hence when Jesus or Paul speak
         of eternal life, this is for Augustine the Biblical conception of happiness, which
         was the central object of the philosophers' investigations, the goal of their
         "sleepless and laborious efforts" (*ibid.* 8.3, cf. 19.1). For the Hellenistic
         philosophical background to these claims, cf. Holte.

17   *Confessions* 1.1.1.

18   A point obscured by the Jowett translation, which translates *paideia* (education) by
         "enlightenment" at the beginning of book 7 (514a). Hence the introduction to the
         Allegory of the Cave should read: "compare our nature, with respect to education
         or lack of education, to this..."

19   *Republic* 518b-c.

20   This dominant metaphor of Augustinian epistemology is introduced in a
         programmatic way, in terms highly reminiscent of the Allegory of the Cave, in
         Soliloquies 1.6.12ff (reason promises to show God to the mind as the sun is shown
         to the eyes).

21   Plato's language of "turning" in this and other texts is translated into Latin as
         conversio, whence our "conversion." Cf. Aubin for the development of this concept
         in Platonist philosophy.

22   In Augustine, the soul's ascent from the cave to the light becomes an ascent within the soul to gaze at the divine Light of Truth above the soul ("by the soul itself I will ascend," *Confessions* 10.7.11). The epistemological details of the ascent are first spelled out in *On Free Choice*, book 2, and are summarized in *Confessions* 7.17.23. The Catholic interpreters of Augustine with whom I disagree have to interpret the one text as "Augustine's proof for the existence of God," and the other as "Augustine's mysticism" — whereas the simple and straightforward reading is, I argue, to see them both as portraying an educative process of growing understanding like the Allegory of the Cave, leading to a vision of the intelligible Light which is neither mysticism nor proof, neither supra-rational experience nor mere external argument, but rather the most inward and most natural fulfillment of the human intellect. For more details cf. Cary, *Augustine's Invention of the Inner Self*, Chapter 5.

23   The mind's dazzlement when it cannot maintain its gaze at the intelligible Sun (derived ultimately from *Republic* 516a) is one of Augustine's most characteristic metaphors. Cf. e.g. *On the Happy Life* §35; *Soliloquies* 1.23; *On the Morals of the Catholic Church* §§3 and 11; *On the Quantity of the Soul* §25; *On Free Choice* 2.42; *On the Teacher* §21; *On the Usefulness of Believing* §4; *Confessions* 7.16 and 7.23; *City of God* 11.2; *On the Trinity* 1:4, 8:3, 12:23 and 15:10

24   *Republic* 516a-b, a progress which Augustine elaborates in *Soliloquies* 1.13.23. This passage, together with the reference to escaping from the cave in 1.14.24, is the strongest evidence that Augustine had firsthand knowledge of Plato's text.

25   *City of God* 8.8 (because the Good is God, true Platonic philosophy is love of God).

26   *Symposium* 210a-212a. Cf. also *Phaedrus* 244a-257b and Plotinus' treatise "On Beauty" (*Ennead* 1.6), which is the treatise of Plotinus most often quoted by Augustine.

27   That Augustine's understanding of love owes a great deal to the Platonist conception of *eros* is commonly acknowledged, but exactly how this affects Augustine's Christianity is a matter of much disagreement (cf. most importantly Nygren and Burnaby).

28   Cf. Augustine's little essay "On Ideas" (= *Eighty-Three Different Questions* §46).

29   *On Free Choice* 2:12.33.

30   This is Augustine's version of the doctrine of divine simplicity, a fundamental principle for him; cf. *City of God* 11.10 and 8.6 (where Augustine shows his awareness of the Platonist origin of this doctrine).

31   1 Corinthians 13:12, a favorite passage of Augustine's.

32   If beatific vision is the *natural* fulfillment of the intellect, then it would follow that "God cannot create intellectual beings without ordering and calling them to the beatific vision" — the thesis associated with Henri de Lubac that was condemned by Pope Pius XII in 1950. The objection is that this thesis "undermines the gratuity of the supernatural order" (*Humani Generis* §26, in Denzinger-Schönmetzer §3891 = Deferrari §2318).

33   In my opinion, all Western Christian thinkers owe Augustine a debt of filial piety, even though he often says what none of us want him to say; cf. my preface to *Augustine's Invention of the Inner Self*.

34   Cf. most importantly *Confessions* 1.18.28 ("in darkened affections lies distance from Your face") — the conclusion of the famous conflation of Jesus' Prodigal (Luke 15:17ff) with Plotinus' Ulysses (*Enneads* 1.6.8). The same point is made

with explicit reference to Plotinus in *City of God* 9.17 ("unlikeness to God is the only separation from him" — an unlikeness which resides not in our immortal nature but in our "craving for things temporal and changeable"). Thus distance in space is a metaphor for distance in will, a heart which is not fully turned toward God in love. For the systematic presence of the imagery of distance, journey, and pilgrimage, as well as Augustine's frequent allusions to the homecoming of Ulysses and the Prodigal Son, cf. O'Connell.

35   An important principle for Augustine; cf. *City of God* 10.22, *Retractations* 1.5.2 (quoting Isaiah 59:2). For the crucial place of this principle in the development of his early thought, cf. Cary, *Augustine's Invention of the Inner Self*, chapter 8.

36   One must beware of loose talk of "the nature/grace distinction." Augustine has a conception of nature and grace (he wrote a treatise *On Nature and Grace*) but he does not have a Thomistic nature/grace distinction, informed by a concept of "the supernatural," i.e. a form of grace that elevates human nature above itself. In Augustine's theology grace heals and helps nature but does not elevate it. For it is natural for the human mind to look above itself and see God.

37   *Summa Theologica* I, 84.4; cf. the whole epistemology of sensible knowledge developed in 84.1-7. Thomas agrees with Augustine that Platonic Forms or Ideas belong in the Mind of God (*Summa Theologica* I, 15.1), but denies that they are the natural objects of the vision of the human mind.

38   Most important here is the interpretation of Augustine's "illuminationism" by Gilson, pp. 77-111, criticized in favor of a frankly ontologist reading of Augustine by the Protestant Ronald Nash, chapters 7 and 8. Gilson's own hesitations about his interpretation are evident on pp. 88, and 92-96.

39   For an introduction to this movement and the official reaction against it, cf. McCool, *Nineteenth-Century Theology*, chapters 5 and 6.

40   For "extrinsicism" and the initial failure of the "New Theology" which De Lubac led against it, cf. the first half of Rahner's article "Concerning the Relationship between Nature and Grace" (pp. 297-310).

41   The key figures in this resolution are Rahner (cf. the second half of his article, pp. 310-317) and von Balthasar (cf. his treatment of the concept of nature in Catholic theology, pp. 257-302 and 343-357). For a brief and lucid introduction to what is at issue in these very dense texts (and in the previously-cited passage from *Humani Generis*, which is the pivotal point of the discussion), cf. McCool, *From Unity to Pluralism*, chapter 10.

42   Cf. esp. the new *Catechism of the Catholic Church*, section 27.

43   For a fuller account of how Augustinian reason became both foundational and unacceptable in Catholic theology, cf. my *Augustine's Invention of the Inner Self*, chapter 5.

44   This is a common thread in John Paul's instructions to Catholic teachers, as can be seen in the opening pages of *The Splendor of Truth*, *Fides et Ratio*, and *Ex Corde Ecclesiae*.

45   Interestingly, this aspect of John Paul II's apostolic constitution on Catholic universities, *Ex Corde Ecclesiae*, is not reflected in the so-called "Brevilacqua document" (draft of 11/98), the American bishops' proposal to implement it. Whereas John Paul depicts education as common search for truth shared by teachers and students, the American Catholic response is to focus on faithfulness to the authority of Catholic teaching. That is to say, when John Paul talks about

reason, American Catholics seem to hear *authority*. (I owe this observation to conversation with members of Villanova University's Core Humanities department, particularly Drs. Abigail Firey and Kevin Hughes).

46   Cf. especially the tone of his directions and exhortations in *Fides et Ratio*, chapters 6 and 7.

47   Historically speaking, the very concept of "fact" is an invention of the 17th century — "like telescopes and wigs for gentlemen," as MacIntyre nicely observes (p. 357). Education can get along without a conception of "facts" — as it did for most of its history — but not without a conception of truth.

48   To be in hell, according to Dante, is to have lost "the good of the intellect," *Inferno* 3.18. The phrase is Thomistic, and refers specifically to God as Truth, as in *Summa Theologica* II-II, 1.3, reply 1.

49   Cicero, *Academica* 2.31.

50   The word "fool" is not simply a term of abuse, but a technical term of Hellenistic philosophy, the negative side of the inherent connection between wisdom and happiness that structures the whole classical philosophical tradition from Plato onwards (cf. Holte). In Stoic philosophy, anyone who is not wise is technically a fool and therefore cannot be happy (hence Augustine as someone who seeks but has not yet found wisdom is willing to be classed among fools in *Soliloquies* 1.4.9 and *Against the Academics* 3.8.17). The usage of a similar term in the Biblical wisdom literature is less severe: the fool is not simply someone who lacks wisdom, but someone who has no desire to acquire it (cf. e.g. Proverbs 1:7, 17,16; 18:2).

51   *On the Trinity* 10.1.1-3.

52   This program of education is laid out in his early philosophical dialogue *On Order* (2.7.24-19.51), its epistemological foundations explored in his next work, *Soliloquies*, and a the accompanying theory of language and interpretation worked out a couple years later in the dialogue *On the Teacher*.

53   Cf. *On Christian Doctrine* 2.6.8 ("what is sought with more difficulty is found with more gladness"), *Against Faustus* 12.7 and 12.14 ("the most hidden meanings are the sweetest") and Epistle 55.21 (the difficult or puzzling passages kindle our love more than the obvious ones).

54   Cf. on this point the astute observations of Brown, pp. 254f, 263 and 275.

55   Teaching of course is the original form of "Platonic love" (cf. the erotic undercurrents between Socrates and his young interlocutors in *Meno, Phaedrus,* and *Alcibiades I*). Augustine's characteristic variation on the theme of teaching as love is his conviction that his writings are a duty of charity required of him by the needs, requests or questions of those for whom he writes (cf. *On the Trinity* 3.1, *On the Merits and Forgiveness of Sins* 1.1.1, and Epistle 101.1).

56   *Phaedo* 67e-69b. By "dualism" I mean specifically soul/body dualism, and any ethics which is based on separating soul from body.

57   *Soliloquies* 1.6.12. This reflects a rather extreme dualism which Augustine later regrets; cf. *Retractations* 1.4.3, correcting a dualist sentiment he seems to have gotten from Porphyry the Neoplatonist.

58   *Phaedo* 78d-81b.

59   For Augustine's adaptation of the Platonist language of purity cf. *City of God* 8.3 (statement of the Platonist theory, attributed to Socrates) and 10.23ff (how Christians attain the purification for which the Neoplatonist Porphyry sought), *On Music* 6.16.51-55 (the four cardinal virtues purify the soul by converting it from

sensible things to intelligible), and *Eighty-Three Different Questions* §12 (purifying the mind in order to see God).

60   *Confessions* 7.1.1. For the epistemological basis of Augustine's turn away from the phantasms cf. *On Music* 6.11.32 and 6.16.51ff, and *On True Religion* 10.18.

61   *Summa Theologica* I, 84.7, citing Aristotle, *On the Soul* 3.7.

62   This turn to the mind — Augustine's inward turn — is hinted at already in *Confessions* 7.1.2, and developed at greater length in 7.10.16 and 10.6.8-27.38.

63   *Confessions* 7.17.23.

64   I state this problem initially in Augustinian rather than Platonic terms: in terms of Truth rather than Form. For the early Augustine the sensible world has not truth but only truth-likeness — a distinction which Augustine thinks is Plato's (*Against the Academics* 3.17.37) and which he makes central to his early epistemology (*Soliloquies* 2.5.8-7.13).

65   Aristotle, *Metaphysics* 1.9 and 13.4.

66   This empirical moment in Plato's thought is present even in the *Phaedo*, 74c.

67   *Confessions* 7.17.23. Cf. likewise *On True Religion* 29.52-30.56 and *On Free Choice* 2.3.8-6.14.

68   *Philebus* 59e-62d.

69   Here I follow the view of Aristotle's development presented by Düring rather than Jaeger. According to Düring, Aristotle was a critic of Plato's doctrine of ideas very early one, while still a member of the Academy. Plato's later dialogues could therefore very well be his response to Aristotle's criticism.

70   *Confessions* 3.4.7-5.9.

71   Neither text is extant, though the reconstruction of *Protrepticus* is, in the opinion of Düring, about 90% complete. For the *Hortensius* as modelled on the *Protrepticus*, cf. the testimonia cited in Ross's edition of Aristotle, 12.26, and Ruch's reconstruction of the *Hortensius*, pp. 18-27.

72   For this setting, see Düring's introduction to his edition of *Protrepticus* (much of this material is also available in his *Aristoteles*). For the rivalry between Plato's Academy and Isocrates' more "practical" and rhetorical school — a rivalry thematic for the whole course of higher education in antiquity — cf. Marrou, p.89ff.

73   This criticism of pagan Platonism, which Augustine develops at length in *On True Religion* 3.3-4.7, seems to have been aimed primarily against Porphyry, the most formidable Neoplatonist critic of Christianity (O'Meara, chapter 10). Cf. the polemic against Porphyry in *City of God* 10.26-32.

74   *Confessions* 7.18.24, *On the Trinity* 4.2.4.

75   Notice how the metaphor of dazzlement concludes the description of Augustine's two visionary experiences in book 7 of *Confessions* (7.10.16 and 7.17.23).

76   This is the message of the first story told in the book which narrates Augustine's conversion (*Confessions* 8.2.3-4.9) — the example of Victorinus, who like young Augustine is a rhetorician and intellectual who must humble himself to join the Church.

77   Cf. *Soliloquies* 1.6.12, *The Usefulness of Belief* 16.34 (purification by authority, so that one may see Truth), and *83 Different Questions* 68:3 ("purified of sin through believing"), and note the persistence of the theme in later works such as *On the Trinity* 1.1.3.

78 This phrase turns up most frequently, of course, in his exegeses of Paul, and perhaps most influentially in *On the Spirit and the Letter*.

79 "...I do as a child who is being taught the Catechism. Every morning, and whenever else I have time, I read and recite word for word the Lord's Prayer, the Ten Commandments, the Creed, the Psalms, etc. I must still read and study the Catechism daily, yet I cannot master it as I wish, but must remain a child and pupil of the Catechism, and I do it gladly." From the first or longer preface to *The Large Catechism* (p. 359).

80 *Philosophical Fragments*, chapter 1.

81 *Theaetetus* 149a-151d.

82 *Meno* 80a-81e.

83 Cf. Augustine's beautiful Christmas sermon on the text "Truth has sprung from the earth" (Psalm 85:11), sermon 185 (in *Sermons* III/6).

84 For a recent proposal about how such a project would look in contemporary terms, cf. Marshall.

85 Cf. Luther's definition of true faith as that which "joyfully embraces this Son of God given for it and says 'He is my beloved and I am His'" (*Theses on Faith* §22, in *Luther's Works* 34:110). We take hold of Christ by believing the Gospel, which is a story about Christ; cf. "A Brief Instruction on What to Look for and Expect in the Gospels," (*Luther's Works* 35:117-124).

86 Matthew 22:38.

87 The assumption of "the basic Christian idea of sin as in very essence selfishness" (p. 649) is the foundation of Nygren's criticism of Augustine's "caritas synthesis," (cf. pp. 476ff). In my judgment, the most lucid argument showing, in effect, why Augustine is right and Nygren is wrong on this score is in Lewis, chapter 1.

88 This is not a metaphor. For Augustine the only motivating forces or efficient causes in the universe are wills (*City of God* 5.9) and the action of a will is always a form of love or its opposite (*ibid*. 14.6ff).

89 This lies behind Augustine's strange statement in *On Christian Doctrine* 32.35 that God uses us, not for his own advantage (*utilitatem*) but for ours.

90 The most important moments in my own college education took place in the classroom where many times I observed professor Richard Stang in the very act of loving a poem. I do not remember very much of what he said about the poetry, for now I read poems with my own understanding — but that is in part because of the love of poetry I learned from him. (Incidentally, Augustine sometimes talks as if there is no truth in poetry — as in *Confessions* 1.13.20-17.27 — but like nearly everyone else I disagree.)

91 *Confessions* 9:2. That his conversion gave him time to study *philosophy* is clear from the writings he produced immediately afterwards, which define themselves as inquiries in philosophy: cf. *On the Happy Life* 1.1-5 ("the port of philosophy in which I am now sailing"), *Against the Academics* 1.1.3ff (fleeing from the windbag's profession, rhetoric, to "the bosom of philosophy"), 2.2.3-6 (Augustine's longing for philosophy and the *otium philosophandi*, the free time to philosophize) and *On Order* 2.15.43-19.51 (philosophy as the culmination of a liberal arts education, leading to vision of God). For the shape of his intellectual project immediately after his conversion cf. Brown, chapter 11, and Cary, "What Licentius Learned."

92   This can be seen in *Confessions* 6.11.18-14.24, where even the crisis brewing over his sex life takes on significance primarily because of the way it obstructs the project of finding the free time needed for serious study. On the thematic importance of this need for *otium* in Augustine's life, cf. Brown, p. 115ff.

93   On young Augustine's ambitions, cf. Brown, chapter 7.

94   That "philosophy" means love of wisdom, not adherence to any particular intellectual school, is fundamental to Augustine (cf. *On Order* 1.11.32 and *Confessions* 3.4.8).

95   For this event, and the end it spelled to the hopes engendered by his conversion, cf. Brown, chapters 14 and 15.

96   One of the most constant themes in Augustine's letters is a sort of groan, with which any professor trying to balance the needs of students and time for scholarship will appreciate: what little time he has for serious thinking or writing is always being claimed by the needs of his flock or his correspondents (cf. e.g. epistles 48.1, 98.8, 118.1-3, 139.3, 213.5).

97   Miller, p. 284.

98   *Summa Theologica* II-II, 32.2.

99   Augustine, epistle 118:23.

References

Aquinas, T. *Summa Theologica*. Westminster, MD: Christian Classics, 1981.

Aristotle. *The Works of Aristotle*. 12 vols. Ed. W.D. Ross. Oxford: Clarendon, 1910-52.

_____. *Aristotle's Protrepticus: an Attempt at a Reconstruction*. Ed. I. Düring. Göteborg: Elanders Boktryckeri Aktiebolag, 1961.

Aubin, P. *Le problème de la "conversion."* Paris: Beauchesne, 1963.

Augustine. Major works in *Nicene and Post-Nicene Fathers*. First Series, reprint edition. Grand Rapids: Eerdmans, 1983.

_____. *Against the Academics*. Ed. J. O'Meara. Ancient Christian Writers series. Westminster: Newman, 1950.

_____. *City of God*. Trans. H. Bettenson. New York: Penguin, 1972.

_____. *Eighty-three Different Questions*. Trans. D. Mosher. Fathers of the Church series. Washington: Catholic University of America, 1982.

_____. *On Christian Doctrine*. Trans. D. Robertson. New York: Macmillan, 1958.

_____. *Retractations*. Trans. M. Bogan. Fathers of the Church series. Washington: Catholic University of America, 1968.

_____. *Sermons*. New Rochelle: New City Press, 1990-97.

_____. *Writings of Saint Augustine*. Vol. 1. Fathers of the Church series. New York: CIMA, 1948. (Contains translations of Augustine's earliest writings, including *On the Happy Life* and *Soliloquies*. *On Order* [*De Ordine*] is disguised under the perversely misleading title "Divine Providence and the Problem of Evil" and *Against the Academics* [*Contra Academicos*] is hard to recognize under the title "Answer to Skeptics." The latter text is badly translated and should be avoided in favor of O'Meara's edition.)

_____. *Writings of Saint Augustine*. Vol. 2. Fathers of the Church series. New York: CIMA, 1947. (Includes *On Music* and *On the Quantity of the Soul* [*De Quantitate*

Animae] under the title "The Magnitude of the Soul.")

Brown, P. *Augustine of Hippo.* Berkeley: University of California, 1967.

Burnaby, J. *Amor Dei: a Study in the Religion of St. Augustine.* London: Hodder and Stoughton, 1938.

Cary, P. *Augustine's Invention of the Inner Self.* New York: Oxford, 2000.

_____. "Believing the Word: a Proposal about Knowing Other Persons." *Faith and Philosophy* 13/1 (1996).

_____. "What Licentius Learned: A Narrative Reading of the Cassiciacum Dialogues." *Augustinian Studies* 29/1 (Jan. 1998) 141-163.

Cicero. *De Natura Deorum, Academica.* Trans. H. Rackham. Loeb series. Cambridge: Harvard, 1972.

Dante. *Inferno.* Italian text with English translation by J. Sinclair. New York: Oxford, 1976.

Deferrari, R. *The Sources of Catholic Dogma.* Translation of 30th ed. of Denzinger (below). St. Louis: Herder, 1955.

Denzinger H., and Schönmetzer, A. *Enchiridion Symbolorum, Definitionum et Declarationum.* 36th ed. Rome: Herder, 1976.

Düring, I. *Aristoteles: Darstellung und Interpretation seines Denkens.* Heidelberg: Carl Winter Universitätsverlag, 1966.

Gilson, E. *The Christian Philosophy of Saint Augustine.* New York: Random House, 1960.

Holte, R. *Beatitude et sagesse: Saint Augustin et le problème de la fin de l'homme dans la philosophie ancienne.* Paris: Études Augustiniennes, 1962.

Jaeger, W. *Aristotle: Fundamentals of the History of His Development.* Trans. R. Robinson. 2nd ed. Oxford: Clarendon, 1948.

John Paul II. *Fides et Ratio: On the relationship between Faith and Reason.* Boston: Pauline, 1998.

_____. *The Splendor of Truth.* Washington: United States Catholic Conference, 1993.

Kant, I. "An Answer to the Question: What is Enlightenment?" (Originally 1784.) In *Perpetual Peace and Other Essays.* Indianapolis: Hackett, 1983.

Kierkegaard, S. *Philosophical Fragments.* Trans. Swenson. Rev. ed. Princeton: Princeton University, 1962.

Leith, J. *Creeds of the Churches.* Atlanta: John Knox, 1973.

Lewis, C.S. *The Four Loves.* New York: Harcourt, Brace, Johanovich, 1960.

Luther, M. *The Large Catechism.* In T. Tappert (ed.), *The Book of Concord: The Confessions of the Evangelical Lutheran Church.* Philadelphia: Fortress, 1959.

_____. *Luther's Works.* 55 vols. Philadelphia: Fortress.

MacIntyre, A. *Whose Justice? Which Rationality?* Notre Dame: University of Notre Dame, 1988.

Marrou, H.I. *A History of Education in Antiquity.* Trans. G. Lamb. London: Sheed and Ward, 1956.

Marshall, B. "What is Truth?" *Pro Ecclesia* 4/4 (Fall 1995) 404-430.

McCool, G. *From Unity to Pluralism.* New York: Fordham, 1989.

_____. *Nineteenth-Century Theology.* New York: Seabury, 1977.

Miller, W. *Dorothy Day: a Biography.* San Francisco: Harper & Row, 1982.

Nash, R. *The Light of the Mind: St. Augustine's Theory of Knowledge.* Lexington: University Press of Kentucky, 1969.

Nygren, A. *Eros and Agape.* Chicago: University of Chicago, 1982.

O'Connell, R. *Soundings in Augustine's Imagination.* New York: Fordham, 1994.

Pius XII. *Humani Generis*. Excerpted in H. Denzinger, *Enchiridion Symbolorum, Definitionum et Declarationum*. 36th ed. Rome: Herder, 1976.

Plato. *Complete Works*. Ed. J. Cooper. Indianapolis: Hackett, 1998.

Plotinus. *The Enneads*. Trans. S. MacKenna. New York: Penguin, 1991.

Rahner, K. "Concerning the Relationship between Nature and Grace." In his *Theological Investigations*. London: Darton, Longman, and Todd, 1961. Vol. 1, pp. 297-317.

Ruch, M. *L'Hortensius de Ciceron: histoire et reconstitution*. Paris: Les belles lettres, 1958.

von Balthasar, H.U. *The Theology of Karl Barth*. San Francisco: Ignatius, 1991.

Wolff, H.W. *Anthropology of the Old Testament*. Philadelphia: Fortress, 1974.

Chapter Five

The Bishop as Teacher

Daniel Doyle, O.S.A.

Introduction

Great teachers are born, not made. This much disputed point might well serve to illustrate the "grace-works" controversy which has engaged Christians since the composition of the *Letter of James,* only to be revisited in the Pelagian controversy and once again in the Reformation, finding its modern equivalent in the "nature-nurture" discussions disputed by educators. The typical Catholic response to such dichotomies is "both-and." Great teachers are born with innate qualities that dispose them to become great teachers: curiosity, memory, analytical and conceptual ability, passion, hunger for truth, a desire to communicate, a love of wisdom. Yet such grace is insufficient unless it is accompanied by skills carefully cultivated and honed through disciplined learning, mentoring, and experience. Expert teachers master words and play with them in ways that invite others to explore and understand the mysteries of our world and of ourselves. Great teachers change the lives of their students. They teach beyond their subject matter. They make a lasting difference. This essay will attempt to illustrate that Augustine's legacy as a teacher is nowhere more apparent than in his teaching the Christian faithful at the Sunday homily. In the first part of the paper I will attempt to summarize the bishop's philosophy of education based on his own training and developed in his many treatises. I will then look at samples of Augustine's preaching, addressing the full range of issues connected with public speaking: use of texts, delivery, audience background, the size of the congregation, audience response. I hope to demonstrate that Augustine was masterful in connecting with his students. Lastly, I will take up the subject of biblical interpretation and application to the everyday concerns of the bishop's congregation.

Augustine's Philosophy of Education

Augustine's philosophy of learning can only be gleaned from a careful reading of his major treatises.[1] Although the value of education for its own sake is recognized as a commonplace in the academy, the bishop had little tolerance for those who pursued learning for its own sake, especially when motivated by selfish ambitions:

And what did it profit me that I read and understood for myself all the books that I was able to get hold of what are called the liberal arts, since I remained the vile slave of selfish ambitions? I enjoyed the books, while not recognizing the source of whatever elements of truth and certainty they contained. For I had turned my back to the light and my face to the things upon which the light falls: so that my eyes, by which I looked upon the things in the light, were not themselves illumined.... Whatever I understood of the arts... I understood because my swift intelligence and keen wits were your gift.[2]

Augustine's distaste for intellectual snobbery and misuse of education is nowhere more apparent than in *Letter 118* to Dioscorus (written in 410 or 411), where he dresses down the ambitious young man for playing intellectual games. Nowhere is Augustine more critical of "the hoary and worn-out falsehoods of so many philosophers."[3] This letter is an important compendium of the bishop's views on contemporary philosophy and rhetoric, including the teachings of the Platonists, the Academics, the Stoics, the Epicureans and Cicero. By 411 the bishop has lost some of his enthusiasm for the subtleties of Cicero's *Dialogues*. Even in Rome few pay any attention to his teaching; in Africa one would have to send all the way to Carthage for a copy. Certainly such knowledge is useless in Greek-speaking cities where the young man resides. Dioscorus would do much better learning the original and complete theories of the Greek philosophers than the derived fragments found among Latin authors. He is nothing more than a shallow dilettante, more interested in impressing others with his cleverness than pursuing wisdom. There is no more deplorable motive for education than that of appearing learned and trying to get ahead. The young man is simply impertinent to ask a busy bishop to explain such subtleties and oblivious to the pressing demands of his ministry which keep him up late nights. Dioscorus gets under the bishop's skin and triggers a hostility that is rarely seen in any of Augustine's other correspondence. Despite his repeated protestations to indulge the ambitious man's questions, Augustine dedicates thirty-four long paragraphs to answering his inquiry. Cicero himself is cited a minimum of five times. Augustine's warning about poor motives for education should echo in the halls of universities for all times: "If it is in order to have a greater opportunity of acquiring temporal riches, of winning a wife, of attaining to high office, and other things of this sort... then it is not fitting for us to help you to that goal; on the contrary, we ought to turn you from it."[4] The only hope for Dioscorus and for all who pursue education as a vehicle to launch successful careers is the school of humility.[5]

With the current fascination in postmodernism gripping faculties of philosophy, theology, classics and literature,[6] Augustine's masterpiece, *Teaching Christianity (De doctrina christiana)*, has received much deserved and renewed attention, particularly in regard to hermeneutic theory and semiotics.[7] Augustine's conversion coincided with his giving up the profession of rhetor, but led to a far wider audience of listeners, the *catholica*. Although trained in the Ciceronian school of rhetoric with its predilection for *delectare* in the famous triptych — *docere, delectare, flectere* (to teach, delight, and persuade) — Augustine came to favor the central importance of *docere* in his role as bishop-teacher. Until the publication of Fortin, a strong consensus had prevailed among scholars of late antiquity that Augustine's work lacked originality and had essentially repeated the views developed by Cicero.[8] Fortin broke ranks with his colleagues and persuasively challenged the *status questionis*, effectively arguing that Augustine had profoundly modified Cicero's teaching on two points: "first, by asserting the priority of the teaching function of the orator over the other two functions, and secondly, by investing the terms *docere* and *doctrina* , which best describe that function , with a meaning that could never have been ascribed to them by Cicero."[9] Cicero is primarily concerned with political and judicial oratory. The goal of teaching is to establish the facts in order to win the case. Plausibility of the argument is more important than its actual truth. The orator is less concerned with the truth than with its appearance: "A plausible falsehood is infinitely more valuable than an unlikely truth."[10] The fact that Cicero avoids the use of the term *doctrina* and prefers the more neutral *docere* in describing the content of rhetoric shows that he is not primarily concerned with philosophical truth in the sense of the Greek *epistêmê*. Bishops — like philosophers — speak ultimately for the purpose of instruction rather than mindless persuasion. It is likely that many Roman orators no longer believed in the gods of the Roman pantheon, yet such personal questioning was put aside in order to fulfill the expectations of their listeners. It was more important to teach the party line than to believe the party line. The better he is able to cover up his personal beliefs, the more successful a speaker he is: "Cicero's perfect orator is a liar, not because he wants to, but because he has no choice in the matter."[11] The bishop does not change the *res* in order to appeal to his listeners, he simply varies the *signa* to better communicate its truth.

In the above mentioned letter to Dioscorus, the bishop mentions how ridiculous it would be to spend all his effort trying to get people's attention, instead of desiring to learn what to teach them.[12] The new convert realized as early as *De ordine* that rhetoric serves an ancillary function in leading people to the truth, the ultimate goal of philosophy. Rhetoric accomplishes this goal not only by teaching, but especially by arousing human emotions and passions through carefully crafted discourse, taking full advantage of appropriate figures of speech.[13] Of course, the bishop will substitute Sacred Scripture as the primary source for samples of eloquence over the standard classical fare that fed him and earlier generations of scholars in late antiquity. This amounts to a complete about-face to the young Augustine's embarrassment at the crude state of Latin he found in the biblical stories. The mature bishop has a completely different assessment: "Where I understand them, it seems to me that nothing could be wiser, nothing more eloquent than the sacred writers."[14] Like a good scotch, certain tastes must be cultivated over time and are only appreciated with age. Eloquence is hollow unless it is accompanied by wisdom. It is more easily acquired by those who have gifted minds. It is more useful for communicating the message of Sacred Scripture than for unlocking its meaning.[15]

In order to make progress in understanding, "we need the mental exercise of wrestling with the text as well as the intellectual satisfaction of discovering what it means."[16] Rhetorical skill is more readily learned by imitation than by artificial studying: eloquence will come more readily to those who read and listen to eloquent speakers than to those who pore over the words of eloquence.[17] If infants learn to become successful speakers by imitating the speech and pronunciation of their parents and family members, why should we be surprised to discover that some people become expert speakers without any formal training. Theoreticians do not always make for the best practitioners. Indeed this same insight can be verified today among Catholic scholars who commonly remark that liturgists often make for the poorest celebrants. They may know their history and theory, but execution of these principles is something else.

The orator's success to a great extent depends upon the image he has been able to cultivate. The successful orator instills confidence in his listener, because he has created a persona that is likable and admired. His own person is a better witness to the truth of his assertions than the arguments he uses. A Catholic bishop, however, is first and foremost concerned with the truth itself, based on the authority of Christ who is the truth. Rather than instill confidence by promoting his own image, he relies on the power of Christ. That is not to say that Augustine is indifferent to the character and moral life of the preacher. Yet his primary goal is not to impress the congregation with his erudition, but rather to instruct them. The source for his knowledge is not the classics of late antiquity, but the sound doctrine of Sacred Scripture, which he obtained through assiduous reading, study and prayer: "The duty to teach is not merely the Christian orator's first duty, it is his highest and in a sense his only duty."[18] His style of delivery must take second place to the clarity of his teaching. Thus preachers are encouraged to rely on the simple style rather than the moderate or grand style, in imitation of Christ who emptied himself of his divinity and became lowly in order to raise us. There are times, however, when it is totally appropriate to employ the other loftier styles as well, depending on the occasion and subject matter. Nothing is to be gained by putting the members of the congregation to sleep. The preacher needs to repeat the truths of faith that have been heard countless times but have fallen on deaf ears. The right turn of phrase might spark the interest of his listeners and persuade them of the need to change and reform their lives. The preacher must know his audience and adapt his discourse accordingly. The goal is clear communication. There are, however, certain things which are better left unsaid, either because they are too complex to deal with in the context of preaching, or because they are too controversial. Such issues should only be tackled or addressed on special occasions and only rarely.[19] The preacher's silence on delicate matters is never to cover-up or conceal. Never is he permitted to speak an untruth no matter how dire the circumstances: this is one issue the bishop never wavered on from the time of his first publication on the subject of lying.[20] Augustine's intransigence on the issue provoked a major falling out with the talented biblical scholar Jerome, whose commentary on chapter two of Galatians attempted to explain Paul's rebuke of Peter on the need for converts to first be circumcised as feigned. Augustine is astonished that Jerome is willing to endorse the acceptability of a falsehood based on nothing less than the authority of Sacred Scripture. Jerome seemed more interested in defending the integrity of Peter and the harmony between the apostles than defending the Gospel as a reliable and credible source of truth. If Paul's rebuke to Peter is only simulated and the story is fabricated, on what basis is the remainder of the Bible to be believed? Elsewhere Augustine characterizes the work of philosophers as untrustworthy, "not...because everything they say is false, but because they rely for the most part on untrustworthy sources."[21]

Fortin astutely observed that Augustine tacitly deleted all reference to "plausibility" (the usual rendering of the Latin *verisimiliter*) in *Teaching Christianity*, while Cicero had emphasized it as the chief merit of a rhetorical argument.[22] The only time the term appears in the work is in connection with teachers of false doctrine. Augustine firmly grounds all Christian teaching in a devotion to truth, regardless of the appearances or consequences.

Augustine's Preaching

Augustine's teaching skills are most evident in his preaching. The bishop's homilies are available to us in three primary collections: the *Sermons*, *The Tractates on John*, and his *Commentary on the Psalms*.[23] Scholars estimate that we are only in possession of one-tenth or perhaps only one-fourteenth of all the bishop's sermons.[24] We have since discovered an additional twenty-six sermons thanks to the discovery of Dolbeau based on a catalogue of manuscripts found in the city library at Mainz in 1990.[25] Scholars owe an enormous debt to the late Benedictine Pierre-Patrick Verbraken for his painstaking work on the authenticity of Augustine's sermons.[26] Adding twenty-six to the original number of 544 reported by Verbraken leaves us a total of 570 sermons which have been preserved. This figure, of course, is debated by other scholars. Manlio Simonetti identifies a total of 870 homilies excluding the recent Dolbeau addition.[27] The bishop generally relied on stenographers to taken down his sermons which tended to be delivered *ex tempore*. He did dictate, however, one section of the *Commentary on the Psalms* and some scholars maintain that he did not actually deliver Homilies 55-124 on the gospel of John. Augustine's sermons are noted for their improvisational character and liveliness. Such improvisation should not be taken for unpreparedness. It appears that Augustine diligently prepared his comments based on the biblical texts, which on Sundays and major feasts were fixed in the lectionary. Apparently the celebrant was free to choose his own readings on ordinary days, where he often preferred to work through a single book of scripture.[28] Reading Augustine's homilies sometimes allows us to reconstruct the readings that were read at that particular liturgy. There were ordinarily three readings: Old Testament, New Testament (almost always from Paul), and Gospel. He generally preferred to preach on only one reading, usually the

Gospel, especially John. His second favorite source for homilies was the psalm which normally was proclaimed between the first reading and the Gospel. On the feast days of martyrs Augustine might comment on the *Passio* of the martyr and on occasion even had read an excerpt from Africa's favorite martyr, St. Cyprian. Sometimes he chose to preach on only part of the liturgy, such as the preface dialogue.[29] The bishop was especially inclined to preach on the two great sacraments, baptism and Eucharist, to the newly baptized who ordinarily were kept in the dark about these mysteries until after their baptism due to the *disciplina arcana*. He was not beyond improvisation, however: when the lector accidently read the wrong text, he would simply adjust and preach on the text that was read.[30]

Augustine is constantly aware of his audience and reacts to their every response. His homilies could be quite lengthy, anywhere from less than one-half an hour, to over two hours, as evidenced in the new Dolbeau collection. The bishop normally sat on the presider's chair as he preached, while the people stood and listened. He sometimes made exceptions, especially during longer sermons, where he might stand at the pulpit while the people rested. His style is often interactive employing expressions like: "... we hear (*audimus*) the apostle say," "Listen to Paul," "Listen to the apostle," "Listen to the Gospel." When trying to explain an especially difficult passage he will frequently say, "Pay attention,"[31] or a more refined, "Would your holinesses please concentrate on what I am saying."[32] It is impossible to cite here all the instances where Augustine asks his congregation to pay attention since the Latin language uses various phrases such as *intendat,* [or *attendat*] *caritas vestra, intendat sanctitas vestra, intendite, attendite, advertite*. The Latin form *attendere*, for example, appears 701 times in the sermons of St. Augustine, excluding the recent Dolbeau discovery; the imperative plural "pay attention" (*attendite*) is used 102 times; the imperative singular is used 189 times.[33] Augustine would often use the second person singular when engaging his congregation (instead of the second person plural), in order to heighten the urgency and immediacy of his message. The tone is usually conversational rather than a monologue. When the people began to lose him, Augustine would frequently repeat himself or summarize the point. And when he had to confront them with difficult moral issues such as adultery he would charge ahead, demanding his listeners to swallow the bitter pill: "whether they like it or not, I will say my piece."[34] Here in *Sermon 9* he criticizes men who readily cheat on their wives and use the lame excuse that they are too weak, while the members of the supposed weaker sex remain steadfast in virtue: "Your chaste wives show you that what you don't want to do can be done, and you say it can't be done."[35] The perversity of human solidarity is such that anyone who gives false witness is abominated, and anyone who steals is considered unjust, while anyone who tumbles in the hay with his maids is admired and his actions are turned into a joking matter. A man who is chaste, on the other hand, is made to feel an oddball and feels ashamed to join the company of those who are not like him: "So this is what human perversity has come to, that someone who conquered by lust is considered a man, and someone who has conquered lust is not considered a man."[36]

The bishop would often pose questions based on the readings, employing the Socratic method that characterized his early work on *The Teacher (De magistro)*: "Who is he [this man] — do you want to know?" (Sermon 22A.7) He often implores the congregation to pray for him as he is preaching, so that he will be inspired and clear in delivering God's Word. Like a good teacher, he knows when he is losing them or boring them with unnecessary details, and he adjusts his delivery accordingly. He is willing to cut short a homily and will urge them to pay attention when the heat is too oppressive.[37] We are uncertain as to whether Augustine had the opportunity to revise his sermons, even though he expressly indicated his intention to do so in the *The Revisions*.

Augustine frequently describes the duty he feels to preach to the people and refers to this responsibility as a "debt" to be paid. Augustine normally preached twice a week on Saturday and Sunday, on major feast days, daily during the Octave of Easter, and sometimes twice a day.[38] We can only conclude that Augustine considered preaching the most important responsibility of a bishop. The bishop's sermons are conveniently organized according to their subject matter: *Se scripturis, De tempore, De sanctis,* and *De diversis.* His brilliant career as a preacher began when he was a simple priest and was asked by his bishop, Valerius, to preach at the regular Sunday Eucharist, an unheard of request for a newly ordained priest at the time. Ecclesiastical customs were broken once again when the talented priest was invited to preach before all the African bishops gathered in assembly. The number of people present in the congregation varied depending on location and occasion. The bishop would often lament the poor turnout for a liturgy when the stadium or amphitheater would be packed.[39] While preaching on the feast of the martyr Saint Lawrence he once remarked: "The martyrdom of Blessed Lawrence is renowned in Rome, but not here; or at least I see that there are very few of you present."[40] Nonbelievers were oftentimes present and he would directly address them. Some had a strong background in Scripture, but most did not. He frequently was a guest speaker outside of Hippo and certainly encountered more sophisticated congregations in urban centers such as Carthage where he was a regular guest. The congregation would readily show its approval and enthusiasm by acclamations and applause. Sometimes the bishop moved them to tears, as occurred before a congregation at Caesarea in Mauretania when he made an impassioned plea for family members to root out conflicts and divisions between relatives, parents, children and siblings. He tells us in *Teaching Christianity*:

> But I realized I was having some effect, not when I heard their acclamations but when I saw them weep. Their acclamations showed they had understood and were pleased; their tears showed that they were really affected... Over eight years have passed since then, and with the help of Christ they have avoided that kind of thing.[41]

Throughout his preaching career, Augustine paid his "debt" with eloquence and passion, devoting himself to the congregations with love and self-sacrifice.

Biblical Interpretation

Augustine's talent as a teacher is immediately apparent in his creative and penetrating interpretation of biblical texts. He would normally comment on only part of the readings, rather than attempt to explain all of the readings. Sometimes the bishop comments on only one reading; on occasion the bishop would only comment on a single detail from the text. His experience, tested over a lifetime of preaching, offers invaluable insight for college professors today who are often faced with commenting on long and difficult classical texts from the canon of western literature. The readings could be difficult, obscure and sometimes dangerous if misunderstood. Some passages should be interpreted literally but never "according to the flesh *(carnaliter)*." He frequently found certain passages especially difficult to interpret, such as a particular line in the creation story (*"aliquantum ad intelligendum spissum est"*).[42] Elsewhere he specifies that the apostle Paul "has spoken obscurely."[43] Other passages are clear and straight forward requiring little comment.[44] Augustine explains the reason for this discrepancy: "...Some things in the scriptures are hidden in darkness and call for study, while others are within easy reach, being proposed with clarity so as to cure whoever wants to be cured."[45] Sometimes the context will clear up an ambiguity. Otherwise they can often be properly interpreted by consulting other passages from the Bible, whether the Old or New Testament. Augustine justified this hermeneutical principle by the basic unity of the Old and New Testaments due to their single principal author, namely God. At times more than one interpretation of a single passage can be given. This poses no problem, so long as neither interpretation conflicts with the creed (*regula fidei*).[46]

At times the bishop will resort to allegory to interpret difficult or ambiguous passages, especially when the literal meaning is clearly untenable, either because it contradicts another teaching found in Scripture or the rule of faith. Augustine's allegorical interpretation may well strike modern ears as odd, forced, or bordering on the bizarre, particularly his *Commentary of the Psalms* where he often appears least rehearsed.[47] This should come as no surprise, since these often were preached at some kind of prayer service outside of the more formal context of the liturgy. The commentaries were driven by the pastoral needs of the flock. The bishop consequently invoked images and metaphors from everyday life. His favorite themes were in direct response to the existential fears, hopes and joys of his listeners, emphasizing the precarious and transitory state of life in this world, where fortunes and health can be lost in a day. His comments on Psalm 106 capture the sobering, stark reality of the human condition: "People are born, people live, people die; while some die, others are born and once again while these others die, others are born. They come, they go, they come, they go without ceasing."[48] He naturally took for granted that David was the author of the Psalms, a view shared by all of his contemporaries. Yet his insights are unique and original and do not appear derived from Hilary, Ambrose or Jerome. There is generally a christological interpretation to the psalms, but always in the sense of the *totus Christus* (the whole Christ, head and body, the Church). Many of these commentaries, in fact, were never preached at all, but were dictated, that is, designed to be read. Simonetti accepts the scholarly opinion of Dom Wilbert, which counted a total of 86 texts that were dictated and 119 that were effectively preached.[49] In the *Commentary on Psalm 64* (Psalm 65 in modern translations) the bishop interprets the mountains in verse 7, "*preparans montes in fortitudine sua*" ("He sets the mountains in place by his strength"), as preachers.[50] Yet the bishop could also be quite conventional in adopting metaphors that were commonly understood in the long tradition of symbolic interpretation. He comments at length in the *Commentary on Psalm 64* on the significance of the two cities Babylonia and Jerusalem, which represent the world and church, respectively. We currently live as captives in Babylonia (*debemus nosse Babyloniam, in qua captivi sumus*), which represents confusion; we aspire to return to Jerusalem, which signifies a vision of peace (*visio pacis*).[51] One of his more brilliant and creative moments in allegorical interpretation is found in his *Commentary on Psalm 41* (Psalm 42 in modern translations), "As a deer longs for running water, so longs my soul for you, O God; I thirst for you O God."[52] In an intimate and conversational manner, the bishop instructs the congregation: "There is another thing which you should take note of about deer" (*Est aliud quod animadvertas in cervo*). Deer generally cross streams in single file, one behind another, each resting its head on the back side of the other. They change places leading the pack as necessary to give each deer the opportunity to rest. So too are Christians to carry each other's burdens, honoring the apostle and fulfilling the law of Christ: *Invicem onera vestra portate, et sic adimplebitis legem Christi*.[53] On the other hand, words that may have an allegorical meaning in Scripture should not always be interpreted allegorically: "Objects that may have an allegorical meaning in scripture do not always have it. Mountains, stones, and lions do not always stand for The Lord, or for something good or something evil. It depends on the context, which is determined by the elements of the of the passage."[54]

There are countless other examples of allegory. In Sermon 4 he explains that the mother of Esau and Jacob gave birth to two sons, the one hairy, the other smooth: "Hairiness stands for sins, smoothness for mildness, that is for cleanness from sins."[55] Later on in the same homily, he expands on his interpretation: "There are bad people in the Church, belonging to Esau, because they too are sons of Rebecca, sons of mother Church, born of her womb, and hairy by persisting in materialistic sins — but still born of the womb."[56] The bishop exhorts his congregation to learn the basic rules of interpretation: "This is a rule of interpretation which I advise you to learn by heart." Certain words, like *saeculum*, always refer to the same thing, namely "sinners" or "lovers of this world/age."[57] Allegorical interpretations are especially useful when trying to understand the significance of numbers, a subject which fascinated both Augustine and his contemporaries. The number seven, for example, is connected with the Holy Spirit, as is the number fifty.[58] The numbers, two, three, four, seven, eight, ten, eleven, fourteen, seventeen, forty, fifty and seventy-seven all have a special significance.[59] "Unfamiliarity with numbers is also the cause of not understanding many things which are put down metaphorically and mystically in scripture."[60]

Teaching Christianity further elaborates on why certain passages are so difficult: "This is all due, I have no doubt at all, to divine providence, in order to break in pride with hard labor, and to save the intelligence from boredom, since it readily forms a low opinion of things that are too easy to work out."[61] We should not be surprised by their occasional difficulty, since the subject they are treating is God: "If you understood, he would not be God."[62] This struggle to understand should be a source of humility, a healthy antidote to the contagion of pride that infects all human beings as a result or original sin. Augustine readily admits when he is unsure about how to interpret a particular passage, and he distinguishs between "knowing" (*scire*) and "conjecturing" (*estimare*). Faith is obviously required for understanding the Bible: "Believe in order that you may understand," citing the Septuagint version of Isaiah 7:9.[63]

Augustine does not avoid difficult questions in his preaching. He felt particularly challenged by tough questions, such as Jesus' assertion that the sin against the Holy Spirit is unforgivable. He not only admits that the question is profound, but concludes: "I have dealt with this most difficult question to the best of my ability, and trust that with the Lord's merciful help I have been able to make some headway."[64] Nor does he shy from tackling cumbersome theological doctrines, including the subtleties of trinitarian questions, employing technical terms such as *substantia*, even though the average person understood this term primarily to mean "riches and material means." Nevertheless, he consistently avoids certain complex questions, such as divine foreknowledge and the subject of predestination. His favorite subjects include all the articles of the Creed, especially belief in God, Christ and the Church. He especially emphasizes the equality of the Son with the Father. In the scriptures it is Jesus himself who teaches us.[65] The inner teacher who dwells within the hearts of the faithful enables the Scripture to be understood: "No one can come to such knowledge without a kind of silent clamor of truth ringing inside him."[66] Augustine will invite his congregation to enter with him into the sanctuary of God: "there perhaps I will teach you if I am able. Or, better, learn with me from him who instructs me."[67] The bishop must first hear the Word of God within himself (*intus auditor*) before he is able to preach it.[68]

Summary

Augustine is a model teacher and applies his natural talent and carefully crafted skills throughout the nearly forty years of his ordained ministry. His success is apparent, as evidenced by his constant appeal over the course of western history. His *Commentary on the Psalms* has nourished generations of monks with *lectio divina*, and his *Sermons* continue to speak with the power and forcefulness of a contemporary political commentator. Entire portions of his sermons could easily be worked into almost any Sunday homily, and his theory of language continues to inspire philosophers and literary critics. Much can be gained by a careful study of his theory which I have only cursorily summarized in the first part of this paper. More important is to see his theory in action, the expert practitioner weaving together words in order to communicate the ineffable Word of God. University teachers have much to learn from Augustine's wise selection of texts and careful attention to detail. Yet he chooses selectively and generally avoids overwhelming his listeners by trying to cover too much. The bishop regularly borrowed from his personal experiences and from the culture which nurtured his own education, but his primary source remained the Word of God. Yet he was far from a biblical fundamentalist or literalist. Augustine did not hesitate to utilize the scientific knowledge of his day and human reason to unlock the meaning of Sacred Scripture, even to the extent of consulting the *Rules of Tyconius*, a Donatist theologian whom most Catholic bishops would have found troublesome. His discourse is liberally sprinkled with biblical citations where the untrained listener cannot distinguish the bishop's words from those of the Word of God. He worked constantly at improving his skills, but never used them simply to overwhelm or impress. He often thought it best that the preacher imitate Christ who humbled himself. Sometimes simple, straightforward prose was entirely appropriate since the goal of teaching is clear communication. Talent and skills are simply a means to an end. That end for Augustine is always love.

Notes

1   The classic loci include his early works, the *Dialogues* of Cassiciacum (including *Contra academicos, De beata vita, De ordine*), the *Confessions*, and *Teaching Christianity*. In the interest of appealing to a wider audience I have chosen to use the English language titles adopted by the very successful, *The Works of Saint Augustine, A Translation for the 21st Century* (ed. John E. Rotelle, O.S.A.; Hyde Park, New York: New City Press, 1990-2000).

2   *Conf.* 4.16.30.

3   *Letter* 118.7 (*Fathers of the Church* 18, 268). The English translations of the Letters of St. Augustine are based on the work of Sister Wilfrid Parsons in the five volumes found in *The Fathers of the Church*, 12, 18, 20, 30, 32 (Washington, D.C.: The Catholic University of America Press, 1953-1981; hereafter abbreviated FC). I have occasionally made minor adaptations in the hope of achieving greater clarity and ease of reading.

4   *Letter* 118.6 (FC 18, 267).

5   *Letter* 118.22 (FC 18, 282): "This way is first humility, second humility, third humility..." Augustine here uses that same literary figure which is echoed today in that hackneyed but effective expression: "In real estate the only thing which counts is location, location and location."

6   See the recently published proceedings of the 1997 Villanova University Conference on Post-Modernism and Religion, *God, The Gift and Postmodernism* (eds. John D. Caputo and Michael J Scanlon; Bloomington: Indiana University Press, 1999). A second Post-Modernism and Religion Conference was held at Villanova in October 1999 on the issue, *Questioning God*. The keynote address was "Forgiveness" by Jacques Derrida and the entire proceedings will be published in the near future.

7   The collection of essays found in *De doctrina christiana, A Classic of Western Culture* (eds. Duane W. H. Arnold and Pamela Brights; Notre Dame: University of Notre Dame Press, 1995) testifies to the importance of this work.

8   Ernest L. Fortin, "Augustine and the Problem of Christian Rhetoric," *Augustinian Studies* 5 (1974) 85-100. Fortin was not the first scholar to call attention to the uniquely Christian character of *Teaching Christianity*. See J. Fontaine, "Aspects et problèmes de la prose di'art latine au IIIe siècle," *Lezioni Augusto Rosatgni*, IV, (Torino, 1968) 32-43. See also Harold Hagendahl, *Augustine and the Latin Classics* (Göteberg, 1967) 567, who argued: "[Augustine's teaching] follows... Cicero's views so closely, often even in the minutest particulars, that it cannot make a substantial claim to novelty and originality..." Also see H. I. Marrou, *Saint Augustin et la fin de la culture antique* (Paris: Boccard, 1938); J. Oroz, "El *De Doctrina Christiana* o la retorica cristiana," *Estudios Clasicos* 3 (1956) 452-459; idem., "La retorical augustiniana: Clasicismo y Cristianismo," *Studia patristica* 6 (1962) 485-95.

9   Fortin, "Augustine and the Problem," 87.

10   Fortin, "Augustine and the Problem," 89.

11   Fortin, "Augustine and the Problem," 91.

12   *Letter* 118.11 (FC 18, 272).

13   *De ordine*, 2.13.38.

14   *Teaching Christianity*, 4.6.9. All the English translations of *De doctrina christiana* are based on *Teaching Christianity, The Works of St. Augustine* (ed. John E. Rotelle, O.S.A.; trans. Edmund Hill, O.P.; Hyde Park: New City Press, 1996).

15   *Teaching Christianity*, 2.37.55.

16   *Teaching Christianity*, 4.6.9.

17   *Teaching Christianity*, 4.3.4.

18   *Teaching Christianity*, 4.12.28, as cited in Fortin, "Augustine and the Problem," 92.

19   *Teaching Christianity*, 4.9.23.

20   See *De mendacio* and *Contra mendacium*, published in 395 and 420, respectively.

21   *Letter* 82.13 (FC 12, 400).

22   Fortin, "Augustine and the Problem," 92.

23   Augustine's preaching is identified by three different technical terms: *Sermo* (Sermon), *Tractatus* (Homily), and *Enarrationes* (Commentaries or Expositions), the latter appearing for the first time in Erasmus's edition. These names sometimes overlap and are interchangeable even though Christine Mohrmann, "Praedicare-tractare-sermo," *Études sur latin des Chrétiens*, Vol. 2 (Rome: 1961) 63-72, has demonstrated that *tractare* and *tractatus* originally referred to exegetical exposition. I am indebted to Cardinal Michele Pellegrino's excellent "General Introduction" to Augustine's sermons found in Edmund Hill's vivid translation of Saint Augustine, *Sermons, The Works of St. Augustine* (ed. John E. Rotelle, O.S.A.; Brooklyn: New City Press, 1990) 13-137. This proved an invaluable source for many of the comments I make throughout this essay.

24 See Pierre-Patrick Verbraken, "Foreward," *Sermons I, The Works of St. Augustine* (ed. John Rotelle; Brooklyn: New City Press, 1990) 11.

25 See Augustin d'Hippone, *Vingt-six sermons au peuple d'Afrique* (ed. François Dolbeau; Paris: Institut d'Études Augustiniennes, 1996), and the important collection of essays on this discovery published in *Augustin, Prédicateur (395-411)*, Actes du Colloque International de Chantilly (Paris: Institut d'Études Augustiniennes, 1998). A convenient summary of the importance of these newly discovered sermons for our knowledge of Augustine is found in H Chadwick, "New Sermons of St. Augustine," *The Journal of Theological Studies* 47 (April 1996) 69-91.

26 See Pierre-Patrick Verbraken, *Études critiques sur les Sermons authentiques de saint Augustin* (Instrumentum Patristica 12; Steenbruggen: 1976).

27 Sant' Agostino *Commento ai Salmi*, a cura di Manlio Simonetti (Fondazione Lorenzo Valla; Arndaldo Mondaodori Editore, 1988) is a very useful introduction and commentary on a sampling of some of the psalms with a facing Latin text.

28 See G. C. Willis, *St. Augustine's Lectionary* (Alcuin Club Collections 44; London: 1962) 5-9.

29 See Sermons 227, 229, and 229A.

30 See Sermon 352.1.

31 Sermon 13.6, "*Haec attendite.*"

32 See Sermon 4.33, "*Intendat Sanctitas vestra quod dicimus.*"

33 *Thesaurus Augustinianus* (Thesaurus Patrum Latinorum, curante CETEDOC; Brepols: Universitas Catholica Lovaniensis, 1989). See entry "*attendere, attendite, attende.*"

34 Sermon 9.3-4.

35 Sermon 9.12.

36 Sermon 9.12.

37 Sermon 99.4.

38 See Agostino Trapè, *St. Augustine: Man, Pastor, Mystic* (trans. M. J. O'Connell; New York: Catholic Book Publishing, 1986) 149.

39 Sermon 51.1-2.

40 Sermon 303.1.

41 *Teaching Christianity* 4.53.

42 See Pellegrino's "General Introduction," to the *Sermons* in *The Works of St. Augustine,* 34, where he cites a fragment published by C. Lambot, "Une série pascale de sermons de saint Augustin sur les jours de la création," in *Mélanges offerts à Mademoiselle Christine Mohrmann* (Utrecht: Spectrum, 1963) 217, line 17.

43 Sermon 164.3.

44 Sermon 32.18.

45 Sermon 32.1.

46 Sermon 7.3-4.

47 Sant' Agostino *Commento ai Salmi*, a cura di Manlio Simonetti. The "*Introduzione*" and notes are especially helpful on a limited sampling of the psalms.

48 *Commentary on Psalm 106*, 20.

49 Simonetti, "*Introduzione*," XXIII.

50 *Commentary on Psalm 64*, 10. *Praeparavit enim magnos praedicatores, et ipsos appellavit montes; humiles in se, escelsos in illo* ("For he has prepared great preachers; he has called them mountains, humble in themselves, exalted in him").

51 *Commentary on Psalm 64*, 1-2.

52 *Commentary on Psalm 41*, 1-3: *Quemadmodum desiderat cervus ad fontes aquarum, ita desiderat anima mea ad te Deus.*

53 *Commentary on Psalm 41*, 4.

54 Sermon 32.6.

55 Sermon 4.14.

56 Sermon 4.31.

57 Sermon 12.2.

58 Sermon 8.17.

59 See Sermons 6.7; 51.32-35; 125.7-10; 260C.2-6; 272B.2-6.

60 *Teaching Christianity* 2.16.25.

61 *Teaching Christianity* 2.6.7.

62 Sermon 117.5.

63 See Sermon 43.

64 Sermon 71.1.38.

65 Sermon 181.1.

66 Sermon 12.4.

67 Sermon 48.8.

68 Sermon 179.1.

Chapter Six

The "Arts Reputed Liberal": Augustine on the Perils of Liberal Education

Kevin L. Hughes

Introduction: Augustine *or* Liberal Education?

Augustine is often cited across denominations as an exemplary figure in the history of what for lack of better terms we may call the Christian intellectual life.[1] At my own institution a recent evaluator of the university's mission statement urged us to take advantage of Augustine in the development of our mission and identity. Thus far, such efforts have usually taken shape in the introduction of Augustine into our core curriculum, the development of an Augustinian Studies concentration, and renewed commitment to the journal *Augustinian Studies* which the university sponsors. All this is in and of itself good. And certainly it is true that we find in Augustine both the depths of Christian commitment and one of the keenest intellects the West has ever produced. No one would deny the significance of his contribution to Christian theology and philosophy. Augustine offers the Christian academy one of the finest models of the integration of faith and reason, and institutions like my own could do worse for a patron.

But there is a certain irony in holding up St. Augustine as an icon for the Christian teacher-scholar. Prior to his conversion, Augustine was an academic, and, one might say, one of the young budding "public intellectuals" of late Roman imperial culture. And yet it seems that his conversion was precisely a conversion away from the world of the academy, first to the private life of philosophical *otium* at Cassiciacum, and then later to priesthood and the episcopacy. Christian conversion is for Augustine an Exodus from bondage, and to "despoil the Egyptians" was to "cram" oneself "with gold and silver and fine rainment," the wealth of pagan culture, as one "came out of Egypt" or abandoned that culture.[2] While much, perhaps, could be pilfered from pagan culture, Augustine leaves little doubt that it should nevertheless be abandoned. So should we speak rather of "Augustine *or* Liberal Education"?

My intention in this essay is to ponder this question in two forms: First, what is Augustine's mature attitude toward the liberal education of his youth and young adulthood? If Augustine indeed rejected "liberal education" in principle, for what reasons? Second, what are the implications of such a view upon the relationship of Christianity and liberal education today? If, in fact, Augustine saw Christian faith and liberal education as disjunctive, what can modern Christian scholars and academic institutions do?

Trafficking in Speechifying: the Perils of Rhetoric and the Academic Profession

Augustine's *Confessions* is ripe with reflections upon his own education and his career as a teacher of rhetoric — in fact, one could argue that education forms one of the thematic centers of the work. The culture into which Augustine is educated and in which he teaches is itself a structure built upon sin, and the story of Augustine's conversion is, at least in part, the story of his departure from it. Usual accounts of Augustine's conversion dwell most heavily upon his attachment to carnal desires, and, indeed, the climactic moment in the garden seems to focus the story upon those particular sins. But Augustine's portrait of his life as a teacher suggests that he sees academia as only a subtle variation on such carnal temptations. From this perspective, the *Confessions* is as much the tale of Augustine's turning away from his liberal education as from his carnal habits.

Augustine's "portrait of a rhetorician as a young man" is rhetorically inflated and not terribly flattering. By his account of his career's beginning in North Africa, Augustine and his friends are nothing better than high-class prostitutes that enjoy their work a bit too much. They are, he says, both seducer and seduced, both deceivers and deceived. The public face of their deception, says Augustine, is through their engagement with the "arts reputed 'liberal.'"[3] His teaching is a practice of mutual seduction and manipulation, of "selling talkative skills apt to sway others because greed swayed me."[4] His greedy consumption of books on the "so-called liberal arts"[5] gains him nothing, despite his naturally gifted intelligence, since he "took care that this excellent part of my substance should be under my control." By claiming his intelligence as his own, by failing to "offer a sacrifice" to God for his gift, Augustine fails to use this inheritance well. Like the Prodigal Son, Augustine leaves his Father,"squanders" his riches in a "distant land," and thus effectively cuts himself off from the riches of wisdom.[6] And yet it should be noted that Augustine's greed is not primarily for wealth or honor. His ambition is particularly a scholarly one:

> I did not want to go to Rome because my friends promised me that there I would command higher fees and enjoy greater prestige — though these arguments were not without force for me; the principal and almost the sole reason was that I heard that young men there study more quietly and are controlled by a more systematic regime of strict discipline.[7]

So his ambition as he journeys to Rome is more intellectual than material, but it is ambition nonetheless. And yet it is this relentless focus upon his own power, intellect, and reputation that pushed him to the forefront of an ambitious profession. In rapid succession, Augustine is able to move from Thagaste to Carthage, from Carthage to Rome, and, after pulling a few strings, from Rome to the imperial courts at Milan.

In the rapid course of this ambitious rise to power, Augustine is continually in search of more sober and reputable students. Augustine "makes a name for himself" in Rome, only to find his aspirations to serious scholarship frustrated yet again by a more sophisticated student conspiracy. Faced with a student boycott, Augustine once again seeks to flee. When word comes from Milan of an opportunity for a rhetorician, Augustine manages to pull some strings among his influential Manichee friends. He is appointed to Milan, a crowning achievement for a young master of rhetoric.

But all his success as a rhetorician, he says, brings him only hollowness, anxiety, and unhappiness. En route to speak to the imperial courts, Augustine encounters a drunken beggar whose simple bliss with a bottle seems to possess a shade of happiness that evades the young rhetor and makes his misery all the more wretched: "He would sleep off his intoxication that same night, whereas I had slept with mine and risen up again, and would sleep and rise with it again . . . How many days!"[8] Augustine was on his way to speak before the emperor, but it seems to him in retrospect only an occasion to "tell plenty of lies with the object of winning favor with the well-informed by my lying."[9] While Augustine and his peers pursue their ambition for "solely the attainment of unclouded joy," he is taken aback to realize that "this beggar had already beaten us to the goal."[10] The emptiness and vanity of his own ambitions hang before his eyes, and he is left with only despair. And yet even so he remains in his profession.

It is only later, after his final collapse and conversion, and in the face of some sort of respiratory illness, that Augustine at last departs the world of the academy for good. His flight puts an end to his "trafficking in speechifying."[11] For Augustine, looking back, the life of a teacher of rhetoric, even in the royal courts of Milan, was little different from that of back-alley weapons merchants and prostitutes. He leaves his post so that "boys who devoted their thoughts not to your law but to false raptures and battles of public speeches, should no longer buy from my mouth the weapons for their frenzy." In resigning, Augustine confesses, "I would . . . return no more to offer myself for sale, now that You had redeemed me."[12] No more would Augustine be a slave to be bought and sold by others or a prostitute who sells himself.

Freed at last from such a profession, Augustine retreats with his friends into the life of philosophical leisure at Cassiciacum. His flight from the city to the countryside reconstructs his intellectual landscape as well. Augustine confesses that God has "laid low the mountains and hills of my proud intellect and made of me an even plain."[13] But it is a gradual process; Augustine fears that the work he produced during his stay still had a "whiff of scholastic pride about it, like combatants still panting in the interval."[14] Cassiciacum was Augustine's "halfway-house" between the ambition of his career and the humility he thought fitting to a Christian person, where he began — but did not finish — unlearning the habits of liberal education.

"Despoiling the Egyptians": the Liberal Arts in *De doctrina christiana*

Augustine gives systematic treatment to the liberal arts, at least insofar as they are useful for understanding Scripture, in *De doctrina christiana*. This work, which Augustine began in 396-397, but did not complete until 426, has been the subject of much debate by Augustinian scholars in this century. Many have seen Augustine's *De doctrina christiana* as a new Christian textbook in the liberal arts. According to a classic argument by Henri Marrou, Augustine intended in this work to produce a new "*culture chrétienne*," using the Bible as a new cultural cornerstone, as Homer was to the Greeks and Vergil was to the Romans. More recently, Eugene Kevane and others have discussed the *De doctrina christiana* as a first attempt to provide a blueprint for a properly "Christian *paideia*."[15] For Frederick van Fleteren, the text provides the "charter for the Christian intellectual."[16] For such scholars, Augustine stands on the cusp of the age, reshaping the classical legacy to form a new, properly Christian, culture. And indeed, the text was received as just such a charter: the great educational manuals of medieval Christendom were essentially adaptations of the *De doctrina christiana*.[17]

Other scholars have wondered whether, in fact, this rather grandiose notion truly reflects Augustine's intention. Christoph Schäublin has argued that "a close reading has shown us that [Augustine] is in no way attempting to preserve — for its own sake — the pagan educational system, not even within narrow limits."[18] Schäublin takes the strong form of an argument against Marrou, suggesting that Augustine would prefer to dispose of the liberal arts altogether. Any use of the rules of discourse or logic or any other art is strictly ad hoc, and, as Peter Brown suggests as well, Augustine wishes such use of eloquence or the arts to be "unselfconscious, unacademic, uncompetitive, and devoted to the understanding of the Bible alone."[19] John Cavadini has taken a more moderate stance toward the subject. According to Cavadini, the *De doctrina* leaves the reader in a tentative but not oppositional relationship to the tools of classical culture, since "there is no culturally unmediated sweetness [of persuasion]," so that even God's Word uses persuasion and eloquence.[20] The Christian stands therefore in some necessary relationship to culture, even if her conversion has released her from being defined wholly by it.

This latter perspective helps make sense of Book Two, where the general approach to the liberal arts seems to be, "Yes, but...," just the sort of tentative relationship which Cavadini suggests. This central section of the *De Doctrina* is the threshing floor of the liberal arts, upon which Augustine is struggling to separate the wheat from the chaff. First, Augustine is quick to dismiss any of the "errors of pagan superstition," which we might refer to as "popular culture." Indeed, he admits that "this is the sort of thing … the pagan poets have been more in the habit of mentioning than of teaching."[21] Augustine seems to feel that even a casual engagement with such things tends towards idolatry. And yet, Augustine refuses to dispose of everything touched by pagan superstition: "still we for our part should certainly not allow such heathen superstitions to make us shun all knowledge of music, if we can snatch anything from it that we can use… After all, it is no reason for us not to learn our letters, just because they say Mercury is their patron god."[22] So, even at the first layer of distinction, Augustine urges prudential judgment and careful distinction of the useful from the superstitious.

Outside of these superstitious arts, Augustine wishes to distinguish further between cultural artifacts that are "superfluous and extravagant luxuries" from those that are "convenient and necessary adjuncts of life."[23] In the former category, Augustine includes most of the plastic and theatrical arts, making exceptions only for "when a difference is made by what is done."[24] The study of the latter Augustine identifies as a "lawful and liberal realm of knowledge."[25] On this level, the Augustinian canons of liberal education finally reduce to the criterion of use. Only those "useful arts" such as grammar, language, writing, and eloquence are "not unlawful to learn."[26]

What I have called Augustine's threshing process he himself discusses with his famous allusion to the "despoiling of the Egyptians" (Ex. 3:22; 11:2-3; 12:35-36). Augustine asserts that the "liberal disciplines … suited to the service of the truth" are the "gold and silver" in the possession of the heathens. These treasures Christians should take for their own use "when they separate themselves in spirit from their hapless company."[27] Augustine fines ample precedent for this practice among the leaders of the Church:

> … for what else, after all, have so many of our good believers done? Can we not see how much gold and silver and fine rainment Cyprian was crammed with as he came out of Egypt, that loveliest of teachers and most blessed of martyrs? Or Lactantius, or Victorinus, Optatus, Hilary, not to mention the living? Or countless Greek writers?[28]

It is important to note that even this image represents conversion as an exodus, a departure from the culture of liberal education and philosophy that had previously enslaved these great figures like Israel under Pharaoh. Any treasures that are taken are piecemeal and cut loose from the web of the oppressive culture left behind. The insights of rhetoric and philosophy will no longer be part of a system or an institution of liberal education per se, but instead be applied *ad hoc* to the understanding of Scripture.

Rhetoric remains for Augustine perhaps the prince of these useful and lawful arts, these despoiled treasures, but in it also lies the deepest temptation. "The discipline of rational discourse, indeed," he says, "is of the greatest value in penetrating and solving all kinds of problems which crop up in holy literature." But it has its dangers: "One must be on guard again a passion for wrangling and a kind of childish parade of getting the better of one's opponents."[29] Indeed, training in the discipline of rhetoric itself can lead one into temptation; the very rules of rhetoric begin to suggest useless indulgence in erudition for its own sake. Augustine far prefers those who learn eloquence by listening and by speaking. Too much emphasis on the rules themselves are akin to step-by-step instruction in the art of walking: those who can already walk have no need of instruction, and those who cannot walk at all have no interest in learning.[30] Such thematic attention to rules and structures constitute "heavy burdens of entirely unnecessary labor."[31] Their only purpose, Augustine suggests, is to "puff up" those who master them, leading them either to trap people "with specious arguments and questions, or else think that by having learned such things we have acquired something great, which allows us to consider ourselves a cut above good and inoffensive people."[32] This thematic attention and obsession with mastery of detail is precisely what Augustine wishes to leave behind as he flees Egypt.

Indeed, this is the root temptation and Augustine's primary reason for caution in approaching the liberal arts. Liberal arts, precisely insofar as they are "liberal" (in our sense of the term, of being unconditioned and for their own sake), can only serve the purpose of self-inflation. The liberal arts may only serve to turn one's narcissistic eye upon oneself and thus "dehumanize you with self-indulgence."[33] Such knowledge cannot help but "puff up." Indeed, Augustine will suggest that all education runs such risks; knowledge, whether of signs or of the "substance of things," "can give us swollen heads and stiff necks, unless we submit them to the Lord's yoke."[34] Education in rhetoric and the arts seems too often to be nothing but a tool for the more effective exercise of pride, an observation to which Augustine's own experience bears witness.

It is perhaps for this reason that Augustine recommends against such an education for "eager and bright young people who fear God and are seeking the blessed life."[35] Perhaps it is also why Augustine refuses so firmly to teach the rules of eloquence, "which I myself learned and taught in the schools," in Book Four of *On Christian Teaching*. He admits very tentatively that there *may* be nothing inherently wrong with these rules, but he states firmly that "even if they are of some use, ... they should not be looked for from me, either in this work or in any other."[36] One can hardly miss the defensive tone in so declarative a statement. Augustine makes it clear that he has fled Egypt. He has cast off the mantle of the liberal educator, and he will never take it up again.

Knowledge Puffs up: the "Splendid Vice" of Liberal Education

How different this vision of Christian learning, how much more ad hoc, than Augustine's plan immediately after his conversion! In these early years, Augustine remained optimistic about the possibilities of education in the liberal arts to lift one to contemplation of God. In *Contra Academicos* (386) Augustine speaks of his conversion as "fleeing to the bosom of philosophy,"[37] and in *De Beata Vita*, he assumes that philosophy is the port that leads to the mainland of the "happy life."[38] His stay at Cassiciacum immediately after his conversion is recorded in a series of philosophical dialogues, written in the classical mode, which, if read together, illustrate the education in the liberal arts at work in the growth in wisdom of Licentius.[39] His departure from Milan is thus not initially a departure from classical culture per se, but rather a retreat into its highest pursuits, the life of philosophical *otium*. Indeed, such a retreat fulfilled, rather than purged, the dream begun when Augustine read Cicero's *Hortensius* at age nineteen. If Christianity transformed this pursuit at all, it was in that the light of Christ had made the pursuit of truth a bit easier. But the pursuit itself was the same: a programmatic ascent to wisdom through education in the liberal arts. Thus it was during this time that Augustine planned his new Christian "encyclopedia" of the liberal arts, the curriculum of which he outlined in *De Ordine* 2, and his *De Musica* was its first installment.[40]

But his mature insight, captured in both *De doctrina* and the *Confessions*, insists that such a program simply would recapitulate the self-indulgence of classical education, which fostered pride and flourished in praise. Sabine MacCormack has suggested that Augustine's disillusionment with the liberal arts stems from the fact that they cannot account for the Incarnation. Specifically, liberal education cannot account for a Wisdom that is so clothed in humility and love that the wise fail to recognize it.[41] In this reading, the liberal arts are useful, but finally inadequate tools for such an ascent to the knowledge of God. But the *Confessions* and the *De doctrina* seem to suggest a stronger objection. In these mature works, Augustine suggests more sharply that the liberal arts themselves can hinder progress in the ascent to God.

The liberal arts actively hinder the "restless heart" in search of God, because they are flawed in their classical Roman foundation. In the *City of God*, Augustine notes that the very structure of Roman liberal education was founded upon the love of praise, by Cicero's own admission! For Cicero, "it is honor that nourishes the arts; it is glory that kindles men to intellectual effort. All pursuits lose their lustre when they fall from general favor."[42] Pursuit of the liberal arts was simply another avenue for the love of praise that, for Augustine, was so central to Rome. As such, they issue forth in a knowledge that cannot help but "puff up" its possessors. To participate in the structures of classical education is to be initiated into the tragic flaw in the Roman character, and thus into the primordial sin of the earthly city, "self-love reaching to the point of contempt for God."[43] Augustine is quick to point out that the love of praise can restrain lower vices and thus might even seem to be itself a virtue.[44] Similarly, liberal education can "sharpen the wits" of its devotees, but likewise can it "make them more spiteful or more conceited."[45] The treasures of truth that this classical culture possessed were of value only if broken out of this cultural constellation, and this is what he intends in "despoiling the Egyptians." Augustine is interested in the jewels of liberal education only when they have been wrested from the crown of classical culture, since this crown is the token of authority in the earthly city alone.

His own experience on the "career fast track" of late antiquity bears witness to this very fact. His early teaching was an exercise in manipulation and seduction for his own ends. At the height of his success, Augustine's only goal was "winning favour of the well-informed"[46] by whatever flattery or sweet rhetoric he might use. Even after he flees this world, his early works bear for him the stamp of a scholar's pride. Liberal education has given Augustine habits of pride from which he must gradually be weaned.

The weaning process, as described in the *De doctrina*, comes through constant meditation upon 1 Cor. 8:1, "Knowledge puffs up; love builds up." This meditation is the celebration of a spiritual Passover that follows the "despoiling of the Egyptians": "For even if he comes forth from Egypt a rich man, still he cannot be saved unless he celebrates the Passover."[47] For Augustine, the Passover represents the cross of Christ, and the cross in turn "encompasses the whole of Christian activity." The treasures of Egypt may only be possessed by one purified through "doing good works in Christ and persevering in adhering to him, hoping for heavenly things, not profaning the sacraments." "Purified through this sort of activity, we shall have the capacity to know also the love of Christ which surpasses all knowledge."[48]

Conclusion

Augustine's hostility toward classical liberal education in his later writings seems clear enough. He found it built upon praise and thus prone to cultivate pride in its masters. His experience as one such master bore witness to this vulnerability, and his conversion to Christianity required a purification, an "unlearning" of so much of his past. If useful skills were still to be found in the liberal arts, they could only be so if they were broken loose from the structures of the Roman culture. Augustine's educational program, if it can be called such at all, is strictly ad hoc and unselfconscious as a "curriculum." It makes use of what tools are available for a particular purpose, and only for that. So far the argument might seem historically remote and specific to a man standing between a dying pagan culture and a new life in the Christian faith.

But Augustine's reflections upon his own culture and education might well lead us to reflect, at least analogically, upon our own. Augustine believes that the sins of self-love that lay at the root of Rome pervade all humanly-established culture as perpetual temptations. If he is correct, then we are prone to them as well, especially in an academy that has distanced itself in principle from "authority of every kind, lay or clerical, external to the academic community."[49] If the academy truly is a supposedly autonomous and self-justifying enterprise, can it possibly avoid self-absorption and self-love? If the academy strives to be "beholden to none," can it avoid the circularity and emptiness of such a stance?

On another level, we might ask if the structures of the Christian university —

hiring, tenure, peer review, promotion, publish-or-perish, and so on — differ in any substantive way from those of an explicitly secular orientation? Usually not. And such structural elements would seem inevitably to recapitulate the competitive, self-conscious, and self-obsessed nature of most academic endeavors. Attending the American Academy of Religion conference seems no different from any other celebrity showcase other professions have to offer, where one's first instinct is to observe the name-tag rather than the person. Such institutions cannot help but incline one toward self-love, pride, and the knowledge that "puffs up," precisely as Augustine suggests.

The reflections of recent scholars like Paul Griffiths offer one of the more Augustinian reviews of scholarly life in recent years. Griffiths critical observations of academic life in recent years have culminated in the conclusion to his book *Religious Reading.*[50] Griffiths suggests that the habits and practices in which we are trained — even our very act of reading in an academic mode, wherein the texts we consider are not the objects of serious loving attention and intellectual contemplation, but rather for manipulation — can amount to nothing more than a science of pride. In the practice of this science, reading is a tool of extraction and manipulation. "This is evident in the case of books," says Griffiths, "by the fact that, if the truth can for a moment be spoken, we frequently don't even read them but refer to them."[51] The academic habits of reading amount to a sort of aggressive consumption not unlike Augustine's own in his youth,[52] and Griffiths argues that the results are similarly destructive.

If Christian scholars are to cultivate different habits that are founded upon love rather than pride, they will have to reflect upon the deep structures of their institutions to discern where their foundations lie. If they rest in exaltation of the scholar's ego or if they continue to result in the relentless anxiety of young scholars in pursuit of a job or of tenure, then they not "liberal" arts at all, and an appropriately Augustinian response would be to reject them altogether. If there is to be any retrieval of liberal education among Christian intellectuals, it must be tempered and disciplined by the practices of Christian discipleship; only then will the intellectual be "gentle and humble of heart, submitting to Christ's easy yoke, and burdened with his light load, being founded and rooted and built up in love, and so not liable to be puffed up by knowledge."[53]

Notes

1   See, e.g., Frederick van Fleteren, "St. Augustine, Neoplatonism, and the Liberal Arts: The Background to *De doctrina christiana*" in *De doctrina Christiana: A Classic of Western Culture* (eds. Duane W. H. Arnold and Pamela Bright; Notre Dame: University of Notre Dame Press, 1995) 14-24, where the text in question is called 'the charter of the Christian intellectual."

2   Augustine, *De doctrina christiana* 2.61 (trans. Edmund Hill, OP, *Teaching Christianity*, New York: New City Press, 1996). All further quotations from this translation unless otherwise noted. (Abbreviated henceforth as DDC.)

3   Augustine, *Confessiones* 4.1.1: *"Per idem tempus annorum novem,...seducebamur et seducebamus, falsi atque fallentes in variis cupiditatibus, et palam per doctrinas, quas liberales vocant..."* Text from Loeb Classical Library edition, with translation from Augustine, *Confessions* (trans. Maria Boulding, OSB; New York: New City Press, 1997), unless otherwise noted.

4   *Confessiones* 4.2.1: *"Docebam in illis annis artem rhetoricam, et victoriosam loquacitatem victus cupiditate vendebam."*

5   *"...artium quas liberales vocant."* Augustine uses the same dependent clause as above (note 4) while shifting the antecedent, underscoring the forced and constructed sense of "so-called" or "reputed" all the more.

6   *Confessiones* 4.16.30: *"Sed non inde sacrificabam tibi. Itaque mihi non ad usum, sed ad perniciem magis valebat, quia tam bonam partem substantiae meae sategi habere in potestate, et fortitudinem meam non ad te custodiebam, sed profectus sum abs te in longinquam regionem, ut eam dissiparem in meretrices cupiditates."*

7   *Confessiones* 5.8.14: *"Non ideo Romam pergere volui, quod maiores quaestus maiorque mihi dignitas ab amicis, qui hoc suadebant, promittebatur – quamquam et ista ducebant animum tunc meum – sed illa erat causa maxima et paene sola, quod audiebam quietius ibi studere adulescentes et ordinatiore disciplinae cohaercitione sedari, se in eius scholam, quo magistro non utuntur, passim et proterue inruant, nec eos admitti omnino, nisi ille permiserit."*

8   *Confessiones* 6.6.10: *Et ille ipsa nocte digesterus erat ebrietatem suam, ego cum mea dormieram et surrexeram, et dormiturus et surrecturus eram; vide quot dies!"*

9   *Confessiones* 6.6.9: "... *quibus plura mentirer, et mentienti faveretur ab scientibus..."*

10   *Confessiones* 6.6.9: "... *nihil vellemus aliud nisi ad securam laetitiam pervenire, quos nos mendicus ille iam praecessiset, numquam illuc fortasse venturos."*

11   *Confessiones* 9.2.2: "... *sed leniter subtrahere ministerium linguae meae nundinis loquacitatis. . ."* (my translation).

12   Augustine, *Confessiones* 9.2: *"Et placuit mihi in conspectu tuo non tumultuose abripere, sed leniter subtrahere ministerium linguae meae nundinis loquacitatis; ne ulterius pueri – meditantes non legem tuam, non pacem tuam, sed insanias mendaces et bella forensia – mercarentur ex ore meo arma furori suo. Et opportune iam paucissimi dies supererant ad vindemiales ferias; et statui tolerare illos, ut solemniter abscederem, et redemptus a te iam non redirem venalis"* (my translation).

13   *Confessiones* 9.4.7: "... *et quemadmodum me complanaveris, humilitatis montibus et collibus cogitationum mearum."*

14   *Confessiones* 9.4.7: "... *iam quidem servientibus tibi, sed adhuc superbiae scholam tamquam in pausatione anhelantibus."*

15   See Henri Marrou, *Saint Augustine et la fin de la culture antique* (4th ed.; Paris, 1958) 331ff; E. Kevane, "Augustine's *De doctrina Christiana*: A Treatise on Christian Education," *Recherches Augustiniennes* 4 (1966) 97-133; idem, "*Paideia* and *Antipaideia*: The *Proemium* of St. Augustine's *De doctrina christiana*," *Augustinian Studies* 1 (1970) 153-180.

16 See, e.g., Frederick van Fleteren, "St. Augustine, Neoplatonism, and the Liberal Arts: The Background to *De doctrina christiana*" in *De doctrina christiana: A Classic of Western Culture* (eds. Duane W. H. Arnold and Pamela Bright; Notre Dame: University of Notre Dame Press, 1995) 14.

17 E.g., Rabanus Maurus, *de clericis*, and Hugh of St. Victor, *Didascalion*.

18 Christoph Schäublin, "*De doctrina christiana*: A Classic of Western Culture?" in *De Doctrina Christiana: A Classic of Western Culture* (eds. Duane W.H. Arnold and Pamela Bright; Notre Dame: University of Notre Dame Press, 1995) 61.

19 Peter Brown, *Augustine of Hippo* (Berkeley: University of California Press, 1969) 267.

20 John C. Cavadini, "The Sweetness of the Word: Salvation and Rhetoric in Augustine's *De doctrina christiana*," in *De doctrina christiana: A Classic of Western Culture* (eds. Duane W. H. Arnold and Pamela Bright; Notre Dame: University of Notre Dame Press, 1995) 164-181. Cavadini suggests, *contra* Brown, that the text represents not a transcending of his education, but a return to rhetoric from the overly optimistic view of philosophy. (On this see Cavadini, note 65, pp. 180-81). I agree with this assessment, with certain reservations, which I hope will be clear in this essay.

21 DDC 2.20.30: "*...quae quidem commemorare potius quam docere adsolent poetae.*" Latin text from *Corpus Christianorum, Series Latina* (CCSL) 32.

22 DDC 2.18.28: "*Sed sive non ita, nos tamen non propter superstitionem profanorum debemus musicam fugere, si quid inde utile ad intellegendas sancta scripturas rapere potuerimus. . . Neque enum et litteras discere non debuimus, quia earum deum dicunt esse Mercurium . . .*"

23 DDC 2.25,38: "*. . . quorum partim superflua luxuriosaque instituta sunt, partim commoda et necessaria.*"

24 DDC 2.25.39: "*Et hoc totum genus inter superflua hominum instituta numerandum est, nisi cum interest, quid eorum, qua de causa, et ubi et quando et cuius auctoritate fiat.*" What would constitute such an exception Augustine never says. It seems, therefore, that most of what we consider the fine arts would end up left upon Augustine's threshing floor as "superfluous." "Art for art's sake" would thus make no sense whatsoever to Augustine.

25 DDC 2.29.45: "*Nam et illud genus iam distinctum ab hoc licito et libero separavimus.*" Such a phrase suggests indirectly that Augustine does not reject the very notion of a "liberal art," but rather what is usually counted as such.

26 DDC 2.25.40: "*Sed haec tota pars humanorum institutorum, quae ad usum uitae necessarium proficiunt, nequaquam est fugienda christiano.*"

27 DDC 2.40.60: "*. . . cum ab eorum misera societate sese animo separat. . .*"

28 DDC 2.40.61: "*Nam quid aliud fecerunt multi boni fideles nostri? Nonne aspicimus quanto auro et argento et ueste suffarcinatus exierit de Aegypto Cyprianus et doctor suauissimus et martyr beatissimus? quanto Lactantius? quanto Victorinus, Optatus, Hilarius, ut de uiuis taceam? quanto innumerabiles Graeci?*"

29 DDC 2.31.48: "*Sed disputationes disciplina ad omnia genera quaestionum, quae in litteris sanctis sunt, penetrand et soluenda, plurimum ualet; tantum ibi cauenda est libido rixandi et puerilis quaedam ostentatio decipiendi aduersarium.*"

30 DDC 2.37.55. Augustine recapitulates this argument when he turns in Book 4 to discuss eloquence in presentation: DDC 4.3.4.

31 DDC 2.40.60: "*. . . sic doctrinae omnes gentilium non solum simulata et superstitiosa figmenta grauesque sarcinas superuacanei laboris habent...*"

32 DDC 2.37.55: "*Ita plerumque citius ingeniosus uidet non esse ratam conclusionem, quam praecepta eius capit, tardus autem non eam uidet, sed multo minus, quod de illa praecipitur, magisque in his omnibus ipsa spectacula ueritatis saepe delectant, quam ex eis in dipustando aut iudicando adiuuamur; nisi forte quod exercitatiora reddunt ingenia, si etiam maligniora aut inflatiora non reddant, hoc est ut aut decipere uersimili sermone atque interrogationibus ament aut aliquid magnum, quo se bonis atque innocentibus anteponant, se assecutos putent, qui ista didicerint.*"

33 DDC 2.26.40: "*Vtilia sunt ista nec discuntur inlicite nec superstitione implicant nec luxu eneruant, si tantum occupent, ut maioribus rebus, ad quas adipiscendas seruire debent, non sint impedimento.*"

34 DDC 2.13.20: "*. . .sed signorum qua non inflari omnino difficile est, cum et ipsa rerum scientia saepe ceruicem erigat, nisi dominico reprimatur iugo.*"

35 DDC 2.39.58: "*Quam ob rem uidetur mihi studiosis et ingeniosis adulescentibus et timentibus deum beatamque uitam quaerentibus salubriter praecipi, ut nullas doctrinas, quae praeter ecclesiam Christi exercentur tamquam ad beatam uitam capessendam secure sequi audeant . . .*"

36 DDC 4.1.2: "*Primo itaque exspectationem legentium, qui fort me putant rhetorica daturum esse praecepta, quae in scholis saecularibus et didici et docui, ista praelocutione prohibeo atque, ut a me non exspectentur, admoneo, non quod nihil habeant utilitatis, sed si quid habent, seorsum discendum est, si cui fortassis bono uiro etiam haic uacat discere, non autem a me uel in hoc opere uel in aliquo alio requirendum.*" This is a fascinating passage that, to my knowledge, has not received sustained attention. The absoluteness of the refusal marks so clearly Augustine's rejection of his past life, and to my ears bears with it the language of temptation akin to his discussion in *Confessions* 10. Is it possible that Augustine experienced the habits of the teacher as a temptation like the habits of lust?

37 Augustine, *Contra Academicos* 1.1.3.

38 Augustine, *De Beata Vita* 5.

39 See Phillip Cary, "What Licentius Learned: A Narrative Reading of the Cassiciacum Dialogues," *Augustinian Studies* 29 (1998) 141-63.

40 See Sabine MacCormack, "Liberal Arts," in *Augustine through the Ages. An Encyclopedia* (Grand Rapids: Wm. Eerdmans, 1999) 492-494.

41 *Retractationes* 3.2 (my translation). Commenting on the early *De Ordine*, Augustine regrets "how much I attributed to the liberal disciplines, arts of which many holy people know little of, and of which certain people who are not at all holy know quite a bit."

42 *De civitate Dei* 5.13; cf. Cicero, *Tusculan Disputations* 1.2.4.

43 *De civitate Dei* 14.28.

44 *De civitate Dei* 5.12.

45 DDC 2.37.55; see above, note 32.

46 *Confessions* 6.6.9; see above, note 9.

47 DDC 2.41.62: "*Ita etiam sentit, quamvis de Aegypto diues exeat, tamen, nisi pascha egerit, saluum se esse non posse.*"

48 DDC 2.41.62: "*Quo signo crucis, omnis actio christiana describitur. . . Per hanc actionem purgati ualebimus cognoscere etiam supereminentem scientiae caritatem Christi . . .*"

49 "Land O'Lakes Declaration," in *American Catholic Higher Education: Essential Documents, 1967-1990* (ed. Alice Gallin; Notre Dame, IN: University of Notre Dame Press, 1993).

50 Paul Griffiths, *Religious Reading: The Place of Reading in the Practice of Religion* (New York: Oxford, 1999), especially Chapter 7.

51 Paul Griffiths, "Does the Gospel Require that the Divinity School Be Closed Down?" Sermon delivered in Bond Chapel, University of Chicago, November 17, 1997.

52 See above, note 5.

53 DDC 2.42.63: "*Hac igitur instructione praeditum cum signa incognita lectorem non impedierint, mitem et humilem corde, subiugatum leniter Christo et oneratum sarcina leui, fundatum et readicatum et aedificatum in caritate, quem scientia inflare non possit. . .*"

PART III
TEACHING AND AUTHORITY
IN AUGUSTINE

Chapter Seven

Augustine's Pedagogy of Intellectual Liberation: Turning Students from the "Truth of Authority" to the "Authority of Truth"

Richard M. Jacobs, O.S.A.

Introduction

Successful pedagogy — and especially, teaching undergraduates well — is riddled with many complexities than oftentimes are made explicit, as good professors — like my colleague to whom this volume is dedicated — recognize all too well. Undoubtedly, communicating disciplinary content efficiently presents professors with one set of challenges, while crafting a learning environment where undergraduates put aside their fears and subject the content of their thought processes to public scrutiny presents a second set of even more vexing challenges (Immerwahr, 1994). Given these and a host of other challenges, it should not prove surprising that lecturing predominates in undergraduate pedagogy and that all too many professors offer their students precious few opportunities to hone their intellectual powers through sustained classroom discourse.

One product of this predominant pedagogical method is students who demonstrate mastery of technical knowledge, pass courses, and receive multiple job offers upon graduation. But, it must be asked, while this product elates consumers, have these professors not failed in their responsibility to initiate their students into the culture of the intellect?

What is it, then, that good professors do to initiate their students into this culture? How is it that these professors enable their students not only to demonstrate mastery of technical knowledge and to pass courses, but also to connect the culture of the intellect with the vital issues arising in their lives in and, more importantly, beyond the Academy? And, at a more intimate and personal level, *why* do these professors do *what* they do?

This chapter focuses upon Augustine's *The Teacher* (*de Magistro*)[1] — written in 386 CE — to consider how one well-regarded educator in classical antiquity, Aurelius Augustine, might respond these questions. In this dialogue, Augustine models not only *what* professors ought to do. In addition, Augustine's pedagogy suggests *why* good professors do what they do.

This chapter first identifies Augustine's normative view concerning what good professors do. Attention then turns to Augustine as he teaches his student, Adeodatus. The purpose for this excursus is to infer from Augustine's pedagogy some ideas concerning why good professors devote themselves to this more complex endeavor (for it is, after all, much easier to instruct students), and to relate these efforts to what is, for Augustine, of primary interest, namely, how professors communicate created truth. This chapter concludes by posing three challenges for professors who would wish to liberate their students' powers of intellect so that they may take delight in the culture of the intellect, that is, by teaching in the spirit of Augustine.

Good (and Bad) Pedagogy: Augustine's Normative View

Augustine sharpens the distinction between what professors do, in a generic sense, and what good professors do, in a specific sense, by modeling throughout *The Teacher* what good professors do. One cannot but notice how Augustine carefully selects and crafts his words in order that his student, Adeodatus, develops his capacity to think for himself. This accomplished, the professor recedes into the background as his student takes a more commanding lead, especially as Adeodatus searches for answers to questions emanating not from Augustine's words but from within Adeodatus' mind. Although the professor remains in the background, he is not absent, for as the student puzzles through the ideas arising in his mind, Augustine raises additional questions spurring spirited discourse between the professor and his student.

It should not prove surprising that for Augustine — in another season of his life, a professional rhetorician — what professors do is craft words with an intentional purpose. For Augustine, words are a medium to remind students, to admonish them, or simply to teach them about reality (1.1). Disciplinary content provides a tool professors use to awaken their students' capacity to think, that is, to perceive, remember, and know truth (5.12-13). However, it is Augustine's intentional use of words that illuminates his pedagogical goal, namely, to sharpen Adeodatus' powers of intellect so that he will be capable of examining his own thoughts against the verities his professor expresses (8.22).

Thus characterized, Augustine's image of the professor (1.1-10.36) is not a rarified historical artifact. For example, in undergraduate programs throughout the nation, countless numbers of professors use words and questions to stimulate student acquisition of disciplinary content. But for Augustine's pedagogy of intellectual liberation, the acquisition of disciplinary content provides a bridge for students to cross the threshold demarcating disciplinary content from discursive thought and so to pass beyond the terrain of words and concepts and to enter into the domain of the intellect. In this realm, students can plumb the depths of human experience, learn to think for themselves, and mature in wisdom. Professors, then, must be careful when selecting and using words, for their meanings should not emerge from the professor's capacity to explain complicated matters but rather from within the students' minds, especially as professors utilize questions to stimulate their students' intellectual powers (4.7).

Figure 7.1 The foundation of Augustine's pedagogy of liberation

For Augustine, a professor selects words that convey meaning:

WORDS — — — — — — — — → **MEANING**:

a professor carefully selects words and formulates questions for students to apprehend the professor's words and questions	the professor's words direct the student's intellect to consider the meaning veiled by the professor's words and questions
students know the words conveyed by the professor	students understand the ideas conveyed by the professor
↓	↓
created material truths	created immaterial truths

These truths are "created" in the sense that they are spurred from "without" (i.e., the professor) and mediated through the sense faculties.

Augustine's pedagogy of intellectual liberation begins with a professor who uses words to stimulate the student's intellectual powers (Figure 7.1). The professor uses words that students perceive, the audible sounds of the words directing their intellects to the idea signified by the words (8.24). These words, then, are authoritative, but only in so far as they direct the students' attention to the idea depicted (10.35). Next, the professor encourages students to take delight in the idea more than in the sounds effected by the words (9.26,27). Consequently, as the professor induces students to examine their thoughts more critically and to articulate the product of their judgments, the professor assists students to hone their capacity to contemplate created material truth — the words — and to savor the delight experienced in contemplating created immaterial truth — the idea signified by the words.

Liberating the students' intellectual powers is a much more demanding endeavor than many believe. For Augustine, the proper *terminus* is reached as students contemplate created truth, make inquiry into their internal thought process, and experience delight as they develop their ability to detect errors without the aid of being told what to think by someone else. As Augustine remarks to Adeodatus,

> I am not at all unhappy about your hesitation, for it indicates a cautious mind. And caution is the best guard of tranquillity [sic]. It is the most difficult thing in the world not to be upset when opinions which we hold, and to which we have given a too ready and willful approval, are shattered by contrary arguments and are, as it were, weapons torn from our hands. It is a good thing to give in calmly to arguments that are well considered and grasped, just as it is dangerous to hold as known what in fact we do not know. We should be on our guard lest, when things are frequently undermined which we assumed would stand firm and abide, we fall into such hatred or fear of reason that we think we cannot trust even the most clearly manifest truth. (10.31)

This, then, is how professors successfully initiate undergraduates into the culture of the intellect using Augustine's pedagogy of intellectual liberation. First, these professors empower their students' capacity to reason. In turn, this exercise provides students with confidence in their ability to reason properly (10.31). And, with additional practice, patience, and persistence, students acquire the refined capacity to assert confidently the created truths they have discovered, resting not in the truth of authority (i.e., the professor) but rather, in the authority of truth (i.e., the students' apprehension of course-related content). Second, through this process professors inculcate the virtue of humility in their students. That is, even though students contemplate created truth, they remain guardedly skeptical of themselves, their thought processes, and their assertions as well. Thus, while professors who use Augustine's pedagogy of intellectual liberation make it possible for their students to assert created truth with confidence, these students do not do so dogmatically. Humility keeps them from clinging pridefully to something they believe to be true but which may, in fact, be false.

Of course, these meritorious accomplishments stand in stark contrast to those outcomes effected by *bad* professors.

In a sermon entitled "On the sheep" (1990) which Augustine delivered nearly two decades after writing *The Teacher*, Augustine the bishop speaks about pastors in their teaching role, remarking that such bad teachers "muddy the waters" as they "...teach distinctly unquietly...they are savage with their learners...[Then, a bad teacher remarks that a student is] bad-tempered, he upsets the student, finding fault with his stupidity, for example, when he is too slow in understanding something, and by upsetting him he stops him understanding as much as he could have done if he had heard it calmly and quietly" (47.9). Augustine then proceeds to pronounce that bad pastors (and, it might be added, their counterparts in the professoriate), "...do this sort of thing in a sour spirit, a grudging spirit, these are the ones who trample down the pastures and muddy the springs. Whatever they may know, they want to know in such a way that others don't know it. Ill-natured, mean-spirited men, driven by a spite straight from hell, bilious of mind rather than body, they have read and they have understood" (47.10). Thus, even though bad pastors may have read and understood much, they are blameworthy, Augustine asserts, because these bad pastors act in the belief that their congregations are inferior to themselves. The conceit of intellectual pride destroys whatever good these bad pastors might have been able to accomplish with their congregations. And so it is with bad professors and their students.

For Augustine, good teachers correct their students' carelessness and stupidity, but they do so without clinging pridefully to their intellectual or moral superiority. Rather, Augustine notes in this homily, these teachers correct their students "out of a real concern for people, and the desire to inspire them with a serious interest in the truth, to instill in them a habit of diligence and application, and to clear their minds, perhaps, of the cloudiness they have contracted from worldly interests, and perhaps by fixing their thoughts on other unprofitable matters they are not able to take in what is of real profit" (47.10).

Two decades prior to delivering this sermon, Augustine specified precisely what he meant by the phrase "what is of real profit," suggesting in *The Teacher* that good professors empower their students to examine their thoughts, to challenge their intellectual adversaries, to remain vigilant in argumentation, as well as to remember their own words (8.24; 9.28). More substantively, as professors lessen their students' dependence upon the truth of authority, helping them to delight in and to act on the authority of truth, these professors form less hierarchical and more egalitarian relationships with their students. That is, as these professors and their students jointly pursue created truth, classrooms evidence spirited scholarly discourse focusing on what professors and students are jointly discovering; and, as they debate these matters, they admonish and correct one another as is necessary. By so doing, the professor and students form a more egalitarian learning community comprised of diverse backgrounds, ages, talents, interests, experiences, and accomplishments bound by the authority of truth.

When the task of initiating undergraduates into the culture of the intellect is perceived as professors and students contemplating created truth and then sharing their apprehension of created truth in the community of the classroom, the pedagogical relationship does not terminate with professors assigning grades and students graduating, ready to begin a new phase of their lives dependent upon the truth of authority. Instead, as professors and undergraduates form intimate relationships within which their words and questions reveal the created truths which they apprehend, professors and students form an educative community. This community is united not only in mind but also in heart, especially as its members engage in scholarly discourse and connect the authority of truth with the vital issues arising in their lives in the Academy. This community and the bonds formed among its members continue beyond graduation and into life, influencing the community's members throughout their lives and wherever they may be. The members of this educative community rest confidently in the authority of truth as they confront the vital issues arising in their lives beyond the Academy. For Augustine, this is *what* professors do as they initiate their students into the culture of the intellect.

Why Professors Do What They Do: Augustine's Conception of Truth

Why, then, do professors do what they do? Why do they devote their energies to initiating undergraduates into the culture of the intellect where satisfaction is derived primarily from disciplined thinking? For Augustine, the love and pursuit of truth — to be a philosopher — motivates professors. Further, the desire to share their love of truth with undergraduates so that they too might love and pursue it throughout their lives is *why* professors do what they do. What, then, is this "truth" that good professors cherish or, dare one say, love?

In *The Teacher*, Augustine suggests that professors enable their students to apprehend created truth in preparation for the revelation of uncreated truth (Figure 7.2). As Augustine demonstrates with Adeodatus, the professor's primary task is to direct students to contemplate created material truth by using words, especially open-ended questions that allow for multiple answers (Immerwahr, 1994). These words engage the students' sense faculties and stimulate inquiry, especially as students consider and evaluate their experience (3.5). The professor's intentional use of words makes it possible for undergraduates to know and understand the disciplinary content serving as the foundation for classroom discourse. At the same time, words are a propaedeutic making it possible for the professor to engage students in a second task, namely, to exercise their powers of intellect by contemplating and valuing created immaterial truth.

Figure 7.2 Augustine's conception of truth

For Augustine, a professor empowers the student's powers of intellect to contemplate created truth in its material and immaterial forms, in preparation for the revelation of uncreated truth by Christ the Teacher:

CREATED TRUTH:	**UNCREATED TRUTH**:
apprehended through the senses	apprehended through contemplation
(the material foundations	(the intellectual foundations
of knowing)	of knowing)
↓	↓
created material truth	
(e.g., factual knowledge)	↓
"secular truths"	
↓	↓
created immaterial truth	*uncreated immaterial truth*
(e.g., research knowledge)	(e.g., philosophical concepts)
"theoretical truth"	"spiritual truth"

In order for students to test the validity of the created material truths asserted by their professors — that is, to assess the truth of authority — students need clear sense perception and careful discernment. For Augustine, these refined powers make it possible for students to esteem created immaterial truth more highly than the material entity from which they derived the created immaterial truth (9.26-27). And, once students contemplate and value created immaterial truth, they can act with confidence, not because their professors, textbooks, or peers — the truth of authority — assert these truths. No, students act with confidence because they apprehend the authority of truth, engage in discourse about it, and desire to act on it.

Augustine's emphasis upon the pedagogical end, namely, for students to behold and to contemplate created truth, reminds professors that initiating undergraduates into the culture of the intellect consists primarily of preparing students to reason properly (10.31). Success in this endeavor will enable students to contemplate and esteem created material and immaterial truths and to proceed from the truth of authority communicated externally to the authority of truth discovered internally. For Augustine, this is what good professors set about to accomplish, for even they are not capable of revealing those uncreated truths which humans must "believe rather than know" (11.37).

Students acquire knowledge and understanding as the consequence of professors who intentionally use their words to develop their student's power of intellect. This penultimate exercise sets the stage — pedagogy is the means — for students to behold and contemplate uncreated truth — Augustine's desideratum — when it will be revealed by Christ the Teacher.

Teaching in the Spirit of Augustine: Three Challenges

Augustine's pedagogy of intellectual liberation raises at least three challenges for professors who would like to initiate undergraduates into the culture of the intellect in Augustine's spirit, even for professors who may not share his conception of uncreated truth.

Challenge 1: Professors Are Servants of Created Truth

Augustine steeps his pedagogical method in the tradition of the Socratic *enlenchus*. In *The Teacher*, Augustine — mimicking Socrates — models a professor who selects his words intentionally to inculcate in his student those intellectual habits that Adeodatus will need if, as a consequence of Augustine's pedagogy of intellectual liberation, Adeodatus is to behold and to contemplate created truth. Augustine's words challenge his student to place into question what Adeodatus is all too quick to believe and, through this interrogation, to enable Adeodatus to be more discriminating. As Adeodatus refines this habit, he learns to test the assumptions underlying the assertions he previously accepted as true.

In *The Teacher*, however, Augustine also expands beyond the Socratic *enlenchus*, using it not as a pedagogical end but as a preparatory phase — a propaedeutic — in the educative process. That is, Augustine selects and uses words intentionally to inculcate intellectual discipline in his student so that Adeodatus will learn to contemplate created truth and to savor the intellectual delight afforded by this discursive activity.

In light of this notion, Augustine challenges those who may be interested in using his pedagogy of intellectual liberation to view themselves as servants of created truth, women and men who allow created truth to inform and to transcend what they do in their classrooms. In contrast, bad professors narrow the educative process to instructing undergraduates, or worse, to entertaining them. Bad professors bring their faulty pedagogical rationale to fruition as they appeal to their students' material sensibilities — for example, good grades, hope of an effusive recommendation, job offers upon graduation — which distract their students away from developing the intellectual disciplines they need if students are to contemplate created truth. In his *Confessions*, Augustine laments of students instructed by professors like these, writing: "To such weakness is a soul reduced when it is not yet anchored in the solid ground of truth. It is tossed and turned, whirled and spun, by every breath of opinion from the mouths of those who think they know, its light is obscured by clouds and it cannot see the truth" (IV.23.107).[2]

Even more egregiously, hubris infects these professors, as they delight in the satisfaction which their students experience through their professor's clever use of words. Placing a higher premium upon adulation and popularity than on their students' acquisition of intellectual discipline, the worst of these professors are puffed up with pride. They falsely believe that they are educating their students when, at best, they are providing instruction in an entertaining way, or, at worst, denying students an initiation into the culture of the intellect.

Few would know more about such bad professors than would Augustine. As a professional rhetorician, Augustine was the "expert" bad professor who crafted his words cleverly in order to dazzle his fellow citizens into believing that what he said was true, whether it was or not. As a proud and haughty practitioner of the propagandist's art, Augustine amassed adulation, fame, and wealth, all the while seeking a more prestigious and lucrative job.

Bad professors are "word vendors," as Augustine characterized his former trade, "selling talkative skills apt to sway others..." (*Confessions* IV.2.93). Sadly, these professors are eking out a comfortable existence by telling their students what to think. In *The Teacher*, Augustine remedies his former abuse by educating Adeodatus to be discriminating about words, to question and test the assumptions underlying assertions, and to take delight in contemplating created truth. In short, Augustine endeavors to liberate his student's intellectual powers so that Adeodatus can learn to think for himself. Augustine — once the expert bad professor — manifests a profound conversion as he models what it means to be a good professor, a humble servant of created truth who bequeaths the culture of the intellect to his student.

Challenge 2: Honesty Characterizes the Pedagogical Relationship

Taken simply at face value, *The Teacher* is a rather tedious dialogue. Unfortunately, this superficial assessment obscures what may well be one of Augustine's singular contributions to discourse considering how professors successfully initiate undergraduates into the culture of the intellect. That is, for Augustine, honesty characterizes the pedagogical relationship which professors forge with their students.

As Augustine and Adeodatus review what transpired throughout the course of their dialogue, the professor reports to his student:

> ...I would have you believe that I have not intended any cheap comedy in this conversation — for even though we may play with words, still that is not to be considered in a childish sense — and that what we are giving our thoughts to is of no slight or ordinary profit; though, if I say that there is a happy life, and that everlasting, to which I desire that God — that is, Truth itself — may lead us by stages suited to our weak steps, I am afraid I shall appear ridiculous for having set out on this great journey by considering not the realities themselves which are signified, but only the signs. So then, you will pardon me if I play this prelude with you, not to do any playacting, but to exercise the powers and keenness of our minds and so prepare ourselves not only to bear, but also to love the warmth and light where the blessed life reigns. (8.21)

Professors interested in using Augustine's pedagogy of intellectual liberation to initiate undergraduates into the culture of the intellect might wonder, how does honesty facilitates this outcome?

To respond to this question, professors might look to the fact that Adeodatus—though a bright and capable student—does not differ all that much from today's typical undergraduate. For example, despite Augustine's zeal, Adeodatus' interest wanes. Like any professor who deals with young adults, Augustine the professor discovers that he must goad his student along (5.14). Adeodatus errs, and when he does, Augustine criticizes and challenges him. The student bristles at his professor's corrections but gradually accepts them (5.15; 6.17). And when Adeodatus airs his frustrations and hopes, Augustine candidly admits his own limitations (10.31). All of this honest give-and-take, the consequence of what Augustine calls "fencing with words" (10.31), breeds the climate of trust necessary for professors to press beyond providing instruction and to initiate their students into the culture of the intellect.

In *The Teacher*, Augustine is honest with Adeodatus concerning his pedagogical intent, especially so when the student ruminates about the created truths forming the content of the professor's lesson. In one particularly telling scene—immediately following Augustine's somewhat brutal interrogation of Adeodatus concerning how words direct the intellect to the ideas of which the words are but signs—the professor does not succumb to his student's demand that the professor respond to the student's question. Augustine retorts: "No! Rather let me ask you the same questions again, so that you yourself may discover where you have erred" (8.22). Augustine's rejoinder illuminates his primary intent, namely, to liberate Adeodatus' intellectual powers to contemplate truth, not to indoctrinate his student to think like his professor. As Augustine later clarifies this point: "If in this case [the student] is led on by the words of the [professor], still it is not that the words teach [the student], but they represent questions put to [the student] in such a way as to correspond to [the student's] capacity for learning from his own inner self " (12.40).

If a professor is to utilize Augustine's pedagogy of intellectual liberation, fostering honesty in classroom discourse must be accorded first place. For Augustine, classroom discourse is relational — not a stultifying monologue or a less formal exchange between a "giver" and a "receiver" (Jacobs, 1993) — engaging professors and students in honest communication concerning what they are thinking as well as their difficulties and limitations in apprehending created truth. In this relationship, honesty makes it possible for professors to express their care and respect for their students and, in the same way, for students to grow in care and respect for their professors. It is this learning environment that Augustine — and those who would wish to teach in his spirit — labors to craft.

Challenge 3: The Subject is the Student's Intellect

Augustine's ideas and contemporary discourse concerning undergraduate education converge on one crucial point: professors are in classrooms to teach their subjects. This area of convergence quickly widens into a gulf, however, when each defines the word "subject."

For many professors, the subject of undergraduate education is the disciplinary content that universities and colleges contract professors to communicate. Under this definition of "subject," professors use various devices to assess how well students have acquired this content. Professors and undergraduates seem pretty satisfied with this arrangement, that is, as long as they achieve other goals (e.g., for professors, to earn tenure, rank, and merit pay increases; for students, to pass courses, graduate, and secure multiple job offers). Yet, according to Augustine, "...people deceive themselves in calling persons 'teachers' who are not such at all, merely because generally there is no interval between the time of speaking and the time of knowing. And because [students] are quick to learn internally following the prompting of the one who speaks, they think they have learned externally from the one who was a prompter" (14.45).

For Augustine, professors are not prompters who orchestrate an educational opera by dictating to their students what they must say. Instead, the subject of education is, for Augustine, each student's intellect. Professors are in classrooms to educate this subject and, by so doing, to liberate their students' intellects to contemplate created truth. Professors utilize the content — the words — of their disciplinary specialties as tools which direct their students' power of desire away from the carnal pleasures mediated by the sense faculties toward the immaterial delight to be experienced in knowing, understanding, and ultimately, in contemplating created truth. As Augustine argues his case,

> ...when [professors] have explained, by means of words, all those subjects which they profess to teach, and even the science of virtue and of wisdom, then those who are called pupils consider within themselves whether what has been said is true. This they do by gazing attentively at that interior truth, so far as they are able. *Then it is that they learn*; and when within themselves they find that what has been said is true, they give praise, not realizing that they are praising not so much teachers as persons taught—provided that the teachers also know what they are saying. (14.45, italics added)

For those who would practice Augustine's pedagogy of intellectual liberation, his notion that the subject of education is the student's intellect reminds professors that *educating* undergraduates involves much more than *instructing* them. While those who practice the latter *introduce* their students to the culture of the intellect by impregnating their minds with various concepts and ideas, those who practice the former *initiate* their students into this culture by empowering their intellects. These professors are successful because they craft learning communities whose members, united in mind and heart in the pursuit of created truth, express and develop the content of their minds with one another against the dictates of created truth.

When the subject of education is disciplinary content, professors use words to instruct students. One-way, unilateral communication characterizes this pedagogical process (Jacobs, 1993), a method especially effective for indoctrination. In contrast, when the student's intellect is the subject of pedagogy, professors focus upon drawing out of their students the inchoate truths residing in their minds. For Augustine, this is where learning begins, as students accept responsibility for "find[ing] that what has been said is true" (14.45) — or, it might be interjected, not true, as the case may be — and engaging in discourse about their discoveries. Highly interactive communication, punctuated by dialogue and shared meaning, typifies classrooms suffused with Augustine's spirit.

Augustine would assert that professors who liberate their students' intellects to act on the authority of truth — in contrast to mindless dependency upon the truth of authority — these are *good* professors.

An Assessment

Augustine concludes *The Teacher* by asking: "For who would be so curious as to send his child to school to learn what the teacher thinks?" (14.45). Of course, anyone using Augustine's pedagogy of intellectual liberation would respond emphatically — like my colleague to whom this volume is dedicated — "No one should!" But, in a world charmed by utilitarianism, many ask in all sincerity, "How can you say that?" These people are adamant in their belief that students come to the

Academy to learn what their professors think in preparation for lucrative careers beyond the Academy.

And so, much like Augustine prior to his conversion, professors busy themselves instructing undergraduates. Perhaps the more interesting professors offer their students entertaining lectures. Even so, Augustine would note, both are word vendors. For them, time — not contemplation — is of the essence, if only because efficiency allows little or no time for the form of play that forges the students' intellectual powers through the crucible of scholarly discourse. Augustine himself noted the importance of play in a remark to Adeodatus: "You will pardon me, therefore, if I play with you to begin with, not for the sake of playing but in order to exercise and sharpen our mental powers so that we may be able not merely to endure the heat and light of the region where lies the blessed life, but also to love them" (8.21).

Sadly though, something else — not just utilitarianism or cleverness — is operative in these classrooms. Were Augustine to survey the current status of undergraduate pedagogy, he would be likely to note that pride governs *what* many professors do. The way they teach, for example, is designed not to initiate students into the culture of the intellect, but to direct their students' attention toward their professors. Taking delight not in liberating their students' intellectual powers to contemplate the authority of truth, these professors endeavor to increase their students' dependence upon the truth of authority.

In contrast, Augustine's pedagogy of intellectual liberation insists that humility motivates good professors. Servants of created truth, these women and men craft learning communities, not for their self-aggrandizement, but to initiate students into the culture of the intellect as a preparation for life. These professors use the luxury of time afforded by the undergraduate years to engage their students in scholarly discourse, to contemplate created truth, and to relate the culture of the intellect with the vital issues arising in their lives. These professors do so by sharing with their students the wealth of knowledge and understanding as well as the wisdom and virtue they possess in abundance. Humility, not pride, characterizes these professors as they bend their wills according to the dictates of "that interior light of truth which effects enlightenment and happiness in the so-called inner [person]" (12.40) and allow created truth to inform their pedagogical judgments. As the ancients used to say, "*Nemo dat quod non habet*" ("one cannot give what one does not possess").

Augustine's pedagogy of intellectual liberation, then, begins with professors and ends with graduates. Early on, professors induce their students into grappling with the "truth of authority," as professors, textbooks, homework, projects, tests, and the students' human experience mediate the truth of authority. Pedagogy presses onward from these foundational elements as professors challenge their students to progress further, namely, to grapple the "authority of truth." It is this intervention — turning students away from their dependence upon the truth of authority and returning them to the authority of truth — that, for Augustine, demarcates professors who simply instruct undergraduates from those who educate them. Pedagogy terminates with graduates, women and men who commence forth into the world possessing the refined capacity to connect the culture of the intellect with the vital issues arising in their lives beyond the Academy.

Notes

1   All quotations in this chapter are taken from *The Teacher* from Peter King's translation (Augustine, 1995).
2   This quotation is taken from Maria Boulding's translation of Augustine's *Confessions* (Augustine, 1992).

References

Augustine. *Against the Academicians and The Teacher*. Trans. P. King; Indianapolis, IN: Hackett Publishing Company, Inc., 1995.
_____. *The Confessions*. Trans. M. Boulding; New York: New City Press, 1997.
_____. "On the sheep." In *Sermons*. Ed. J. E. Rotelle; trans. E. Hill; Brooklyn, NY: New City Press, 1990. Pp. 298-326.
Immerwahr, J. "The Socratic classroom: Classroom communication strategies." *Journal of Management Systems* 6 (1) (1994) 37-44.
Jacobs, R. M. (1993). "Road maps to navigate school communication." *Journal of Management Systems* 5 (2) (1993) 1-14.

Chapter Eight

The Limits of Augustine's Personal Authority: The Hermeneutics of Trust in *De utilitate credendi*

Felix B. Asiedu

Introduction

"We depend on appraising the testimony and authority and general ethos of other people, as they appraise the testimony and authority of still others, who in turn depend on others . . . and no one can say where these circles of trust end, except of course when societies and universities destroy themselves by losing the arts of determining when trust is justified." So states Wayne Booth, a distinguished teacher and master rhetorician, in his Ryerson Lecture at the University of Chicago in 1987 on "The Idea of a University as Seen by a Rhetorician."[1] Booth's sentiments, expressed in the language of testimony, authority, trust, and the arts that justify such trust capture many of the elements in the thought of Augustine, another rhetorician of a much earlier age, whose personal anxieties and reflections about the nature of truth often led him to emphasize the need for trust as a prerequisite for knowledge.

Because Augustine makes most of his arguments in the context of justifying religious belief, and in particular belief in the Christian religion, his notion that authority, belief, or faith always precedes reason (or knowledge) easily give his assertions an air of dogmatism, and so he can easily be dismissed. Yet at the heart of Augustine's arguments lies the basic contention that discourses on the nature of true religion share with any general hermeneutics of education the element of trust: trust not only in a teacher's authority, but also in the desire of the inquirer to seek knowledge in sincerity and in truth. Invariably, both the person who seeks to learn an art (or a skill) and the one who seeks to know the truth in religion need to find a teacher who can be a guide towards the desired end. Neither activity can begin without a prior conviction, however formed, in the authority of the teacher. If one claims, as Augustine certainly does, that in matters of religion authority precedes reason, one is simply pointing out what is always necessary to any form of education or instruction. For Augustine, trust is foundational in all forms of inquiry and human knowing. The inquirer or seeker, trusting in the authority of the teacher, and beyond that, in the community of learning, builds a body of knowledge and puts to the test what he or she acquires. Without such an understanding of a learning community, true learning is nearly impossible.

Augustine, as we will see in his *De utilitate credendi*,[2] assumes that those who belong to the Catholic community of which he is a part, constitute a learning community with recognized teachers who should be trusted to teach the Christian religion, and that it is to these trustworthy teachers that any inquirer seeking to know the truth about the Christian religion ought to turn and not to imposters and charlatans. Leaving aside for the moment Augustine's insistence on belonging to the right community as opposed to the Manichaeans, his former co-religionists whom he now considers misguided and untaught, we may pose the following questions.

What happens when trust is broken? What becomes of the nature of teaching authority? Can the teacher, once he has lost the trust of his students, ever regain it? How can it be regained? These questions are also implied in Booth's allusion to what obtains when societies and universities lose the arts, which justify trust. This is a scenario which is all too prevalent at the most basic level of human social interaction and communal life, whether it is the relationship between spouses, parents and children, or even among friends. Trust is indispensable, and even in some contexts where it may be grossly misconstrued as loyalty, the basic idea is unmistakable. In matters of religious belief and practice we might say it is paramount, and those who exercise teaching authority in any particular tradition cannot fulfill their vocations without it. So how can a teacher who moves from one community to an alternative community establish his credibility and regain the trust of those who once trusted him or her?

This brings us back to Augustine's *De utilitate credendi*, a work written to one Honoratus, whom Augustine had managed to persuade to become a Manichee during their student days in Carthage, when Augustine was an unabashed apologist and evangelist for the Manichaean religion. By the time Augustine wrote the *De utilitate credendi*, he was deeply ensconced in the Catholic church. Not only was he no longer a Manichee, he was not simply any ordinary Catholic. He was a priest and a teacher of the church. He, the former Manichaean apologist, now served as an apologist for Catholic Christianity, and had the unenviable task of undoing some of the deeds of his past. Augustine now had to retrieve from the ranks of the Manichees the friends he had persuaded to go along with him into what he could now generously describe as a vain superstition. Behind the *De utilitate credendi*, then, lies the issue of Augustine's trustworthiness. Could Augustine again be trusted by his friend?

So little is known about Honoratus that it is difficult to say how Augustine's efforts appeared to him. It would be intriguing if indeed the Bishop Honoratus who is the recipient of one of Augustine's last letters (Ep. 228; ca. 428/429) was in fact the Honoratus who had been the focus of *De utilitate credendi* some three and a half decades before. But we can have no such assurances and one must simply wonder as to whether Augustine succeeded in persuading his friend. It is of some importance, however, that in so much of this apology Augustine does not present himself as the teacher that Honoratus should seek, but rather as a fellow traveler who had once given him wrong directions but who now seeks to set him on the right path. The mood of *De utilitate credendi* gives Augustine's argument, and indeed the title of the work, a kind of pragmatism that is otherwise not his metier. The central arguments, however, can be found throughout the works written before Augustine entered the priesthood in 391.

From *De moribus ecclesiae catholicae* to *De utilitate credendi*

In his much earlier *De moribus ecclesiae catholicae*, his first work written after his baptism in April 387, Augustine's attitude towards the Manichees bristles with a sense of disbelief as to why his former co-religionists remained adamant in their beliefs when they lacked so much foundation. Augustine is at his most irrepressible when describing what he considers the intrepid objections of the Manichaeans to Catholic teaching and common sense. Words like foolish, foolishness (*insipiens, stultus, stultitia*), shameless (*impudens*), absurd (*absurdus*), madness (*dementia*), ignorant (*ignorantia, imperitus, indoctus*), vain (*vanus, vanitas*), blindness (*caecus, caecitas*) superstition (*superstitio*), impious or impiety (*impius, impietas*),[3] come relatively easy to him whenever he turns his attention towards the Manichaean religion of his own past,[4] and there are times when he almost despairs of persuading them.[5]

In *De moribus ecclesiae catholicae* Augustine pleads with his putative audience to listen to Wisdom, because she does not disappoint, for Wisdom prevents no one who desires her:

> Who ever seeks her early will have no difficulty; for he shall find her sitting at his doors. To think, therefore, upon her is perfection of wisdom; and whoever watches for her shall quickly be without care. For she goes about seeking such as are worthy of her, showing herself favorably disposed to them in the byways, and meets them in every thought. For the very beginning of her is the desire of discipline and the care of discipline is love; and love is the keeping of her laws; and paying attention to her laws is the assurance of incorruption; and incorruption makes us near to God. Therefore the desire of wisdom brings one to the kingdom.(*De moribus ecclesiae catholicae* 1.17.32. BWA 1:334-335)

This very extensive excerpt from Wisdom 6:12-20 easily fits into the thematic explorations of Proverbs 2-9 where Wisdom, also in feminine persona, goes into the streets and alleys in search of the simple-minded and the foolish, beckoning them to follow her ways. She is depicted as standing in the "public square" declaiming to anyone who would listen, yet few seem to take heed. Augustine's apology tries to make plain the way of beatitude to those who are inclined to think it all a secret (*occultus*),[6] accessible to a few, and enjoining them to seek a more open and unencumbered path. Augustine's posture also foreshadows the prospect that much of his own efforts might prove ineffectual, and that the shelter of the most chaste bosom of the Catholic church (*firmissima fide sanctissimo ecclesiae catholicae*) to which he implores the Manichees to enter may still be without them. Dogged hostility can easily nullify his position.

Over and over again in *De moribus ecclesiae catholicae* Augustine describes the Manichees as a misguided lot (or something worse) who, in their ignorant peregrinations, reject proper instruction. "What more do you want?" Augustine asks at one point. "Why are you so fierce in your ignorance and impiety? Why do you pervert the untutored with your noxious persuasions?" (*De moribus ecclesiae catholicae* 1.17.30). Augustine's ensuing acknowledgment of the difficulties people have in understanding the Old Testament, with its many undignified expressions, some of which must be taken figuratively and so on, concedes the general cast of Manichaean objections to the biblical tradition, even if Augustine believes the details of their criticism can be answered (*De moribus ecclesiae catholicae* 1.17.30). His concession also has an element of a retrospective, since these were the same difficulties that had led him away from the *superstitio* of the Catholics to the Manichees in the first place (*De utilitate credendi* 1.2ff.; *Confessions* 3.5.9). And then, as if to pose the troubling question of the workings of divine providence, he wonders why the Manichees have been allowed to go on in their ignorance for so long. The retort he offers turns on the view that the apostle Paul predicted the emergence of heretical groups: "There must be many heresies so that those who are approved among you may be made manifest" (*opertet multas haereses esse, ut probati manifesti fiant inter uos* [1 Corinthians 11:19]). For *De moribus ecclesiae catholicae* Augustine expresses a modest goal: he wants to make the Manichees want to understand (*ut intelligere aliquando cupiatis*), for if wisdom and truth are not sought wholeheartedly, with all of one's strength, they cannot be had (*De moribus ecclesiae catholicae* 1.17.32).

"But don't bark at me," Augustine exclaims, "I too was a dog and received my just reward: the rod of correction instead of the food of teaching" (*De moribus ecclesiae catholicae* 1.18.33). How seriously Augustine thought he could persuade by resorting to such a characterization is interesting to ponder, since Augustine also uses Matthew 15:26 (do not give what is holy to dogs) as a preface for his own remarks. The Manichees, Augustine contends, lack the desire for instruction, that love which asks, seeks, and knocks (*De moribus ecclesiae catholicae* 1.17.31). So while Wisdom promises that those who ask receive and those who seek find (Matthew 7:8), the Manichaeans have barred themselves from this very way of life. There is no desire on their part for wisdom and diligent inquiry (*amore sapientiae diligentiaque quaerendi* [*De moribus ecclesiae catholicae* 1.17.32]) which would lead to knowledge, but only shameless obstinacy (*impudentissima pertinacia* [*De moribus ecclesiae catholicae* 1.29.60]). If only they would listen to Catholic teachers with the same kind of peaceable disposition and zeal that Augustine himself claims he lent to their teaching, he is convinced they would not need the long years of questionable tutelage he received from them. In no time they would be able to sort out the difference between truth and vanity (*De moribus ecclesiae catholicae* 1.18.34).

Obviously incensed by Manichaean insistence that reason be met with reason and not by appeal to the authority of the Catholics and their scriptures, Augustine nevertheless accepts the terms, all the while objecting that it is wrongheaded, since in all forms of education and instruction authority precedes reason (*De moribus ecclesiae catholicae* 1.2.3). *De utilitate credendi* assumes this standpoint, that all instruction depends on authority. But unlike his characterizations of the Manichees in the *De moribus ecclesiae catholicae*, Augustine cannot approach Honoratus as an *insipiens*. After all, it is Augustine who had persuaded Honoratus to become a Manichee in the first place (*De utilitate credendi* 1.2). There is a significant change in tone.

As would be expected, Augustine's posture in *De utilitate credendi* is extremely deferential. In the way he goes about arguing for the credibility of Catholic Christianity, Augustine lays out the complicated task of a teacher whose previous authority as a Manichaean apologist would have to be discounted in order to accord him the hearing he now required as a teaching authority in the Catholic church. For Augustine to achieve his purposes, Honoratus would have to be persuaded of Augustine's trustworthiness while discounting Augustine's much earlier evangelistic campaigns as a Manichee. Honoratus would also have to grant that Augustine himself had not been deceived a second time as he appears to have been misled the first time when he was persuaded by the Manichees. And then, of course, Honoratus would have to be interested enough in the apparently intractable questions about true religion, the happy life, and the good of the soul.

Much of what Augustine does in *De utilitate credendi* is to establish his credibility. And for this reason he carefully recounts the various stages he went through before finally returning to Catholic Christianity. Augustine's narrative sets before his friend the specific events and changes that had taken place since the time he had been in Honoratus' company in their school days. Consequently, he provides in *De utilitate credendi* some of the most extended details about his conversion in all the works that precede the *Confessions*.

Surprisingly, Augustine does not use his characteristic formula, "unless you believe you will not understand" (Isaiah 7:9), even though much of what he presents in *De utilitate credendi* serves to make that very point: believe, then you will understand what is you have believed; trust in competent teachers so you may learn of the mysteries of the Catholic faith. Curiously, Augustine also makes no reference in *De moribus ecclesiae catholicae* to Isaiah 7:9 in that pre-Vulgate form in which he quotes it and deploys with such disarming rhetorical effect throughout his works: unless you believe you will not understand (*nisi credideritis non intelligetis*). On the other hand, the passage appears in Book 1 of *De libero arbitrio* which Augustine claims to have written at about the same time that he wrote *De moribus ecclesiae catholicae*, during his second stay in Rome in 388.[7] Given the general provenance of both *De libero arbitrio* 1 and *De moribus ecclesiae catholicae*, it is also surprising that Augustine uses it in the former and not the latter. The absence of Isaiah 7:9 from *De moribus ecclesiae catholicae* and *De utilitate credendi* therefore needs explaining, since it would have supported Augustine's arguments perfectly. Augustine's unease about having to begin with *ratio* in *De moribus ecclesiae catholicae* 1.2.3 might suggest that he had not come upon Isaiah 7:9 as a handy rubric for his entire attitude towards belief and understanding. But this may be doubtful.

It is possible that the presence of Isaiah 7:9 in *De libero arbitrio* 1 is an indication of later editorial activity in a work that took longer to complete: 388-395 for *De libero arbitrio* as compared to 388-390 for *De moribus ecclesiae catholicae*. But there is every indication that Augustine was aware of what he could make of Isaiah 7:9 from very early on. The formula adopted from Isaiah 7:9 appears in a number of Augustine's works spanning the years 389 to 397: *De magistro* 11.37 (389), Augustine's exposition of Psalm 8 (c. 391/392), the *De diversis questionibus* LXXXIII 81.2 (388-396), *De fide et symbolo* 1.1.1 (393), *De doctrina christiana* 2.12.27 (396), *De agone christiana* 13.14 (396), as well as the definitive anti-Manichaean tome, the *Acta contra Faustum Manichaeum* 4.2; 12.46; 22.53 (397).

Although an argument could be made that almost all of these references come after the final redaction and publication of *De moribus ecclesiae catholicae* and suggest that Augustine may have came to the peculiar use of Isaiah 7:9 sometime after publishing *De moribus ecclesiae catholicae*, it seems far more likely that Augustine opted not to use Isaiah 7:9, partly because it celebrated the very point of Manichaean criticism of Catholic teaching. This would explain its absence from almost all of his explicitly anti-Manichaean writings, with the sole exception of the late and definitive *Contra Faustum*. Not citing Isaiah 7:9, however, does not mean that Augustine did not in fact articulate an understanding of belief in accord with what the formula expresses. This much is self-evident in *De utilitate credendi*.

The Sincere Search for Truth and Falling into Error

One of the first things Augustine does in *De utilitate credendi* is to separate Honoratus from the general band of the heretics (*heretici*), as he deems the Manichees. When he gives his reasons for writing, Augustine does so in terms of an outstanding debt he owes Honoratus: "If I thought, Honoratus, that there was no difference between a heretic and one who follows heretics, I should judge that my tongue and my pen alike should remain quiescent in this matter. But there is a great difference" (*De utilitate credendi* 1.1). And the difference is that Augustine thinks of a heretic as someone who for some vainglory or temporary benefit propounds falsehoods or follows false and new opinions, persisting in his error even when shown the truth. But one who follows a heretic does so because of a delusion or an appearance of truth or piety in the heretic. If he has taken up his pen to write, it is because Honoratus is following a falsehood and Augustine cannot keep from his friend what he has discovered about the truth: "Nothing is easier, my dear friend, than to say or even to think that one has discovered the truth. How difficult it really is you will, I trust, recognize from this letter of mine" (*De utilitate credendi* 1.1: LCC 291). But what were the difficulties?

Augustine reminds Honoratus that he fell among the Manichees for "no other reason than that they declared that they would put aside all overawing authority, and by pure and simple reason would bring to God those who were willing to listen to them, and so deliver them from all error" (*De utilitate credendi* 1.2). And he continues:

> What else compelled me for nearly nine years to spurn the religion implanted in me as a boy by my parents, to follow these men and listen diligently to them, than that they said we were overawed by superstition and were bidden to believe rather than to reason, while they pressed no one to believe until the truth had been discussed and elucidated? Who would not be enticed by these promises, especially if he were an adolescent with a mind eager for truth, but made proud and garrulous by the disputes of learned men in school? Such they found me then, scorning what I took to be old wives' tales, and desirous of swallowing and holding the open and sincere truth which they promised. But again, what reason kept me from wholly cleaving to them? For I remained in the grade they call "hearers" so that I might not give up worldly hopes and duties. The reason was that I observed that they were more clever and ready to wit in refuting others than firm and sure in proving their own doctrines. (*De utilitate credendi* 1.2: LCC 292)

Augustine is bound to give all these details about the motives behind his many turns and how he finally made his way back to the motherly confines of Catholic Christianity. He describes himself as a famished infant at his mother's breast: "Why do I speak of myself, who was then a Catholic Christian, and who have now, nearly exhausted and parched after my long thirst, sought again with all avidity the breasts which nourished me, and weeping and deeply groaning, have pressed them, that there might come forth sufficient to refresh me in my present state and bring back hope and salvation? Why do I speak of myself?" (*De utilitate credendi* 1.2: LCC 292).

But speak of himself he must. So much depends on his personal credibility that Augustine will have to do more than just give a sampling of what took him through nine years with the Manichees and now to his new position as a teaching authority in the Catholic church. What could be more dramatic than that the child of a devout Catholic mother, who had openly flouted her authority and derided her religion as mere superstition, would now be found in the church, not on its fringes or even as a catechumen, but with the mantle of a teacher and an expert on the true religion?[8] Augustine recalls what he managed to do for the Manichaean cause, "You were not yet a Christian when you were, by my exhortation, with difficulty induced to hear and find out about these men whom you violently detested," and he finds a way to explain how Honoratus was persuaded to join them, "What else delighted you, I pray you to recall, save their great presumption and the promise of reasoned doctrine?" (*De utilitate credendi* 1.2: LCC 292).

Now that he has returned to the Catholic church, Augustine must retrieve Honoratus from the error into which he plunged his friend. The question is, where does Augustine derive the authority or the conviction to persuade someone he once led astray? He claims that as impressionable young men they were tricked, something he now knows is relatively easy to do with people who are "moderately educated." The Manichees were like tricky fowlers who deceive birds to fall into their traps (*De utilitate credendi* 1.2: LCC 292-293).

In *De moribus ecclesiae catholicae*, Augustine urged the Manichees to seek out qualified Catholic teachers. Here in *De utilitate credendi*, Augustine does not appeal to his own standing as a Catholic teacher. He does, however, appeal to his sincerity: "God, to whom the secrets of my conscience are known, knows that in this little book I am doing nothing in malice, but in the hope that my words may be acceptable in proof of the truth" (*De utilitate credendi* 2.4: LCC 294). Augustine is making up for the lost time, no doubt, offering the admission that he led Honoratus into error, so now he should also be taken seriously when he says that he would like his company on the straight path:

> As eyes which are scarcely opened after a long period of darkness and blindness turn away from the light which, nevertheless, they desire, especially if one try to point them to the sun, so, in my case, I do not deny that there is an ineffable and unique spiritual good visible to the mind, but I confess with weeping and groaning that I am not yet fitted to contemplate it. Nevertheless, he will not leave me if I make no pretense, if I follow the path of duty, if I love truth and friendship, if I am filled with anxiety lest you be deceived. (*De utilitate credendi* 2.4: LCC 294)

Duty, friendship, and the love of truth: these are the things that capture something of the delicate task that Augustine has before him. Duty compels him to undo the regrettable consequences of his previous zeal for the Manichaean religion. Friendship demands that he long for Honoratus to share in what good Augustine believes he has found himself. The love of truth compels him to recall his friend from error. So if he makes no pretense of his love for God, truth, and the bonds of friendship, it is because these are the very things which have led him to write to Honoratus. And he has some hope that he will succeed in turning his friend from error. Augustine adopts a very moderate tone and nowhere pretends to be urging his own ecclesiastical authority as the basis for his argument. All the same, he is bent on presenting an argument that he thinks persuasive, and not simply following trifling commonplaces (*De utilitate credendi* 1.3).

As the first part of this argument, Augustine attacks the Manichees' censure of the Old Testament (*De utilitate credendi* 2.3), maintaining that there are many who are indeed ignorant of what the scriptures contain. Moreover "not many have the power to defend them in an equally popular way, because of the mysteries they contain. The few who know how to do this do not love public controversy with its

consequent publicity. Hence they are unknown except to those who seek them out"
(*De utilitate credendi* 2.3: LCC 293). Augustine presents the four senses of
interpretation he had learned from Ambrose as the most wholesome way of
overcoming these difficulties (*De utilitate credendi* 3.5). But he leaves it to the
Manichaeans to sort out their own difficulties about all the many interpolations they
allege in the scriptures (*De utilitate credendi* 3.6), though he thinks they would be
making a bolder and more transparent statement if they simply claimed that those
who wrote the scriptures were untruthful. Their posturing is the more disingenuous
because they have yet to produce uncorrupted exemplars to prove their charge. One
does not need wisdom to detect such falsity, Augustine asserts, all one needs is an
ordinary heart (*De utilitate credendi* 3.7) to be able to see from where the
Manichaean calumny derives. If one should err, as the Manichaeans prove
themselves to be doing on a grand scale, better that one err with the whole human
race (*omnia gentum*), rather than with the Manichees. If there is anyone anywhere
who knows the true religion, then one is duty bound to go find out. If there is a
dispute, then one is compelled to look for the most able and noteworthy teachers
who are acceptable by all without question (*De utilitate credendi* 7.15: LCC 303),
since no one who has any sense about what he seeks ventures in his studies without
the proper books or teachers.

"Am I sending you fables. Am I compelling you to believe rashly?" (*De utilitate
credendi* 7.14: LCC 303) Augustine asks. The juxtaposition of wisdom (*sapientia*)
and fables (*fabulae*), rash belief and the compelling force of Augustine's words,
recall so much of Augustine's Manichaean past. But he is not content in leaving his
apology to Honoratus on this level. It is not only Manichaean error about scriptural
interpretation which misleads the unwary, but the fact that they have missed entirely
the whole focus of true religion: "No one doubts that he who seeks true religion
either believes already that the soul, which is to profit by religion, is immortal, or
at least hopes to gain that belief from religion itself" (*De utilitate credendi* 7.14:
LCC 303). It is (or should be) first and foremost about the soul and its destiny.

In the place of Manichaean notions of deferred responsibility for human acts,
Augustine says simply that "our soul is ensnared and plunged in folly and error, but
seeks the path of truth, if there be any" (*De utilitate credendi* 7.14: LCC 303). This
is everyone's experience, Augustine insists, and if Honoratus does not recognize this
universal impulse, then he must already be in possession of the good life and
Honoratus would be a true friend to share with Augustine what wisdom he has
discovered. If, on the other hand, Honoratus recognizes in himself the folly and
ignorance of the soul, then he should join Augustine in the search for truth. If he
believes truth can be found only among a very few, then he must know in advance
what truth is (*De utilitate credendi* 7.16: LCC 303ff.). If Honoratus counters that
"he is compelled by the force of truth" to make such a conjecture that truth can be
found only by a few, then he does not know what he is looking for (*De utilitate
credendi* 7.16: LCC 303). Either way, truth becomes for him something of whose
reality he has some intimation. And as long as he acknowledges this, then he is

bound to seek it from the most authoritative teachers. So we are back to authority. That is why people go to Cicero to learn about rhetoric and not a less competent authority, Augustine observes (*De utilitate credendi* 7.16: LCC 303-304). And yet few succeed in learning what is prescribed even by the learned.

Augustine suggests that the inquiry into true religion has exactly this same character of looking for a teacher and discovering that perhaps the many who go for instruction do not all come out well equipped for their tasks (*De utilitate credendi* 7.17: LCC 304ff.). The Catholic church may be no different. There are the multitudes who flock to it, most of them unlearned, but that does not mean there is no one who can expound its mysteries. And it behooves someone like Honoratus to inquire from those who are able to teach it, instead of objecting that the multitude scared him away, as if it is from them that he or any other inquirer would learn. If, on the other hand, Honoratus should claim that no teachers can be found to teach him the true religion, what better reason would he have for traveling even further afield, if his journey's end is the search for truth and the happy life. Augustine reminds Honoratus of how rash they were in their judgments of Catholic Christianity in their student days. He claims they did not search near and far: "Instead, by our arbitrary judgment we unhappy youths condemned a religion which might have proved to be most holy, and at any rate was still an open question, a religion which has taken possession of the whole world" (*De utilitate credendi* 7.17: LCC 305).

Augustine also reminds Honoratus of the unimpressive meeting with Faustus of Milevis (*Confessions* 5.3.3; 5.6.10-5.7.13) shortly before Augustine left for Rome, pointing out that while Faustus' "coming to explain all our difficulties was held out to us as a gift from heaven" ((*De utilitate credendi* 8.20: LCC 306), it proved a terrible disappointment. "No one knows better than you how I sighed for the truth" (*De utilitate credendi* 8.20: LCC 307), he reminds Honoratus. Augustine goes on to describe how his brief phase of Academic skepticism prepared him for his eventual return to Catholic Christianity (*De utilitate credendi* 8.20: LCC 306-307). Doubting almost everything, he still could not believe that truth was entirely out of reach, when he reflected on the powers of the human mind. The question became one of authority: which authority did he have to believe amid the many? And amidst tears and prayers he found his way back to the Catholic church. Augustine recounts all this to spur Honoratus towards similar judgments, but he admits that the Manichees can make a similar showing. They too promised the same consolations to the troubled and anxious soul of Augustine at an earlier period (*De utilitate credendi* 8.20).

Augustine, however, insists that there is a difference. The Manichaeans are not to be trusted when they promise to be able to explain their most obscure doctrines by reason, as they bring the charge against the Catholic church that it imposes on its adherents the "yoke of belief" (*De utilitate credendi* 9.21: LCC 307). What seems so commendable on the part of the Manichees turns out to be something altogether different. While a person delights in such promises, he forgets what his true needs are and does not realize that true religion cannot advance without the "weighty command of authority." Things must first be believed so that one may later gain understanding, if one conducts one's self properly (*De utilitate credendi* 9.21: LCC 308). Augustine's "unless you believe, you will not understand" is clearly implied here.

Besides, Augustine argues, even the person who inquires into the true religion would have to be believed not to be an imposter by the one who has knowledge in order for any teaching to take place. So the inquirer elicits belief on the part of his teacher. Is it then too much to ask that the seeker also believe in order that he might understand what he is taught (*De utilitate credendi* 9.22)? What Augustine does not add, which is more than relevant to his situation, is whether there are any criteria for changing one's mind. Since it is in the nature of education that sometimes one is taught falsehoods or half-truths, at what point can teaching authority be questioned? Certainly the student must begin his studies by trusting the authority of the teacher, but what happens if the inquirer comes to know differently and changes his mind? After all, isn't this what Augustine's departure from the Manichees and his disaffection with Academic skepticism imply? Could not a skeptical reader demur by saying that Augustine was merely a restless soul who was not satisfied with what he had received, but always sought something new, and once he found it, insisted that it was the truth?

Augustine admits that the common reproach heaped on the credulous might well be brought against him: "If the mistrustful man is at fault because he suspects everything he does not know, how much worse is the credulous man?" (*De utilitate credendi* 9.22: LCC 308). He tries to obviate the objection by saying that it is neither estimable nor worthwhile to be too credulous on the one hand or mistrustful on the other. The mistrustful person doubts too much, while the credulous one does not doubt at all. Augustine is convinced that the one who believes is not to be deemed credulous on any account, since such an attitude assumes that believing and being credulous are two forms of the same vice, like being a drunkard and being drunk on one occasion (*De utilitate credendi* 10.23: LCC 309). Moreover, it is ignoble to be so mistrustful of what one does not know as to desist from inquiring into what the true religion might be. The conversion narrative he presents is also predicated on his love of truth, and he believes this precludes any criticism about his credulity.

If the objection is made that belief is permissible in lesser things but is to be shunned entirely when religion is at issue, Augustine counters that if that is the case then it will have to be admitted that no friendships are possible, since one needs to be believed and trusted in friendship. Augustine's response does not quite meet the objection. However, in a possible allusion to his role as a teacher in the church, Augustine observes that if a "master is not blamed for trusting the slaves who serve him," then it is unfair "that God's ministers should believe us when we profess to be sincere but that we should be unwilling to believe them when they instruct us" (*De utilitate credendi* 10.24: LCC 311). And nothing is more fitting than to make one's self fit for receiving the truth by believing the things God has appointed to prepare the soul for its end. If, after all that Augustine has urged for his friend's consideration, Honoratus still thinks it blameworthy to believe and presumes that reason alone suffices for the happy life, then he would do well to notice that all knowledge implies belief, because all knowledge depends on some form of authority. Authority is invested in those who teach any discipline and Honoratus would be doing nothing preposterous by deferring to the authority of Catholic teachers. But isn't Augustine asking too much?

Knowledge, Belief, and the Hermeneutics of Trust

In matters of religion, he contends, two kinds of people are to be praised: those who have found the truth and who must be judged entirely blessed, and those who seek it properly and earnestly (*De utilitate credendi* 11.25: LCC 311).[9] There are, however, three classes of human beings that are to be deplored. First, those who do not know but think they know: these are the opinionated ones. Then there are those who know they do not know but who are not seeking in such a way as to find. And then there is a third class who know they are ignorant but have no interest in finding out. Augustine assumes that Honoratus is not to be counted among these three groups of people (*De utilitate credendi* 11.25: LCC 311-312).

If knowledge and opinion stand at the opposite ends of the epistemological spectrum, then belief occupies a middle position, sometimes faulty and erroneous but at other times true (*De utilitate credendi* 11.25: LCC 312). And Augustine has every intention of defending the nature of Catholic belief along this spectrum: "Believing is blameworthy if one believes anything unworthy of God or if one believes too readily a man. In other matters, if anyone believes anything, knowing that he does not know it, there is no fault committed" (*De utilitate credendi* 11.25: LCC 312).

Belief is what we hold on the basis of well-founded authority; knowledge (*scientia*) is what we gain through the use of reason. Our opinions we owe to neither reason nor authority, but to error. Once something is believed it can be understood and at that point ceases to be a matter of belief only. "But belief does not imply knowledge and opinion never does," since the latter is simply indifferent to reason (*De utilitate credendi* 11.25: LCC 312). For Augustine, opinion is self-justifying error founded on one's own authority.

Those who have found the truth believe the truth, while those who are earnest seekers believe upon authority. Those who think they know, but do not know what they talk about, simply believe their own opinions. Those who are ignorant but neither desire to know nor seek in such a way as to find believe nothing. The important fact is that everyone believes something by believing their own opinions or on the authority of others (*De utilitate credendi* 11.25. LCC 312-313). Hence there is a profound need to determine who it is one can trust.

Augustine notes, for example, that one has to believe one's parents, saying that it is on the mother's authority that people know who the father of a child is (*De utilitate credendi* 12.26: LCC 313). Who would not be thought blameworthy for not loving his parents, because he did not believe them to be his and he feared he might be loving those who might not be his parents? he inquires (*De utilitate credendi* 12.26: LCC 313). He continues that "nothing would remain stable in human society if we determined to believe nothing that we could not scientifically establish" (*De utilitate credendi* 12.26: LCC 313). Augustine sets belief and trust against what can be established by demonstration or reasoning.

In the "knowing and worshiping of God" (*De utilitate credendi* 12.27: LCC 314), we are dealing with what cannot be scientifically established, so a completely reasoned account without any appeal to authority is unthinkable. Not even the Manichees can do what they promise, so they are not to be believed who tell us not to be believe, and promise to give us from the start a reasoned account.

When the human capacity for wisdom enters into the problem of religion, it is more likely that most are in the role of the fool than of the wise man, though few would openly concede that they are fools. The wise man here is not someone clever or skilled, but rather one who has a "clear and strongly established knowledge of God and man" (*De utilitate credendi* 12.27: LCC 314), and lives and conducts his life in a way that answers to that knowledge. All others, no matter how skilled, ignorant, excellent or depraved their manner of life, Augustine numbers among the foolish. From this, no one with moderate intelligence can miss the point that it is more "useful and helpful to obey the precepts of the wise" than for the fool to live by his own whims (*De utilitate credendi* 12.27: LCC 314). "The wise man alone does not sin. The fool sins in all that he does except when he obeys a wise man, for then his actions proceed from right reason" (*De utilitate credendi* 12.27: LCC 314). Without explicitly stating it, Augustine includes the best of the philosophers among the foolish, for he does not credit the philosophers with clear and strongly established knowledge of God.

The most commendable life for all who are foolish, all who have not attained a clear and settled knowledge of God and human affairs, is to follow those who have already found it. So rather than spurning belief as the stuff of ignorance and mere opinion, belief has its own legitimacy if it involves following the lead of those who know and love God. It is clear, of course, that the person who follows a wise man, as Augustine has it here, is not his own master, since he depends on another's wisdom. Augustine insists that "if our heart is set on the good religious life, there is nothing for us so long as we are foolish, but to seek out wise men and to obey them, so that we may not suffer the domination of the folly which is in us, and may in time escape it altogether" (*De utilitate credendi* 12.27: LCC 314). This much is what is involved in *De moribus ecclesiae catholicae* when Augustine speaks of the biblical tradition as the voice of Wisdom and those who passed on that tradition as people who were in all probability wise. This is the only posture that is praiseworthy when one is in search of the happy life. The wise man stands between the folly of human beings and the pure truth of God, and he imitates God as much as it is granted to him, while the foolish man does his best when he imitates a wise man (*De utilitate credendi* 15.33: LCC 318).

"So long as he remains a fool, no one can with absolute certainty discover a wise man, by obeying whom he may be delivered from the evil of his folly" (*De utilitate credendi* 13.28: LCC 315). But in Augustine's phenomenology it would be more appropriate not to believe that true religion exists and to be indifferent to the search for such an end, than to suppose that it exists but it requires no belief or authority: "For my part I judge that believing before reasoning, if you are not able to follow reasoning, and cultivating the mind by faith in order to be ready to receive the seeds of truth, is not only most wholesome, but is indeed the only way by which health can return to sick minds" (*De utilitate credendi* 14.21: LCC 316). In such matters as the quest for truth, many appear wise who are in fact fools (*De utilitate credendi* 15.33: LCC 318). Honoratus must, therefore, choose between the two: either to remain among those who appear wise but are not, or to join those who trust in credible teachers in the hope of understanding the truth.

If people find it unthinkable that they should be asked to believe, Augustine reminds Honoratus that the Wisdom of God demands just this. Christ himself demanded "faith above everything else and before everything else, because those with whom he was dealing were not yet able to penetrate to the divine secrets" (*De utilitate credendi* 14.32: LCC 318). Faith, then, is whatever trust one places in the Teacher. The miracles of Jesus served "no other purpose than that men should believe in him," and in so doing he led the foolish by faith, so that those who did not know the truth might come to a recognition of it (*De utilitate credendi* 14.32: LCC 318). And in this Christ shows how far the divine mercy extends and the heights to which human frailty could be set (*De utilitate credendi* 15.33: LCC 319). The inquirer cannot understand the teacher unless he trusts him: "To wish to see the truth in order that you may purge your soul is a perverse and preposterous idea, because it is precisely in order that you may see, that it has to be purged" (*De utilitate credendi* 16.34. LCC 320). Augustine has more to say on the evidential force of miracles, but his justification of belief stands independently of that argument.[10]

Learning what and whom to trust: that is the central theme of *De utilitate credendi*. In his *De vera religione*, written shortly before the *De utilitate credendi*, and also to his friend and patron Romanianus (another person whom Augustine had persuaded to become a Manichee), Augustine noted at one point that "the trustworthiness of temporal things whether past or future can be believed rather than known by the intelligence," and that the challenge we face lies in "our duty to consider what men or what books we are to believe in order that we may rightly worship God," because in this lies our salvation (*De vera religione* 25.46). In other words, each one has the burden of finding out what is believable and trustworthy. But upon what criteria? Later on in that same work he offers his hermeneutics of trust, a disposition towards inquiry which is supposed to provide the guarantee that the search for truth would not prove fruitless:

> Let us then make clear to ourselves what faith we ought to repose in history and what
> in intelligence; what we ought to commit to memory, not knowing that it is true but
> believing all the same; where is the truth that neither comes nor passes away but abides
> the same; what is the mode of interpreting allegory, believed to have been spoken in
> wisdom through the Holy Spirit; whether it is enough to allegorize things that have been
> seen in ancient days and in more recent time, or is it to be applied to the affections and
> nature of the soul, and to unchangeable eternity . . . When we have come to know that
> one truth, all puerile impudence is driven from our minds and holy religion comes into
> its own. (*De vera religione* 50.99: LCC 275-276)

Mention of allegory and what modes of interpretation are appropriate for what kinds
of texts draws attention to the very textual nature of mediated tradition. For it is
primarily in written texts that are to be found the deposits of tradition and testimony.
To know where to repose one's trust is therefore unquestionably a matter of textual
interpretation, historical imagination and moral insight. Augustine raises this very
prospect here in *De utilitate credendi* when he asserts that unless there are shared
beliefs between a writer and a reader, true communication is nearly impossible (*De
utilitate credendi* 4.17). A certain form of trust is required between the author and
the reader in order for any meaningful understanding to take place. For Augustine,
it is not only divine speech which requires prior belief in order that one might gain
understanding. This is the essential character of all human communication. It
should, therefore, not be seen as an extraordinary prerequisite to demand that people
trust what is written about God in order to gain understanding of the divine.
However, by acknowledging the need for commonality between the writer and his
readers as a necessary condition for communication, Augustine might appear to be
suggesting that in the absence of such commonality there is no place for dialogue
or understanding. But that would be far from his purpose.

As he notes elsewhere, when the mind deals with things not present to our
senses, "we do not speak of the things themselves, but of images derived from them
and implanted in our memory" (*De magistro* 12.39: LCC 96). But these memorials
belong to us privately: when we speak of them, those who hear us simply have to
believe us, for they do not have access to them directly (*De magistro* 12.39: LCC
96). Then there are those things which we come to know by thinking and the
exercise of reason. If other people hear us speaking they are enjoined to come to
understanding by their own use of reason, what Augustine calls the contemplation
of truth (*De magistro* 12.40: LCC 96-98). So understanding assumes at least two
minds going through their own operations, mediated by signs from the one who does
the signifying at any given time.

The words that are spoken may not properly reflect the mind of the speaker, if
he is not sure of what he speaks, but those who are not intent on deceiving their
hearers try as much as possible to have their words conform to what goes on in their
minds. And various phenomena like slips of tongue, people saying something other
than what they planned to say, or giving a speech they had recited to themselves at
an importune time, all point out the difficulty of speech approximating to what has

been thought in the mind (*De magistro* 13.42: LCC 98). The problems are compounded when we read:

> First, [the reader] may accept as true what is false, and what the writer knew to be false. Secondly — though this is not obvious but no less deadly — they may accept as true a false opinion actually held by the writer. Thirdly, they may understand some truth from another's writing, which the writer himself did not understand. In this kind of error there is no little advantage. (*De utilitate credendi* 4.10: LCC 298)

The writer has his difficulties too: "either one may write usefully and be misunderstood or both the writing and the understanding may be at fault, or the reader derives an advantage while the writer meant something quite different" (*De utilitate credendi* 5.11: LCC 300) The best situation is when good things are written and are understood without difficulty by those who read, but this is seldom the case:

> For it often happens that the writer's views are sound and the reader's also, but the latter holds it in a different sense, sometimes in a better sense, sometimes in an inferior sense, but always profitably. But when we share the views of our author and they are suited to promote good conduct, the cause of truth is served in a high degree and no place is left open for falsehood. Now, when we have to do with very obscure matters this kind of relationship between author and reader is extremely rare, and in my opinion it is not a case where clear knowledge is possible but only faith. How can I find out the intention and meaning of an author who is absent or dead, in such a way that I could give evidence as to them on oath? (*De utilitate credendi* 5.11: LCC 300)

As long as two minds are at work, the possibilities of misunderstanding are enormous.

Behind all these words is the idea of interpretation as bearing witness, as if giving testimony under oath. But it is not the giving of testimony under oath about the writer, but about what is written. So the presence of the author would not necessarily make such a witness any less risky, since the author could deliberately mislead even when in person. Similarly, the signs, which constitute the written text, may also be intended to mislead. For Augustine, the truth of what is written is independent of who does the writing, so the author's character has no bearing on trying to sift the truth, though it is "most honorable to believe that an author was a good man, whose writings were intended to benefit the human race and posterity" than to think otherwise (*De utilitate credendi* 5.11).

Bearing Witness to Truth

Augustine would like Honoratus to extend to him the kind of goodwill that one would extend to another in the expectation of learning something new. In short, Honoratus must reckon Augustine to have been a fool in his Manichaean days. But is the appeal to Augustine's sincerity enough to vouch for the truth of what he says, and for the credibility of the religion he now defends? Augustine seems to think so. But herein lies a problem. If, in typical Manichaean fashion, Honoratus had come do despise or mock Catholic claims that its teachings ought to believed and its teachers trusted (*Retractationes* 1.14.1), why should he pay any heed to Augustine? Augustine seems to believe that a reminder of how they used to be in the past and what presumption characterized some of their most important judgments should be warrant enough for Honoratus to reconsider where he now stands as a Manichee.

It is noteworthy that Augustine does not mention in his *Retractationes* whether Honoratus was persuaded by the *De utilitate credendi* to abandon the Manichees. So while we may never know just what Honoratus made of Augustine's arguments, we have every reason to wonder as to the limits of Augustine's personal authority in this particular instance. There is reason also to suspect that Augustine's success in getting Manichees to abandon their faith and join him among the Catholics were few and far between. The most notable example we have is that of Felix the Manichaean Elect, Augustine's interlocutor in the public disputation which took place in 404 (*Acta contra Felicem Manichaeum*), in the aftermath of which Felix declared his Manichaean religion anathema and may have become a Catholic.

In the other direction, there is the case of Augustine's friend and patron Romanianus. In spite of the various entreaties towards philosophy (*Contra academicos*) and true religion (*De vera religione*) which Augustine sent his way, Augustine gives no indication that Romanianus ever joined the Catholic church. It is conceivable that Romanianus may have abandoned the Manichees without necessarily ending up among the Catholics as Augustine had. There is also the telling example of Licentius, Romanianus' son, once a student of Augustine's at Cassiciacum. Licentius, perhaps like his father, managed to shake off Augustine's influence to the latter's disappointment (Ep. 26).

If success were to be deemed the measure of truth, then Augustine's attempts at trying to persuade his former co-religionists suggest that the argument based on trust (and authority) could only go so far. To say this is not to intimate any inherent weakness in Augustine's contention that trust and authority precede all forms of instruction. What it underscores is that trust only serves as a prerequisite for meaningful dialogue. The real and perceived differences which obtain between peoples and societies and among individuals within given societies may still remain even when there is a great deal of trust, especially when the subject at hand is "true religion" or the ultimate end of human life.

Augustine's sincerity may well have restored Honoratus' trust in him without necessarily persuading the latter of the rightness of Augustine's newfound beliefs. Augustine seems to have recognized this. There may be some indication of this in the tone and content of Augustine's anti-Manichaean writings which appeared after the *De utilitate credendi*. We find in works like *Acta contra Fortunatum Manichaeum* (392), *De duabus animabus contra Manichaeos* (392/393), *Contra epistulam quam vocant fundamenti* (396), *Contra Faustum Manichaeum* (400), *De natura boni contra Manichaeos* (399), and the *Acta contra Felicem Manichaeum*

(404) a concerted effort to refute specific Manichaean doctrines, with a thoroughness and comprehensiveness that is at times unrelenting and even tedious.

One may also detect in a number of these works an expression of sympathy, somewhat different from the tone of his first anti-Manichaean work, the *De moribus ecclesiae catholicae*. Whereas in the *De moribus ecclesiae catholicae* of 388 Augustine seems to tire of Manichaean obstinacy, in *Contra epistulam quam vocant fundamenti* of 396, for example, he begins with a reminder of where he himself had been, something akin to his retrospective in *De utilitate credendi*, and he underscores how difficult it is to unlearn one's errors. The words of sympathy are meant in part to secure a hearing. However, Augustine's words seem genuinely cognizant of the difficulties entailed in acknowledging that a way of life to which he had been devoted was in fact not worth what he once thought it was:

> Let those who rage against you who know not with what labor the truth is to be found and with what difficulty error is to be avoided. Let those rage against you who know not how rare and hard it is to overcome the fancies of the flesh by the serenity of a pious disposition. Let those rage against you who know not the difficulty of curing the eye of the inner man that he may gaze upon his Sun, — not that which you worship, and which shines with the brilliance of a heavenly body in the eyes of carnal men and of beasts — but that of which it is written through the prophet, 'The Sun of righteousness has arisen upon me;' and of which it is said in the gospel, 'That was the true Light ,which gives light to every man that comes into the world.' Let those rage against you who know not with what sighs and groans the least particle of the knowledge of God is obtained. And, last of all, let those rage against you who have never been led astray in the same way that they see that you are. (*Contra epistulam quam vocant fundamenti* 2.2, NPNF 4, 128-129)

To any Manichee reading these words, Augustine appears at his most empathetic, almost as if Augustine is recalling his own difficulties as a Manichee and the troubles he endured as he tried to free himself from error. He casts himself as a most sympathetic controversialist who knows not only the error from which he is calling his former co-religionists, but one who would rather join in sharing their grief than participate with those who would rage against them.

This is a remarkable posture, given that in the much earlier *De moribus ecclesiae catholicae* Augustine seemed to strain for sympathy, asserting at one point, somewhat reluctantly, that the love of God compelled him to extend the utmost goodwill to his Manichaean neighbors. Whatever he might feel about them, the Manichees were his neighbors after all. And since the Manichees also believed that one should love God and neighbor (*De moribus ecclesiae catholicae* 1.28), Augustine would not even be commendable in their eyes if he did otherwise. In the midst of disputing Manichaean objections that the Old Testament is centered on fear, Augustine replies that it was mere ignorance, since the commandment to love God and neighbor came out of that same part of the scriptures the Manichees maligned. Augustine also argues that fear and love belong together: the former restrains while the latter instructs. The one constrains from error, the other leads into the truth. Augustine claimed that he did not want to be at fault by not helping the "Manichaean his neighbor" when it was in his power to do so. He intended no harm to the Manichees, and so was free of the one sin, but would be guilty of another if he remained silent.

And because the love of neighbor is "a sort of cradle of our love of God" (*quasi cunabulae caritatis dei* [*De moribus ecclesiae catholicae* 1.26.50]), and it is out of the cradle of benevolent love that one should expect to progress orderly to the love of God, every one stands in all his loves between God and his fellow human beings. And "no one should think that while he despises his neighbor he will come to happiness and to the God whom he loves" (*De moribus ecclesiae catholicae* 1.26.50). Augustine does not have the option of indifference, and least of all towards the Manichees: "would that it were as easy to seek the good of our neighbor, or to avoid hurting him, as it is for one well trained and kind-hearted to love his neighbor" (*De moribus ecclesiae catholicae* 1.26.50). Goodwill is not enough: "They either rise together to fullness and perfection, or while the love of God is first in beginning, the love of our neighbor is first in coming to perfection."[11]

Augustine believed that he was required to dispense not only *disciplina* for the good of his neighbor's soul, but also *medicina*, whatever was needful for the neighbor's bodily health either in preserving or restoring it. Both preventative and curative measures were necessary, and he saw his *De moribus ecclesiae catholicae* as an exercise in the curative discipline which the Manichees sorely needed in order to unlearn their ignorance. Hard insensibility on his part towards his former co-religionist, "which is very different from the calm of a rational serenity" (*quam rationis tranquilitate serenantur*) was not an estimable response (*De moribus ecclesiae catholicae* 1.27.54). Augustine believed, however, that he was allowed a certain "rational serenity," if he felt no special love for the Manichees. But whatever the case, he needed to act out of goodwill (*voluntas bona*), desiring that they partake of that good which had become his. He gladly acknowledged that the disposition of "thoughtfulness and prudence" (*ratio atque prudentia*), which this special benevolence requires, is given by God (*De moribus ecclesiae catholicae* 1.26).

One cannot mistake how different Augustine's mood is in *De utilitate credendi* where he reminds Honoratus of the reasons which led him into error and how he now seeks to retrieve Honoratus from the error into which he plunged him. The words of self-reproach Augustine uses in *De utilitate credendi*, tinged with all the elements of confession and regret, underline much of what he acknowledges at the opening of *Contra epistulam quam vocant fundamenti*, where he continues to restate his past errors and his new-found desire to bring other Manichees into the joy he believes he has found:

> For my part, I, — who after much and long-continued bewilderment, attained at last to the discovery of the simple truth, which is learned without being recorded in any fanciful legend; who unhappy that I was, barely succeeded, by God's help, in refuting the vain imaginations of my mind, gathered from theories and errors of various kinds;

who so late sought the cure of my mental obscuration, in compliance with the call of the all-merciful Physician; who long wept that the immutable and inviolable Existence would vouchsafe to convince me inwardly of Himself, in harmony with the testimony of the sacred books; by whom in the end, all those fictions which have such a firm hold on you, from your long familiarity with them, were diligently examined, and attentively heard, and too easily believed, and commended at every opportunity to the belief of others, and defended against opponents with determination and boldness, — I can on no account rage against you; for I must bear with you now as formerly I had to bear with myself, and I must be as patient towards you as my associates were with me, when I went madly and blindly astray in your beliefs. (*Contra epistulam quam vocant fundamenti* 3.3, NPNF 4, 130)

But as always in these anti-Manichaean works, the irrepressible Augustine insists that for all these reasons enunciated he is owed a hearing. The terms he sets in *Contra epistulam quam vocant fundamenti* are very much what he states in *De utilitate credendi*. He comes not as a competent authority, but as a fellow inquirer convinced that if the truth is sought, Catholic teaching will be vindicated: "Let neither of us assert that he has found truth; let us seek it as if it were unknown to us both. For truth can be sought with zeal and unanimity if by no rash presumption it is believed to have been already found and ascertained. But if I cannot induce you to grant me this, at least allow me to suppose myself a stranger now for the first time hearing you, for the first time examining your doctrines" (*Contra epistulam quam vocant fundamenti* 3.4, NPNF 4, 130).

Augustine assumes all along that the true source of his authority and the credibility of Catholic teaching lay not so much with the competence of its teachers, but in the Teacher, namely Christ. When he refers Honoratus to consider that Wisdom himself demanded faith before understanding, Augustine is content to rest his case there. As he stated earlier in *De moribus ecclesiae catholicae* 1.18.13, it is the Lord himself who teaches us how to live, and it is this witness that distinguishes the Catholic Christians from both the Manichaeans and the philosophers. Wisdom, personified in Proverbs 2-9 as a woman entreating the simple-minded to seek her, has now appeared in fact. So all those who pretend to love wisdom, be they philosophers or Manichees, would do better simply to heed the words of the Teacher, because reason cannot attain to what the christological event attests to and the way of beatitude which the Christian religion provides.

Without the spirit of inquiry and the desire to pursue the truth to which Augustine appeals over and over again in *De utilitate credendi*, the insistence on trust and authority as prerequisites for true knowledge falls on deaf ears. If Honoratus does not find what Augustine presents in *De utilitate credendi* any the more convincing, then, as Augustine understands it, true friendship and the longing for truth should compel Honoratus to seek the truth, and once he has found it, to be willing to share it. To know and to love the truth and to be unwilling to share it freely is not to possess the truth as one ought to:

What then you aim at in yourself you must aim at in your neighbor, namely, that he may love God with perfect affection. For you do not love him as yourself, unless you try to draw him to that good which you are yourself pursuing. For this is the one good which has room for all to pursue it along with thee. (*De moribus ecclesiae catholicae* 1.26: BWA 1:343)

Even if the ultimate goal of persuading Honoratus to leave the Manichaean religion and become a Catholic Christian did not materialize, Augustine's emphasis on trust seems an eminently laudable objective, which can never be overstated. When tied to his emphasis on the spirit of inquiry in the search for truth, it provides the two most important elements for any philosophy of liberal education. To seek the truth in sincerity, to bear witness to the truth, and to share the truth with as many friends as possible who are seeking the same end: these are the essential attributes that preserve the bonds of trust necessary for a truly liberal education. It may very well be that without these three elements "the arts of determining when trust is justified" to which Wayne Booth calls attention in his reflections on the "Idea of a University" will always remain tenuous at best.

Notes

1   Wayne C. Booth, *The Vocation of a Teacher: Rhetorical Occasions, 1967-1988* (Chicago: The University of Chicago Press, 1988) 324-325.

2   A note on the translations. For the *De utilitate credendi* and *De vera religione* I have used J. H. S. Burleigh's translation found in *Augustine: Earlier Writings* (The Library of Christian Classics; Philadelphia: Westminster Press, 1953), henceforth LCC. For the *De moribus ecclesiae catholicae* I have used R. Stothert's translation in the Nicene and Post-Nicene Fathers, reprinted in Whitney J. Oates, ed., *The Basic Writings of St. Augustine*, vol. 1 (NewYork: Random House, 1968), henceforth BWA. For the *Contra epistulam quam vocant fundamenti* I have used the Nicene and Post-Nicene Fathers (Grand Rapids, MI: Eerdmans, 1987), henceforth NPNF. In some instances I have made slight modifications without indicating them.

3   Such descriptions of the Manichees appear in various places in *De moribus ecclesiae catholicae* (1.1-2; 2.3; 7.11; 10.16-17; 17.30-32; 21.38; 29.59-60 etc.). The definitive *Contra Faustum* has a good many of these characterizations.

4   I should note that public disputation tempered Augustine's attitude somewhat, though one can also detect in these performances his annoyance and irritation at certain Manichaean tendencies and attitudes in *Acta contra Fortunatum Manichaeum* (392) and *Acta contra Felicem Manichaeum* (404). For a general survey of Manichaean interests in public debate see Richard Lim, "Manichaeans and Public Disputation in Late Antiquity," *Recherches Augustiniennes* 26 (1992) 233-272.

5   In fact Augustine's spirited argumentation in *Contra Faustum Manichaeum* (400) and the nature and complexity of his long relationship with Faustus (*Confessions* 5.3.3ff.) indicates just what difficult task Augustine had set himself. Something of that difficulty is already presaged in his earlier encounter with Fortunatus (*Acta contra Fortunatum Manichaeum*). Cf. Richard Lim, "Manichaeans and Public Disputation in Late

Antiquity," 256-266.

6   Cf. H. C. Peuch, *Le Manicheisme: son fondateur, sa doctrine* (Paris, 1949) 81-82; cited in G. Bonner, *Augustine: Life and Controversies* (Philadelphia: Westminster Press, 1963) 161.

7   Augustine knew two versions of the verse. In *De doctrina christiana* 2.7.17 he provides the alternate Vulgate version, "if you will not believe, you shall not endure" (*si non credideritis non permanebitis*), which he would not have had prior to Jerome's translation. The citation of the Vulgate version may also be an indication of Augustine's later revision of the earlier draft of *De doctrina christiana* Books 1 & 2 (396) when he came to complete the entire work in 427.

8   Leo C. Ferrari, "The Young Augustine: Both Catholic and Manichee," *Augustinian Studies* 26 (1995) 109-128, argues that Augustine had remained a catechumen during his nine year tenure among the Manichees. This appears to contradict Augustine's entire attitude toward Catholic Christianity during this period.

9   Augustine corrects the first part in *Retractationes* 1.14.2, that complete blessedness is not to be had here. But actually his words do not intimate this, except he is on the lookout lest he be deemed to be offering what might sound Pelagian.

10   In any event, he sees miracles as producing two effects: either causing wonder or producing good will and gratitude. Both effects are meant to lend credibility to the one who produces them, so again it becomes a question of legitimating authority.

11   R. J. Canning in a series of studies has explored the relationship between the love of neighbor and the love of God in Augustine. That Augustine thinks of the relationship in dialectical terms seems to me unquestionable. See the following: "The Distinction between love of God and Love for Neighbour in St. Augustine," *Augustiniana* 32 (1982) 5-41; "Love of Neighbour in St. Augustine. A Preparation for or the essential moment of love of God?" *Augustiniana* 33 (1983) 5-57; "'Love your neighbour as yourself' (Matt. 22.39): Saint Augustine on the Lineaments of the Self to be loved," *Augustiniana* 34 (1984) 145-197; "Augustine on the identity of the neighbour and the meaning of true love for him 'as ourselves' (Matt 22, 39) and 'as Christ has loved us' (Jn 13, 34)," *Augustiniana* 36 (1986) 161-239; "The Unity of Love for God and Love of Neighbour," *Augustiniana* 37 (1987) 38-121.

Chapter Nine

Limit and Possibility:
An Augustinian Counsel to Authority

Mark J. Doorley

Introduction

As a political character in the fourth and fifth century Roman empire, Augustine of Hippo had sufficient opportunities to reflect on the nature of leadership, both in the Empire and in the Church. From the evidence of his letters and texts such as *The City of God*, it is clear that Augustine considered it his responsibility to engage the leaders of the day, challenging them to cultivate the wisdom necessary to rule justly. This Augustinian brand of political wisdom was radical. It demanded of the leader humility and piety. This was not the counsel of the Roman tradition, nor was it readily acknowledged as a more responsible approach to leadership. However, Augustine refused to back down, and continued to call for a reform of the political leadership so that it would be more responsive to the needs of the people, particularly the powerless ones.

Is Augustine's counsel limited to the leaders of Late Antiquity? Can humility and piety be the virtues of a contemporary leader? Do contemporary people who are in positions of authority exercise that authority with humility and piety? One need not look far to find that Augustine's counsel continues to garner for itself disregard, even ridicule. Humility might find its way into the persona of particular individuals, but it is used to conserve power, rather than as a genuine response to one's life. The virtue of piety is left to the private life of the individual, rather than as an important component in one's ability to rule justly. Augustine is still the minority, radical voice.

This essay is an argument in favor of Augustine's counsel about wisdom in the contemporary world. What seems lacking in so many areas of human interaction, particularly in the lives of those whose responsibilities effect so many, is an attitude of humility and an awareness of the transcendent.[1] Some may claim that humility and piety are private virtues. Their place is in the home, with one's family. However, humility and piety in the public realm are required by the reality of human experience. To relegate these virtues to the private life of individuals is to deprive those same individuals of resources for wise leadership.

The essay will proceed in the following way. First, we will look at several

Augustinian texts which will elucidate Augustine's reasons for his counsel of humility and piety. Second, we will look into the epistemological claims of Augustine, focusing on the activity of human judgment. What will become clear is that an analysis of human judgment provides reasonable grounds for affirming the existence of a transcendent reality. Such an affirmation need not be circumscribed by religious dogma, but it can provide a much needed corrective to the achievements of human creativity. We ought to be humble and pious, not because the great Augustine of Hippo counseled such, but because human experience provides reasonable grounds for such virtue. The leader who approaches his or her responsibilities with humility and an awareness of what is beyond him or her, in terms of knowing, will be a leader who is willing to admit error, who is willing to listen to all voices, and who is committed to acting, albeit cautiously, for the good of all.

Augustinian Texts

The City of God, *Book V*

In Chapter 12 of this book, Augustine begins to list the qualities of the Roman leader. First and foremost, he was "passionately devoted to glory." This glory was achieved through his military exploits which aimed at making the empire sovereign over all her neighbors and enemies. It was this desire for praise and glory that kept in check their "other appetites" (*City of God*, 5.12). The good and the wicked alike pursue glory, but only those who merit glory are good leaders. It is not merely the domination of others through the exercise of power that merits one honor and glory; it is the way in which one pursues this domination. It is only those who strove to attain honor and glory by honorable means who merit the praise of the people. So, Augustine concludes, "glory, honor, and power must be the consequences of virtue not its antecedents" (*City of God*, 5. 12).

Augustine recognizes that the love of praise checks other appetites. Lust, greed and viciousness are among those vices that are often checked by the love of praise, because yielding to their tempting voices would jeopardize the praise that one has earned. Insofar as the love of praise checks worse vices, it is a virtue. But this cannot be the end of the story for Augustine. He goes on in chapter 14 to make clear that the love of praise must itself be checked because it can blind one to the truth to which one must be more deeply committed. "...if things which are themselves good and right 'lose lustre' because of general disfavour, then the love of human praise itself should be ashamed, and yield place to the love of truth" (*City of God*, 5.14). The love of praise might cause a leader to overlook an injustice in order to protect his "treasure," namely the praise and honor of the people.

The love of praise can also blind one to the true recipient of all praise, namely, God. Augustine compares the Roman citizen who seeks glory with the Christian martyr. The Romans sought glory in order to preserve their country. Their aim was a kingdom in this life. If they died in that search for glory, they could count on the praise of the survivors. The Christian martyr, on the other hand, sought the glory of God, not his or her own glory. Insofar as they received praise for their constancy in the faith, they redirected that praise to the God who enabled them to be constant in the face of death. The Roman does not redirect the praise he receives from the people for his deeds. He is the actor, the one responsible for his own success. It is this sense of self-sufficiency, coupled with the deserving praise and honor, that concerns Augustine about political leadership. The desire for glory and the satisfaction of that desire can quickly corrode the virtue of human beings in positions of power.

In chapter 19 of Book V, Augustine discusses the distinction between ambition for glory and ambition for domination. The person who seeks glory is "anxious for the good opinion of enlightened judges." The person who seeks domination regards as irrelevant the good opinion of these same judges. He may, however, want to appear to possess the good moral qualities that the person seeking glory possesses. For example, the person seeking glory may love the truth and may desire to be known as an honest man. The person seeking domination may hate the truth but dissemble in order to be known as a lover of truth, hence, making his domination more complete. The good person is limited by love of the truth; the corrupt leader has no such limit, hence he or she is far more dangerous.

In this same chapter, Augustine describes the truly virtuous person. It seems here that he has moved away from the secular ruler toward a Christian ruler. It will be helpful to quote this description in its entirety. What is clear is the challenge of balancing the demands of Christian piety with the realities of political life:

> ...if he is a truly good man, he does not regard the salvation of his fellow-men as of no importance. For so great is the righteousness of one who has his virtues from the Spirit of God, that he loves even his enemies; and such is his love even for those who hate and disparage him, that he wishes them to be reformed so that he may have them as fellow-citizens, not of the earthly city, but of the heavenly. As for those who praise him, though he takes little account of their applause, he does not undervalue their love; he does not want to deceive those who praise him, because he would not want to play tricks on those who love him. And for that reason his ardent concern is that praise should rather be given to him from whom man receives whatever in him is rightly deserving of praise. (*City of God*, 5.19)

The good ruler receives praise, but he understands that the praise is not for him, but for God who enables him to accomplish the good things he does. What is more, Augustine sees that the ruler must be concerned about the temporal **and** eternal welfare of his enemies, his detractors, his competitors! As Augustine moves from a discussion of Roman leadership to the Christian leadership, the scope of concern broadens from the welfare of the Roman state to the welfare of all peoples, including one's enemies. The motive for this broader scope is that the point of departure for all action is God's perspective, not that of one's country. With the introduction of Christian faith into the life of the ruler, Augustine charges that a much broader perspective must inform the ruler's approach to political realities.

In Chapter 24 of Book V, Augustine describes the happy Christian ruler. Again, allowing Augustine himself to speak is the simplest way to understand him:

> We Christians call rulers happy, if they rule with justice; if amid the voices of exalted praise and the reverent salutations of excessive humility, they are not inflated with pride, but remember that they are but men; if they put their power at the service of God's majesty, to extend his worship far and wide; if they fear God, love him and worship him; if, more than their earthly kingdom, they love that realm where they do not fear to share the kingship; if they are slow to punish, but ready to pardon; if they take vengeance on wrong because of the necessity to direct and protect the state, and not to satisfy their personal animosity; if they grant pardon not to allow impunity to wrong-doing but in the hope of amendment of the wrong-doer; if, when they are obliged to take severe decisions, as must often happen, they compensate this with the gentleness of their mercy and the generosity of their benefits; if they restrain their self-indulgent appetites all the more because they are more free to gratify them, and prefer to have command over their lower desires than over any number of subject peoples; and if they do all this not for a burning desire for empty glory, but for the love of eternal blessedness; and if they do not fail to offer to their true God, as a sacrifice for their sins, the oblation of humility, compassion, and prayer. (*City of God*, 5.24)

The characteristics of the happy ruler listed here contradict the characteristics which are celebrated in the great Roman rulers. Compassion, gentleness, humility, and the recognition of God's omnipotence are the virtues of the good Christian political leader. Augustine is introducing a new way of thinking which would undermine the cult of the emperor with which his readers were all too familiar. To undermine that cult further he gives the examples of Constantine and Theodosius.

The more important of these two examples seems to be Theodosius, because of the degree of humility which he was called upon to practice during his reign. In chapter 26 of Book V, Augustine recalls the details of the incident which led to the event to which he wishes to draw the readers' attention. Theodosius made a horrible mistake in judgment which resulted in the death of numerous people. At the request of his bishop, the emperor appeared at the scene of this massacre, prostrated himself before the citizens of that town, and asked forgiveness. He did penance in such a fashion "that the people of Thessalonica, as they prayed for him, wept at seeing the imperial highness thus prostrate, with an emotion stronger than their fears of the emperor's wrath at their offence" (*City of God*, 5. 26). In thus prostrating himself, in admitting his mistake, Theodosius breaks from the traditional model of Roman leadership. He remembers that he is but a man, prone to mistakes in judgment, and able to repent for those mistakes. In thus repenting he appealed to his people on a basis more profound, and indeed, stronger, than the fear with which they at first received him. However, Augustine points out that Theodosius' repentance was motivated by his faith in God and the authority of his bishop, rather than in some

Machiavellian attempt to manipulate his people. That his repentance did lead to a more peaceful political situation is but a fortunate byproduct of the emperor's Christian piety.

In Book V, Augustine presents the reader with two competing pictures of leadership. The one is Roman and is characterized most succinctly by the desire for glory and praise, a glory and praise that rest in the person of the ruler. The other picture of leadership is Christian. The Christian leader understands that he rules by God's favor and that his rule must always be secondary to that of God. He understands his humanity and his capacity to make mistakes. He understands the potential dangers of human praise and glory although he appreciates their value in the political arena. He is humble and compassionate toward all, particularly his enemies. This is a very different ruler than that with which Augustine's readers were accustomed.

What justification does Augustine offer for this new description of a ruler? Why ought a reader take him seriously? Why should a ruler follow his prescriptions? Augustine begins to answer these questions in Book XIX of *City of God*. He also offers his own experience as bishop in Book X of *The Confessions*. A discussion of these two texts begins to suggest a substantial argument for the kind of wisdom Augustine advocates for those in positions of authority.

The City of God, *Book XIX, Chapter 6*

In this chapter Augustine offers an epistemological justification for the humble character of the political leader. In this chapter he focuses on the judicial function of government, although his reflection can be generalized to all moments of judgment. The judge has the duty to ascertain the guilt or innocence of the accused. He is committed to discovering the truth. "How pitiable, how lamentable do we find [the judges]! For indeed those who pronounce judgement cannot see into the consciences of those on whom they pronounce it." How can the judge ever be certain about the truth of the matter? Yet, he must make a judgement! Herein lies the misery of the human condition. The judge can never know with certainty the guilt or innocence of the accused, yet he has a duty, given him by society, to make a judgment. In order to remedy his ignorance he resorts to torture. To save the innocent he must torture them in order to ascertain the truth. "In view of this darkness that attends the life of human society," Augustine asks, "will our wise man take his seat on the judge's bench, or will he not have the heart to do so?" He is constrained by the "claims of human society."

Augustine finds the situation described above "a mark of human wretchedness." Surely the judge does not intend to harm the innocent, yet the epistemological limitations of human life in society may lead to that which he does not intend. It is a necessity of social living that judgements must be made. It is a necessity of human nature that certainty about the guilt or innocence of another person cannot be assured. This dual necessity ought to be grieved by mature reflection. The judge ought "to hate the necessity in his own actions and ..., if he has the wisdom of devotion, ... [to cry] out to God, 'Deliver me from my necessities!'" The wise judge sits on his bench in "fear and trembling," prudent in the manner in which he searches out the truth, but always seeking the mercy of God for his possibly mistaken judgments.

This discussion focuses on the judge and the accused. However, is it not also quite applicable to many moments in daily life when human beings must make judgments about other people? Human beings make judgments about their spouses, their children, their parents, their relatives, their employer, their employees, the bus driver, and their teachers. We make judgments about each and every person with whom we have a relationship. And those judgments occur in the "darkness" of our human condition. We cannot know the conscience of the other person. We cannot predict with certainty what will happen the next moment, the next day, the next week. Yet we must make judgments. We must attend to the words and actions of those in our lives. We must be thoughtful about those words and actions, cautious in make judgments about their meaning. We must always be open to the possibility of error, to the possibility of misunderstanding or inattention on our part. This human condition requires from us a humble attitude in our interaction with others because of our recognition of this miserable truth.

A wise leader, political or otherwise, must be sensitive to the double necessity that Augustine points to in this text. The characteristics that were discussed in the previous section are justified if one appreciates the bind that this double necessity creates for the leader. He or she cannot be the touchstone of certainty, because he or she is always human, and as human, caught in a veil of ignorance that cannot be fully lifted. If and when an error is uncovered, the wise leader acknowledges it and asks forgiveness. This request for forgiveness arises not out of a sense that the error occurred out of malice, but out of a sense of the frailty of humanity that the leader shares with those who are led. It is almost a reminder that all human beings can make the same mistake; that all human beings need to be more prudent, more humble.

To emphasize the misery of the necessity of political judgments Augustine turns to a discussion of the just war in chapter 7 of Book XIX. A just war is waged in order to respond to the injustice of another nation. The wise man does not countenance the waging of war, but he recognizes the need to wage war in the face of injustice. War is an awful reality that brings tragedy to the lives of the citizens of the country. However, it is a necessary evil. Augustine "recognized that in a world of finitude there are tragic things that happen and morally murky decisions to be made. Goods can conflict; hence, the tragedy of necessary wars."[2] The leader who wages such a war will "lament the fact that he is faced with the necessity of waging just wars." Unlike the Roman leaders who waged war as an arena in which glory could be earned, the Christian leader enters into war only as a way to combat injustice on the part of the enemy. The Christian leader knows that war is miserable, forced upon him or her by the injustice of the enemy. There is no glory to be found in waging war, only misery, yet a necessary misery. Again the attitude is one of profound awareness of, and respect for, the inevitability of human misery. What one can do is avoid adding to the necessary misery by one's own irresponsible judgments and decisions.

Confessions, *Book X*

The inability of judges to read the hearts of men and women and the inevitability of war are marks of the human condition in society. One might think that at least one can be sure of one's own self, sure of one's own intentions. However, Augustine is also aware of the ignorance that often reigns in our claims to self-knowledge. In the *Confessions* Augustine recounts his own life, investigating the motives for the various decisions of his life. However, in Book X he admits that knowing one's own motives is a very dicey business. Can one ever know oneself completely? If Augustine cannot know himself completely, then to what extent can we trust his investigation into the motives of his life's actions? If it is so difficult to know oneself, how much more difficult it must be to judge another person in a court of law?

By Book X, Augustine has surveyed his life up until the present moment in which he finds himself a priest and bishop of the Church. He has relied on his memory in this confession which has revealed not only the sins of his life and their root, but also the grace of God at work in his life. Confession is both a recounting of one's faults, but also a praising of the God who works good in each of us. In the beginning of Book X, Augustine points out that his confession falters under the conditions of its telling. In other words, he can only talk about what he knows. "No one knows what he himself is made of, except his own spirit within him, yet there is still some part of him which remains hidden even from his own spirit" (*Conf.* 10.7). Only God knows the entirety of a human being's self. The human being cannot know what will happen today or tomorrow, which temptations will be resisted and which surrendered to. Augustine then says, "let me confess what I know about myself, and confess too what I do not know, because what I know of myself I know only because you shed your light on me, and what I do not know I shall remain ignorant about until my darkness becomes like bright noon before your face" (*Conf.* 10.7). To be "before the face" of God is to be in heaven. This cannot be experienced in this life. Therefore, perfect self-knowledge can never be achieved in this life. There will always be some things about ourselves that we cannot know.

But Augustine knows much about himself. This Book X is a painstaking look at his current faults and the sources of greatest temptation to him. Significant sources of temptation for him are the five senses and an avid curiosity. However, arguably, what seems to be the greatest source of temptation for him is the desire for approval, particularly because of his role as a public figure. "The enemy of our true happiness therefore lies in wait for those of us who by reason of our official position in human society must of necessity be loved and honored by our fellows" (*Conf.*

10.58). In these words one can almost sense the anxiety of Augustine as he thinks about the many ways in which his actions merit for him the gratitude, praise and honor of people. Yet such gratitude, praise and honor **are** merited. They are genuine sentiments which rise in response to the good acts of the bishop and priest. "Are we to lead evil lives in order to be rid of it [public approval] and so test our ability" (*Conf.* 10.60)? Augustine dismisses such a possibility as "crazy," but he also is sensitive to how corrosive such genuine public sentiment can be to the soul of someone like him who craved such approval in his youth.[3]

Augustine finds himself in a difficult position. He does not want to commit the sin of pride, but he also is a public figure who is prone to say and do things that will warrant the praise and honor of the people. He cannot stop doing good things. He cannot forbid people to offer him praise and honor. However, he can confess. He can admit his previous frailty in the realm of human approbation. He can offer up his praise for God who is the author of the good words and actions for which the people praise him. Augustine can confess his own tendency to relish the praise of his people. To what end? So that they can pray for him (*Conf.* 10.62). They can pray for him and, in praying for him, see themselves and see God working in their lives through Augustine who shares his self with them.

Here is a bishop of the church who willingly bares his soul to his people, asking for their prayers. He does this not only for his own good, but also because of his profound awareness of his own humanity. He is their leader; they depend upon him for guidance and strength. However, he is human and prone to the same weaknesses as they are. He offers them guidance and strength, yes, but these are mediated through the shared belief in God, active in and through the community, crystallized, as it were, in the leader, the pastor. What one has here is a profoundly different model of leader than that offered by the Romans. Augustine's readers would recognize immediately, and perhaps be shocked by, the radical departure from tradition which his account suggests. A leader who recognizes his limitations, who recognizes the ultimate authority of God, who is willing to bare his soul to those who look to him for strength and hope: this is not the emperor who sought glory for himself. This is a leader for whom glory is reserved for the One by whom all things are possible.

Foundations for an Augustinian Wisdom of Authority

Augustine was a player in the political world of the North Africa Roman Empire. One need only read through the many letters that Augustine wrote to various Roman officials. The bishop occupied a peculiar place in the political hierarchy of the empire. He was the voice of the voiceless. The measure of a person's success in getting things done through the bureaucracy of the empire was the weight of one's voice. There were many people in the empire, most conspicuously the poor and the imprisoned, who had no voice. The bishop became their champion in the political realm. Augustine was a very effective *vox populi*.

An issue which received great attention from Augustine was the Roman practice of capital punishment. What is most evident in Augustine's letters in regard to capital punishment is his constant reminder that the horizon of political judgment is not this world or this empire. Often the legislator imposes the death penalty in order to safeguard the law and order of the empire. However, the empire is not the ultimate good. Augustine reminds the recipient of his letters that there is something more valuable at stake in the case of a convicted criminal, namely his eternal salvation. For Augustine, one must always keep in mind the ultimate good of those to be affected by one's judgments. Capital punishment does not function in the best interest of the one affected by this action. Any chance for repentance, hence eternal salvation, is snuffed out by such a final act.

In Letter 153 Augustine responds to Macedonius, a provincial ruler of North Africa, who wonders why Augustine might consider it his duty to intercede for the life of a criminal. Macedonius claims that to intercede for the criminal is to approve his crime. The following is part of Augustine's response to that claim:

> In no sort of way then, do we approve of the sins which we wish to be corrected. Nor do we wish what is wrongly done to remain unpunished because it is pleasant. But in our pity for the man, whilst we abhor the vice or crime, the more it displeases us, the less we wish the man guilty of it to die unrepentant. For it is easy and natural to hate the wicked because they are wicked, whilst it is a rare thing and a kind thing to love them because they are men, so as at once to disapprove of the sin whilst approving of the nature committing it, and thus to hate sin the more because it stains the nature you love. He, then, who persecutes the crime to save the man is not linked in iniquity but bound by humanity. This life alone is the only place of correction. After it, every man will have what he has gained for himself during the course. Hence charity for the human race compels us to mediate for the guilty, lest they so finish this life in temporal punishment as, after it, to endure unending punishment.[4]

For Augustine, the critical issue is the eternal status of the human being. He is also sensitive to the fact that human beings are capable of great misery, yet are good in their nature. As we have seen in the prior section of this paper, the "darkness" that marks humanity can lead a person to make horrible judgments and to commit abominable deeds. However, it is precisely this "darkness" that ought to hold the hand of the executioner, not only, as we saw in the prior section, because no judgment is certain, but also, as Augustine claims above, because the horizon of our judgments is not this world, but eternity.

Augustine calls for wisdom from the leaders of his time. He challenges them to remember that they are but human, as are those who are at their mercy, not only in the criminal justice system but in the entire political economy. It seems from what we have examined thus far that Augustinian wisdom grows out of two related claims: the epistemological limitations of human judgment and the eternal *telos* of human activity. What can be taken from the context within which Augustine lived and wrote that might enrich a contemporary notion of political wisdom?

It seems that the epistemological limitation of human judgment can be recognized in our contemporary contexts, in many variations, without much argument. It is the second claim about human nature that demands an argument. What I would like to do in the following pages is link these two claims in such a way that an acceptance of the first is an implicit acceptance of the second. What will be clear is that what Augustine meant by "God" and "eternal salvation" must be understood today in a way that he might not accept, but which will maintain the basic insight that those terms expressed for him. What I want to argue is that an awareness and acceptance of one's epistemological limitations is the condition that must be fulfilled before one can uncover the transcendent dimension of one's life.

What is it that one knows when one claims that one knows? Skeptics say that we cannot know anything. Idealists claim that we can only know our mental constructions. Empiricists say that knowing is whatever can be verified in the sense data. Is this knowing? What all three of these schools of thought have in common is that they are experiencing a world of data, both sense data and the data of consciousness. They are all asking questions of this data and theorizing as to their meaning. Finally, they are passing judgments on the various theories that have resulted from their theorizing. The skeptics judgment is that no judgment is possible. The idealist's judgment is that his or her judgments concern the world-as-it-appears to him or her rather than the world as it is. The empiricist's judgment is that only measurable data is available for knowledge. There is disagreement as to the content of the judgment, but there is uniformity in terms of the process by which the judgment was achieved.

Human beings have experiences; they raise questions about their experience; they theorize about those experiences; finally, they "marshal and weigh" the evidence in order to judge which theory is the most able to explain their experiences.[5] Human beings have an enormous urge to understand what is going on in their worlds. Moreover, they want to understand their world correctly. It is to achieve correct understanding that human beings must resort to judgment. Whether one is a strict skeptic, a convinced empiricist, or an idealist, one must make judgments. And these judgments are not arbitrary. A person who claims to know something about the world is not going to preface her remarks by saying something to the effect: *What I am going to say is only true for my world*. On the contrary, when we come to know something about the world, even if that something is that nothing can be known, we always have good reasons for our claim. These putative "good" reasons provide a basis for the claim that it is the human activity of judging that is most prone to be effected by the "darkness" of which Augustine spoke.

Anyone who makes any claim about the world is engaging in the activity of judgment. If the activity of judgment is particularly vulnerable to the "darkness" of the human condition, then all human claims will be subject to the human condition. So, it is possible, for any given judgment about the world of one's experience, that a person could be mistaken. Everyone has experienced a mistake in judgment.

Usually the mistake becomes apparent when an action pursued in accordance with one's judgment turns out to be harmful or in some way wrong. We go back over the process by which we arrived at the decision to act and often find that our choice rested upon a mistake of judgment. Just as we have all experienced mistaken judgment, we have all experience correct judgment. When is a person not mistaken? When does one arrive at reasonable grounds for making a judgment in a particular situation? To answer these questions one must understand what in fact is occurring in the act of judgment.

Experience, whether remembered or current, gives rise to questions for human beings. Granted human curiosity is a function of its encouragement or discouragement by a variety of personal, familial, social and/or cultural factors. However, spontaneously, human beings are curious about what is happening around them. The questions which arise are met by possible answers, theories about what is happening. This, too, is a function of one's intellectual capacity which in turn is a function of various social and cultural factors. However, theorizing, coming up with possible meaningful answers to one's curiosity, is a spontaneous human characteristic. Finally, human beings are not satisfied with possibilities, with theories. Human beings want to know what is true, what is the case, what is "really" happening around them. This is the arena of judgment. In judging the reasonableness of whatever intelligible possibilities have occurred to him or her, the human being must judge which most completely explains the elements of his or her experience.

A woman might feel a lump in her breast one morning as she showers. Immediately she becomes anxious to discover the nature of this lump. She meets with her doctor who examines her and offers her several possible diagnoses. This woman is not content with the doctor's exercise in creativity. She wants to know what the lump means. What is it? She might seek advice from other doctors. She might go to specialists. She will exhaust all reasonable means available to her so that she can be fairly certain about the nature of the lump in her breast. She is engaging in the process of marshalling the evidence and weighing it in order to make a judgment about her experience.

Certainly this woman's desire to know what the lump in her breast means is affected by her anxiety about her own health, the reality of death, the anxiety of her loved ones, and other factors. However, the series of activities which she pursues in order to discover the meaning of her experience is the same series of activities which all human beings pursue whenever they wonder about the meaning of their experience. This set of activities functions in the physics laboratory just as much as it functions in the kitchen of a five star restaurant. It functions on the playground, in a nuclear submarine, in a marriage. Human beings want to know what is the case, what is occurring, in their world.

The act of judgment is an insight into the relationship between the conditioned, its conditions, and the fulfillment of those conditions. The conditioned is the possible meaning of one's experience. In the example of the woman who discovered a lump on her breast, the conditioned might be that the lump is cancerous. This is called a conditioned because it is correct if and only if the conditions which would make it correct are fulfilled. So, for "the lump is cancerous" to be a correct statement, the various conditions identified by medicine must be fulfilled. The role of the medical team is to verify whether or not the conditions necessary for this conditioned to be correct are in fact fulfilled. Only when the fulfillment of these conditions is verified can one say to the woman: The lump which you have in your breast is cancerous. The act of judgment grasps the conditioned, the relevant conditions of this conditioned, and the fulfillment of the conditions.

What must be noted immediately is that the fulfillment of the conditions is not a necessary fulfillment. If and only if one understands the conditions of the possible explanation of one's experience, and if and only if those conditions happen to be fulfilled, can one make the judgment that such and such is the case. A person may not be capable of understanding what the conditions are, or of understanding the process by which one can verify whether or not they are fulfilled, however he or she can trust the experts, much as one trusts one's parents to teach him or her how to drive safely. It may be very difficult to ascertain whether or not the conditions are fulfilled. This does not necessarily mean that one must not make a judgment. It means that if one makes a judgment, the judgment is made with the proviso that it may be proven to be mistaken when further evidence is acquired. The theory of evolution is exactly that: a theory. It is verified to a high degree by the data that scientists have collected. However, no one has made the claim that it is certain. It is highly probable, but not certain. Judgment is the action by which one can say, with good reason, either probably or certainly, what is the case in one's world. What is the case in one's world is not necessarily so. It is so because the conditions happen to be fulfilled. Their fulfillment is itself merely a probable occurrence.

A conditioned whose conditions happen to be fulfilled is a virtually unconditioned. So, judgment ascertains whether or not a conditioned is virtually unconditioned, that is a conditioned whose conditions are fulfilled. A virtually unconditioned is not an unconditioned. It only acts as if it is unconditioned because its conditions are fulfilled. What, then, is an unconditioned? An unconditioned is something that has no conditions. If it has no conditions, it necessarily exists. The virtually unconditioned is contingent for its existence or occurrence on the fulfillment of its conditions. An unconditioned has no such limitation. However, does such a necessary thing exist? This is the traditional question about God's existence and it has emerged in a study of human judgment: "...the [virtually unconditioned] pertains to this world, to the world of possible experience, while the [unconditioned] transcends this world in the sense that its reality is of a totally different order."[6]

The virtually unconditioned is an element of all human knowing. Implied in the virtually unconditioned is the unconditioned itself: God The question, then, lies within the horizon of human beings. The term "horizon" refers to the range of relevance operative in any particular human being. Literally, one's horizon is that beyond which one cannot see. In this context, one's horizon is the limit of one's questions. If the question of God were outside the human horizon, then it would not occur to the human being; it would make no sense. The fact that the question is asked, and the fact that so many people spend so much energy in the attempt to answer it with a "no," indicates that it is very much within the horizon of human conscious activity. It is not a nonsensical question. It lies within the dynamism of the desire to know, which animates the human being to understand correctly what occurs, or what is, around him or her:

> Man's transcendental subjectivity is mutilated or abolished, unless he is stretching towards the intelligible, the unconditioned, the good of value. The reach, *not of his attainment*, but of his intending is unrestricted. There lies within his horizon a region for the divine, a shrine for ultimate holiness. It cannot be ignored. The atheist may pronounce it empty. The agnostic may urge that he finds his investigation has been inconclusive. The contemporary humanist will refuse to allow the question to arise. But their negations presuppose the spark in the clod, our native orientation to the divine.[7]

The attainment of the unconditioned is beyond human ability, however the question about it is not. Questions demand answers. The human desire to know demands satisfaction even in regard to questions whose answers do indeed lie outside human ability. Human beings grasp the virtually unconditioned. Human knowledge is conditioned knowledge. It is absolute insofar as conditions are fulfilled. It is not absolute insofar as the fulfillment of conditions is neither necessary nor guaranteed. Yet within the horizon of human conscious activity there is the question of the unconditioned, a question with an answer beyond human capability. There is limit to human knowing, but there is also a beyond.

The question about the unconditioned is like any other question. It indicates a limit in one's achieved knowledge, but it simultaneously moves the questioner in the direction of an answer. Questions mark both a limit and a way beyond the limit. Questions remind the questioner of his or her limited knowledge. However, they also make the questioner aware of a "beyond," an "other," toward which, by the dynamism of the questions themselves, the questioner may move.

The "beyond" that questions reveal places my achieved knowledge in question. This placing in question is not radical in that it discounts my achieved knowledge. This placing in question proposes the possibility that my knowledge and my projects are limited, not complete, in error, misplaced, or wrongheaded. This "beyond" calls into question what I think is valuable, what I choose to do. I may still have to choose, and act, but I choose and act aware of the "beyond," allowing the possibilities of the "beyond" to influence the choices and actions that I make. This is similar to what Augustine was getting at in his letters of capital punishment and what he calls the miserable condition of humanity. The judge does not know the conscience of the accused, nor does he know what God intends for this individual. This limitation of his knowledge implies the possibilities of the "beyond." If he goes ahead with the execution, he should do so fully aware of the possibility that he is mistaken in judgment. The proper response to the existence of limits is humility which the proper response to the possibilities of the "beyond" is something like piety.

When Augustine wrote of the necessity for political judgment, yet the inevitable "darkness" that accompanies human knowing, he was setting up the ground for his call that all leaders be humble. The leader must remember that he is but a human being. The leader who claims omniscience, who refuses to take criticism, who will not even discuss the possibility that he or she has made a mistake: this leader is inauthentic. His or her claims are contrary to reasonable judgment about human knowing. Augustine praises Theodosius for his humility in recognizing his mistake in judgment and for placing himself under the yoke of the Church in doing penance. What is important here is the possibility of making a mistake, the admission of a mistake when it occurs, and the attempt to make amends. Augustine claims that this is the ideal Christian ruler. Can a 20th century person accept Augustine's description of the ideal ruler?

The person of wisdom is open to the possibility of mistake. He or she is committed to the truth. He or she also wants to do what is good. Do not these qualities mirror what the 5th century bishop called for? It seems that they do. While Augustine calls for an explicit acceptance of the Christian God, it does not seem that such need to be the case. Implied in the human activity of judgment is the question of the beyond; however, the details of any proposed answer do not seem to be limited. The possibility of error in judgment and the recognition of a "beyond" call for a particular kind of wisdom on the part of the person in a position of authority. This leader must be aware of his or her limits, must be able to admit mistakes, must be able to ask forgiveness, must be willing to make amends. This is a leader in the mold of Augustine's Theodosius.

Conclusion

The wisdom of the leader grows from the soil of human facticity and human transcendence. These two seem strange bedfellows at first glance. However, as our investigation of the texts of Augustine and our discussion of human judgment have shown, they are inextricably linked in the concrete human person. The drive to understand the universe is an unlimited one, yet the conditions for the satisfaction of that drive are such that understanding will always be limited. This is not to say that a limited understanding is not a valuable understanding. The quest for knowledge is an honorable one. Indeed, it is a necessary one, particularly for the person who is called upon by his or her community to make judgments that affect others. Human knowledge is marked by limited achievement and unlimited possibility. The limited character of human knowledge ought to elicit humility in the human person. Similarly, the unlimited possibility of the universe ought to elicit a kind of reverence for that unlimited possibility, a reverence which is manifested in the manner in which one offers a practical solution to a problem.

Augustine challenged the leaders of his day to remember their humanity and their eternal salvation. In their humanity they would find a reason for caution and prudence in judgment. In their eternal salvation they would find another reason for prudence, namely the perspective of God, which calls into question quite often the priorities of institution and/or family. What seems a good decision from the perspective of the State is often, from the perspective of eternity, a very unreasonable and irresponsible one. Augustine does not counsel despair in the face of limited human cognitional achievement, but he does counsel humility in light of the propensity of error.

In contemporary political bureaucracies, one rarely hears a counsel of humility in the face of limited human cognitional achievement and human orientation toward the absolutely transcendent. However, the need for such a counsel is nonetheless clear. The claim is warranted by experience and by an examination of the activity itself that human judgment is not the source of absolute certainty. Human judgment can enable us to know our experience. However, this knowledge is contingent on conditions being fulfilled, and the fulfillment of such conditions is far from being guaranteed. Insofar as the conditions are fulfilled, one achieves knowledge. Yet there is a limit to the knowledge that can be achieved. Those limits are functions of being human, being in space and time, being subject to desires that would push us away from the demands of intelligence and reason. However, just as there are limits, so too there is a beyond. Questions demand answers, and insofar as the conditions are fulfilled, those answers are achieved. However, even unanswered questions leave the human being with an awareness of what is beyond his or her achievement. If this were not so, how would we know that we know anything? An awareness is not a knowing, but it is enough to cause us to question what we think we know. It is enough to suggest that perhaps there is more going on in any situation than our own desires or hopes. The possibility of this "more" is precisely the transcendent, which Augustine named God, and which we name the "Infinite" or the "Other."

One need not be a Christian in order to recognize the relativizing role of the transcendent. The transcendent need not be God. It could also be one's country, one's planet, one's universe. However, a recognition of the transcendent does force one, if one is responsible, to question his or her judgments and decisions. Rather than follow through on a policy of capital punishment, the leader might raise questions about the good of the community, the good of the person. He or she might raise questions about the eternal destiny of the person to be executed. Of course, once the questions have been raised, the same course of action may be indicated. However, the course of action is pursued with the awareness that one might be wrong, precisely because the conditions of the conditioned are such that only a more or less probable judgment can be made. One could be wrong.

The Augustinian counsel is not to drop out of politics or to avoid situations in which one must lead other people. The counsel is that a wisdom born of self-reflection is necessary in order for a human being to lead well. Self-reflection will lead to a recognition of the conditional character of human knowing and to the transcendent dimension of that knowing, such that there is always already a "beyond" that beckons us to take into account what may be beyond our capacity to know. To recognize the simultaneously conditioned yet transcendent character of human knowing supplies a much needed corrective to the tendency of human beings, when in positions of authority, to forget who they are. This forgetfulness leads to the abuse of power which Augustine sought to address in his texts. It also leads to the abuse of power which we so often witness in our own day.

An element of a solution to the necessity for leadership is to challenge those who want to hold positions of authority in society, in business, in government to affirm their humanity and to recognize as constitutive of their humanity an orientation to a "beyond," the content of which is something to be revealed, but whose function is universal: there is always an "other," there is always more, to call into question the decisions of the day.

Notes

1   An awareness of the transcendent is roughly equivalent to Augustine's piety. This equivalence will be explained later.
2   Jean Bethke Elshtain, *Augustine and the Limits of Politics* (Notre Dame, IN: University of Notre Dame Press, 1995) 51.
3   Here is, in part, the existential source of Augustine's misgivings about political leadership that are so evident in *The City of God*.
4   Augustine, "To Macedonius (A.D. 414)," in *Letters of St. Augustine* (trans. Mary H. Allies; London: Burns and Oates, 1890) 277-278.
5   See Bernard Lonergan, SJ, *Collected Works of Bernard Lonergan*. Vol. 3: *Insight: A Study of Human Understanding* (eds. Frederick E. Crowe and Robert M. Doran; Toronto: University of Toronto Press, 1992) 296-342.
6   Bernard Lonergan, *Method In Theology* (Toronto: University of Toronto Press, 1971) 102.
7   Ibid., 103 (italics mine).

References

Arendt, Hannah. *Love and Saint Augustine*. Chicago: University of Chicago Press, 1996.
Augustine. *City of God*. Trans. Henry Bettenson. London: Penguin Books, 1984.
_____. *The Confessions*. Trans. Maria Boulding, O.S.B. Hyde Park, NY: New City Press, 1997.
_____. *Enchiridion of Faith, Hope, and Love*. Trans. J. Bo. Shaw and Introduction by Thomas Hibbs. Washington, DC: Regnery Publishing, Inc., 1961.
_____. *Letters of Saint Augustine*. Selected and translated by Maria H. Allies. London: Burns and Oates, 1890.

_____. *The Political Writings*. Ed. Henry Paolucci. Washington, DC: Regnery Publishing, Inc., 1962.

_____. *The Works of Saint Augustine: A Translation for the 21ˢᵗ Century*. Ed. John E. Rotelle. Volume III/10: *Sermons*. Trans. Edmund Hill, O.P. Hyde Park, NY: New City Press, 1995.

Babcock, William S. Ed. *The Ethics of Saint Augustine*. Atlanta, GA: Scholars Press, 1991.

Banner, William Augustus. *The Path of St. Augustine*. Lanham, MD: Rowman & Littlefield Publishers, Inc., 1996.

Donnelly, Dorothy F. Ed. *The City of God: A Collection of Critical Essays*. New York: Peter Lang, 1995.

Elshtain, Jean Bethke. *Augustine and the Limits of Politics*. Notre Dame, IN: University of Notre Dame Press, 1995.

Lonergan, Bernard. *Collected Works of Bernard Lonergan*. Eds. Frederick E. Crowe and Robert M. Doran. Volume 3: *Insight: A Study of Human Understanding*. Toronto: University of Toronto Press, 1992.

_____. "Dialectic of Authority." In *A Third Collection: Papers by Bernard J. F. Lonergan, S.J.* Ed. Frederick E. Crowe, S.J. New York: Paulist Press, 1985.

_____. *Method in Theology*. Toronto: University of Toronto Press, 1971.

Chapter Ten

Augustine and English Protestants: Authority and Order, Coercion and Dissent in the Earthly City

Andrew R. Murphy

Introduction

I begin with several basic and, I think, uncontroversial statements about Augustine's view of life in the earthly city. Earthly flourishing — realized in the goodwill of human friendship, the commission of charitable acts toward neighbors, or the love exhibited within the family, for example — represents a lesser good than the eternal peace that awaits the saints, but a good nonetheless. Earthly peace is a prerequisite for human flourishing: we can not become all we are meant to become if we live in fear of being harried out of our homes or subjected to arbitrary violence.[1] Even as he radically de-emphasizes the value of earthly *vis-à-vis* eternal peace,[2] though, Augustine affirms the importance of civil order, the way in which the church's safe passage through history depends upon and is intermingled with the peace of the earthly city.[3] Order in earthly society thus provides a grounding for the church to live out its mission. But earthly peace also serves a host of nonchurch institutions, as they go about creating and sustaining meaningful lives in the midst of this fallen world.[4] So although a "lower" good, and useful purely in instrumental terms, earthly peace and order are to be preserved and nurtured: parents, teachers, clergy, and magistrates all play a role in creating the conditions in which humans can flourish.

This essay explores how important earthly peace and order were to Augustine by considering a specific example of threatened disruption to that peace: his position on the coercion of heretics during the Donatist controversy. I consider how this Augustinian view intimates that of later orthodox Protestant thinkers by examining 17th century English debates over religious toleration. I do not posit an *identification* of the Donatist controversy with these later debates: Donatists were not seeking religious liberty, nor were all those calling for toleration in early modern England exclusively concerned with church purity (though many were). In these later debates, echoes of both Augustine's defense of orthodoxy and Donatist objections to imposition are heard, arguments that reiterate the ongoing significance of this devotion to civil peace and the rejection of purity as an earthly ideal.

Coercion and the Donatists

The Donatist schism had its root in a reaction to perceived church impurity, against the perceived liberalism of the Catholic church in readmitting those who were branded *traditores* during the Diocletian persecution (more specifically with the election of Caecilianus as bishop of Carthage in 312). By its failure to purge itself of these unforgivable members, Donatists charged, the church polluted itself and justified their separation from it.[5] In the Donatist context, then, Augustine's position sought to defend a sort of theological and ecclesiastical latitudinarianism, while Donatists insisted that the church be purged of any and all imperfections.[6] By the time he became involved in the dispute, the schism had been gathering in intensity for some time. Augustine's position rejects those who seek institutional purity here on earth, and who are willing to sacrifice the many and considerable temporal goods for the sake of that purity. He argued that schism violated Jesus' and Paul's teachings about the unity of the church, and represented the placing of such unlikely purity ahead of the bond of Christian love and unity. The evident Donatist willingness to employ violence further weakened their case in Augustine's eyes, leading directly to his endorsement of imperial intervention and, later, his famous call for Donatists to be "compelled to come in." The social and political upheavals that accompanied the schism, in his view, illustrate the dangers of those who would sacrifice civil peace for the elusive perfection of a blemish-free church.

Augustine was, of course, not opposed to coercion in principle, and, although initially opposed to the practice,[7] he did come to support a variety of measures against heretics. His support for coercion in the Donatist controversy was fourfold: 1) the schism (indeed, virtually all schism) was indefensible, sinful, and contrary to Scripture, setting the search for an elusive purity above Christian love; 2) coercion could be efficacious, if not by virtue of its force (or threatened force), then by the broader effect of making heretics reconsider their views, and thus potentially freeing the mind from erroneous opinions; 3) only the affliction of the righteous constituted persecution; and 4) the Donatist resort to violence justified their suppression.

Rejecting Donatist calls for a pure church, Augustine in this sense appears more "liberal" than the dissidents he advocated persecuting. We should also note that Augustine personally attempted to mitigate the punishments carried out on individual Donatists.[8] The main elements of the theory of coercion, however, were firmly established in the context of his struggles with Donatism.

Let us take the four main arguments in turn. First and perhaps most prominently, Augustine decried schism as a renunciation of the Christian unity advocated by Jesus and Paul. Those initiating schisms ignored Jesus' command to let the tares and wheat grow together until the last days, and refused to acknowledge that the church, while on earth, is *always* a mixture of wheat and tares:

[W]ithin the communion of the sacraments of Christ, there are gathered to the glory of His name even those who are wicked, and who persist in the obstinacy of error; whose separation, however, as chaff from the wheat, is to be effected only in the final purging of the Lord's threshing-floor. These do not destroy those who are the Lord's wheat — few, indeed, when compared with the others, but in themselves a great multitude; they do not destroy the elect of God, who are to be gathered at the end of the world from the four winds, from the one end of heaven to the other.[9]

On this understanding, by their separation over the issue of *traditores* and by perpetuating the division for so many years, Donatists privileged perfection and purity over church unity. Referring to the origins of the schism, Augustine argued that

even if the charges had been true which were brought by them against Caecilianus, and could at length be proved to us, yet, though we might pronounce an anathema upon him even in the grave, we are still bound not for the sake of any man to leave the Church, which rests for its foundation on divine witness, and is not the figment of litigious opinions, seeing that it is better to trust in the Lord than to put confidence in man.[10]

Elsewhere, Augustine argued that impurity in the church does not touch the salvation of the members more generally, but only those who participate in such impurity:

[It is] beyond question that no man in the unity of Christ can be stained by the guilt of the sins of other men if he be not consenting to the deeds of the wicked, and thus defiled by actual participation in their crimes, but only, for the sake of the fellowship of the good, tolerating the wicked, as the chaff which lies until the final purging of the Lord's threshing-floor. These things being so, where is the pretext for your schism? Are ye not an "evil generation, esteeming yourselves righteous, yet not washed from the guilt of your going forth" [from the Church]?[11]

Thus the original schism itself was illegitimate, and schism more generally was contrary to Paul's emphasis on church unity.[12]

Joined to this strong condemnation of schism and schismatics was Augustine's corresponding call for church unity: "You say, however, 'Why seek to have us joined to you, if we be thus stained with guilt?' I reply: Because you still live, and may, if you are willing, be restored."[13] "Let peace be concluded in the virtue of Jerusalem,," he wrote elsewhere, "which virtue is Christian charity; to which holy city it is said, 'Peace be in thy virtue, and plenteousness within thy palaces.' Let them not exalt themselves against the solicitude of their mother..."[14]

It is important to note, secondly, that Augustine did *not* believe — as apparently imputed to him by Vincentius[15] — that force could bring about genuine religious belief. Still, he argued that we should not underestimate the effect that coercion or the threat thereof might have; given propitious circumstances, it could set the conditions for a reconsideration of previously-held views or dogmatically-asserted customs, which could pave the way for a change of heart or mind:

How many [Donatists] were bound, not by truth...but by the heavy chains of inveterate custom... How many supposed the sect of Donatus to be the true Church, merely because ease had made them too listless, or conceited, or sluggish, to take pains to examine Catholic truth! How many would have entered earlier had not the calumnies of slanderers...shut them out! How many, believing that it mattered not to which party a Christian might belong, remained in the schism of Donatus only because they had been born in it... To all these classes of persons the dread of those laws...has been so useful... [Some] say: We knew not that the truth was here, and we had no wish to learn it; but fear made us become earnest to examine it when we became alarmed, lest, without any gain in things eternal, we should be smitten with loss in temporal things: thanks be to the Lord, who has by the stimulus of fear startled us from our negligence, that now being disquieted we might inquire into those things which, when at ease, we did not care to know! Others say: We were prevented from entering the Church by false reports, which we could not know to be false unless we entered it; and we would not enter unless we were compelled: thanks be to the Lord, who by His scourge took away our timid hesitation, and taught us to find out for ourselves how vain and absurd were the lies which rumour had spread abroad against His Church.[16]

Augustine even uses the example of Paul as one who was "coerced" by God into conversion.[17]

Thirdly, Augustine noted, claims of persecution required a righteous cause, something the Donatists did not possess. Jesus pointedly praised those who were "persecuted for righteousness' sake" and not simply those fact who were suppressed by magistrates:

If to suffer persecution were in all cases a praiseworthy thing, it would have sufficed for the Lord to say, "Blessed are they which are persecuted," without adding "for righteousness' sake."...In some cases, therefore, both he that suffers persecution is in the wrong, and he that inflicts it is in the right. But the truth is, that always both the bad have persecuted the good, and the good have persecuted the bad: the former doing harm by their un-righteousness, the latter seeking to do good by the administration of discipline; the former with cruelty, the latter with moderation; the former impelled by lust, the latter under the constraint of love.[18]

If schism was an unjustified sundering of the church's unity, then cries of persecution simply did not apply. Although Augustine does point out that heretics strengthen the church,[19] this does not change the fact that they are heretics, and are to be entreated and, if necessary, compelled to return to the church.[20]

Finally, Augustine points out that Donatists engaged in frequent acts of violence and threatening behavior against Catholics and members of society more generally. Indeed, the first Catholic appeals for imperial intervention were not in the interest of compelling them to return to the church, but rather sought imperial protection from the attacks of the roving bands of Donatist Circumcelliones. Initially, Augustine hoped that "although the madness of the Donatists was raging in every direction, yet we should [only] ask of the emperors to ordain that those who either preached the Catholic truth with their voice, or established it by their study, should no longer be exposed to the furious violence of the heretics."[21] Still, the situation worsened:

> among the Donatists herds of abandoned men were disturbing the peace of the innocent for one reason or another in the spirit of the most reckless madness. What master was there who was not compelled to live in dread of his own servant, if he had put himself under the guardianship of the Donatists? Who dared even threaten one who sought his ruin with punishment? Who dared to exact payment of a debt from one who consumed his stores, or from any debtor whatsoever, that sought their assistance or protection? Under the threat of beating, and burning, and immediate death, all documents compromising the worst of slaves were destroyed, that they might depart in freedom. Notes of hand that had been extracted from debtors were returned to them. Any one who had shown a contempt for their hard words were compelled by harder blows to do what they desired. The houses of innocent persons who had offended them were either razed to the ground or burned. Certain heads of families of honorable parentage, and brought up with a good education were carried away half dead after their deeds of violence, or bound to the mill, and compelled by blows to turn it round, after the fashion of the meanest beasts of burden.[22]

Even if their disunity and lack of charity did not condemn them, Augustine argued, the Donatists' resort to violence fatally undermined their claims of persecution. Taken along with his argument that force in the service of truth could, given fortuitous circumstances, prove efficacious, Augustine's case for coercion was sealed.

Augustinian English Protestants and Early Modern Orthodoxy

If purity-inspired schism threatened social order and traditional church structures in Augustine's dispute with the Donatists, events in seventeenth-century England reinforced the fears of orthodox Protestants on broadly similar grounds. From the turmoil of the Civil Wars of the 1640s through the Revolution of 1688, religious and political debate over issues of coercion, dissent, authority, and persecution raged in England. Hundreds of years and a continent away, then, radically different kinds of Christians struggled with issues of dissent and coercion. A consideration of their arguments gives us a renewed appreciation of the difficult task of creating and sustaining fragile societies, along with the reaction against earthly perfection and purity that characterized the orthodox position, a position that continued to owe much to Augustine.[23]

Unity

Defenders of orthodoxy and uniformity continued to point out that claims for the toleration of heterodox opinions, and the schism to which such claims almost certainly led, were contrary to Biblical teachings. Just as Christ had called for the apostles to love each other and to "be one; as thou, Father, art in me, and I in thee" (John 17:21), so had Paul and other early church leaders enjoined Christians to unity. Such injunctions appear throughout the epistles; for example, Matthew Newcomen took Phillipians 1:27, in which Paul calls for the church to "stand fast in one spirit, with one mind striving together for the faith of the gospel," as a sermon text. Bewailing the divisions in the church as contrary to Christian principles, he claimed that church unity was not "a mere *Idea Platonica*" but had existed concretely in the church's past.[24] Proclaiming that "justice is not contrary to meekness," Samuel Rutherford argued that Paul's calls for humility and unity do not rule out the suppression of heresy.[25] During the Restoration, the great examples of this uniformitarian position are Stillingfleet's *The mischief of separation* and *The unreasonableness of separation*.[26] Stillingfleet supported comprehension — the relaxation of the parameters of acceptable Anglican doctrine — to encompass various dissenting groups (most notably Presbyterians) on some points, as a necessary step to secure Protestant unity. This move toward inclusion never extended to the toleration of more heterodox or radical sects, however; these Stillingfleet condemned as lacking charity and a commitment to Christian unity.

The underlying basis for many of these discussions of unity lay in the contested notion of *adiaphora*, or "indifferent" things in religious worship. Defenders of orthodoxy argued that schism on the basis of admittedly indifferent matters was unjustified and contrary to Pauline injunctions to Christian unity.[27] If separation for the sake of "greater purity" is sanctioned, where will such schism end, asked Stillingfleet.[28] If the differences between Anglicans and Dissenters were only over indifferent things, "why should they be so unreasonable as to separate from us, and to make or continue a perpetual breach for things of little moment?"[29] Why could Dissenters' "tender consciences...not dispense with a few innocent and harmless ceremonies of the Church of England, from which they differ in things not necessary to salvation?"[30] Misguided insistence upon church purity, they asserted, had led sectarians to destroy the church's unity.

The Psychology of Belief

Seventeenth-century English dissenters often raised the psychological view that belief could not be forced because it was a faculty of the understanding, not of the will, and thus beyond human control.[31] Thus, setting aside all Scriptural arguments, persecution was ineffective and doomed to fail: one could make people *do*, but not *believe*, some article of faith. Persuasion, not coercion, was the way to deal with spiritual errors. John Musgrave suggested that "in that which consisteth in the persuasion of the heart, corporal violence prevaileth no more than the vapor of wind that blows, to hinder the heat of the fire."[32]

Similar sentiments were expressed by Jeremy Taylor, William Walwyn, Leonard Busher, and Richard Overton, all of whom separated the understanding from the will, placed matters of religion and belief in the former, and therefore ruled out attempts at compulsion in matters of conscience.[33] Since God is "to be glorified in a free and voluntary obedience of his rational creatures,"[34] force is to be abjured, since it can not bring about the true and voluntary belief demanded by God. "It is not in our power to believe as we please," one author wrote, and since "our errors are not voluntary, we ought not to be punished for them."[35] Not only does persecution violate Christian charity, Buckingham argued, but it is "contrary to sense and reason...[and] absurd to attempt to convince a man's judgment by anything, but reason."[36]

In addition to the psychological argument about will and understanding, religious dissenters increasingly emphasized the necessity of subjective assent in matters of faith, an approach that in their minds forswore coercion. When John Cotton referred sardonically to "some point of doctrine which you believe in conscience to be the truth, or... practicing some work which in conscience you believe to be a religious duty," Roger Williams replied that one is persecuted regardless of whether one's beliefs or practices are true or false.[37] William Walwyn declared bluntly that "though the thing may be in itself good, yet if it do not appear to be so to my conscience, the practice thereof in me is sinful."[38] In *A new quaere*, Saltmarsh cited Paul's epistle: "Let every man be fully persuaded in his own mind," wrote Paul (Romans 14:5), and Saltmarsh heartily concurred, denouncing coercion as antithetical to both Scripture and human psychology.[39]

Still, this argument for toleration did not entirely address the political question at hand, since their opponents rarely argued that one could coerce an individual into holding a given belief. Augustine himself, as we have seen, did not assert that one could force an individual to believe something, claiming rather that, through punishment or coercion, an individual might see the error of his or her ways and thus reconsider of his or her own accord. George Gillespie echoed the Augustinian position, arguing that, as a result of punishment, a heretic may "be at least reduced to external order and obedience, being persuaded by the terror of civil power, which may and doth...prove a preparation to free obedience."[40] In their view, "a little smart" might make individuals reexamine false beliefs and increase their receptivity to the truth.[41] It was true that force or the threat thereof might only make hypocrites, but this in itself was not an argument for liberty of conscience, since over the long run "[those holding erroneous beliefs] may profit so much by what they hear and see, as to be convinced of the folly of their former way..."[42]

The Objective Notion of Persecution

Echoing Augustine's insistence that persecution required true belief (that those punished for unrighteousness are not persecuted), orthodox Protestants in seventeenth-century England stressed the objective nature of conscience. In response to the argument about subjective assent, defenders of orthodoxy reasserted the traditional understanding of conscience and persecution, presenting conscience as "God's deputy within us," a "lump of divinity" in the human soul.[43] Persecution, on this account, lay not simply in forcing an individual to do something he preferred not to do with regard to religion, argued Maurice, but "an inflicting, of outward temporal evils, for the exercise of true religion." Thus French Protestants, and not English Dissenters, were persecuted, for they suffered for "a religion, which we verily believe to be true."[44] Assheton defined persecution similarly, as "an inflicting, of outward temporal evils, for the exercise of true religion."[45] Since Anglicans required nothing that was contrary to Scripture (indifferent matters being just that, indifferent, and binding once commanded by the sovereign), there could be no persecution in suppressing Dissenters.[46]

Thus it was considered possible for an individual to believe something objectively mistaken and against the will of God, and thus to have an erring conscience. Out of "some tenderness of conscience," then, Rutherford saw toleration as threatening to bring in a "liberty of sinning."[47] Elsewhere Rutherford stated flatly that "all that conscience saith is not Scripture."[48] To the argument that conscience *per se* binds an individual to perform the dictate of that conscience, Rutherford responded by again raising concerns about the potential for anarchy and disorder: "This poor argument will conclude against all laws of magistrates, against murderers, bloody traitors...the King forbids the English Jesuit to stab the prince...doth the supreme magistrate compel this Jesuit to sin?"[49] If conscience were to mean anything, it had to denote something more than personal whim or fancy: otherwise conscience is merely (as a satirical observer put it) simply "a theological scarecrow" designed to shield an individual from the ethical and legal constraints of living in human society.[50] The orthodox notion of erroneous conscience stressed fallen human nature and drew strength from the empirical, historical arguments about the past consequences of religious division and dissent. In this view, what was often passed off as "conscience" was in reality little more than opinion, whim, fancy, or desire, the tendency of people "to follow after novelty and new-fangledness."[51]

The Violence of Schismatics

Behind the orthodox opposition to the subjectification of conscience lay recurrent concerns about violence, anarchy, and the potential for theological dissent to lapse into licentiousness. William Prynne saw Independent or congregational church government as "a seminary of schisms...[and] a floodgate to let in an inundation of all manner of heresies, errors, sects, religions, destructive opinions, libertinism and lawlessness among us..."[52] The link between heresy and social chaos, for Prynne, was direct and causal. If compulsion in matters of religion was unacceptable, it was difficult to see how coercion could be acceptable in any other area of human endeavor: "if liberty be granted in these [e.g., heresy, false prophets], we know no cause why men that can in such a handsome way pretend conscience for it, should be denied liberty to run into excess and riot."[53] As Gillespie put it, "the very nature of the argument [that compelling against one's conscience compels one to sin] driveth universally against the compelling of any man to do anything which is against his own conscience."[54]

Late-seventeenth-century defenders of orthodoxy in England had one great advantage over earlier generations: they could draw upon the events of the 1640s and 1650s as examples of the mischief that schism and schismatics can visit upon a society. The history and events of the Civil War years proved enormously effective rhetorically. Advocates of uniformity branded religious dissidents as the political and religious heirs of the rebellious spirit that had borne fruit in the English Civil Wars and execution of King Charles I. They often suggested that the unrest of the past fifty years could be traced back to Puritan restless rebelliousness from the earliest days of the Elizabethan church settlement: "Those that strained at the cap and surplice, could well enough digest rapine, sacrilege, and regicide," argued one.[55] Linking claims for toleration to advocacy of popular sovereignty and other extreme political positions, Henry Maurice pointedly stated that the danger to the state had already been displayed

> by an unnatural and unfortunate rebellion, by the deliberate and solemn murder of a most excellent and merciful prince, by a heavy and tedious tyranny of many years, by several conspiracies since the Restoration, by association against the succession of His Majesty, and a formed project of rebellion...in short, by the incessant working of a turbulent spirit...Experience has found [faction and claims of conscience] to be inseparable companions in the bodies of our Dissenters.[56]

William Falkner linked those advocating religious liberty with the murder of Charles I.[57] The continued chorus of religious dissent must surprise anyone "but merely versed in the transactions of these 40 last years," wondered one author; while another pointed to "the fresh bleeding wounds of these three nations" as an argument for unity in church and state.[58]

More generally, this evocation of the 1640s and 1650s equated toleration and religious dissent with social anarchy, licentiousness, and chaos. The public allowance of diverse religious practices "doth naturally improve into contentious disputes, and those disputes (if not restrained) break out into civil wars..."[59] Contempt for magistracy soon follows contempt for ministry, and were the magistrate to grant toleration, individuals would soon claim conscience for "anything concerning God and man, how holy or just so ever it were, that did dislike him..."[60] The specifically religious implications of this argument lay in the claim that the anarchy toleration brought in would lead to the collapse of morality and the triumph of irreligion and license: "when men may do anything they think right, they will go near to think any thing right," wrote Thomas Ashenden during the Exclusion Crisis.[61] Connecting toleration with popular sovereignty, Falkner linked both with "anarchy" and "irreligion," claiming that if this view of conscience and its prerogatives were to triumph, it would destroy civil government, and "we should live as among wolves."[62]

Conclusion

It is important to reiterate that fourth-century Donatists were *not* making claims for liberty of conscience; nor were later English thinkers always more "liberal" than their interlocutors, as was the case with Augustine and the Donatists. Still, in their promotion of church unity, their insistence on an objective notion of conscience and persecution, and their concern for the potential for religious disputes to issue in violence, the early modern English thinkers examined herein reiterate some of the basic themes Augustine articulated in his justification of coercion of the Donatists. Insofar as the Augustinian position influenced the broader Christian tradition in its approach to heresy and schism in the intervening years, it is not surprising, then, that English religious dissidents so often accused their Anglican opponents of persecution and "popery."[63]

My aim in this paper has not been to *justify* Augustine's position on coercion,[64] nor the position of English orthodoxy during the seventeenth century. Neither has it been to *criticize* Augustine's position.[65] Certainly we can gain an understanding, and a valuable one, of the dynamics of church and state as they manifested themselves in these two contexts, and appreciate the real danger with which religious dissent and schism were viewed by their respective opponents, without claiming that the Augustinian position is one we ought to endorse. Indeed, the extraordinary religiosity of Americans, founded in and abetted by the separation of church and state, depends entirely on a *rejection* of Augustine's invocation of civil authority to promote church unity and "compel them to come in." Still, the defenders of orthodoxy (be they Augustinian or seventeenth-century Anglican) did have good reasons to be suspicious of religious dissenters, given the fact that they had been implicated in the execution of a king, and that Donatist Circumcelliones were thought to have pillaged communities throughout northern Africa.

The debates canvassed in this essay did not take place in an isolated, philosophical vacuum, where audiences selected the most persuasive arguments on the basis of analytic rigor or aesthetic appeal. Instead, they were — and in our own day, they continue to be — political arguments, often advanced in times of great social upheaval and, indeed, civil war. Augustine and his early modern heirs considered the many blessings of temporal life — families and friends, teachers and students, and the rhythm and flow of everyday life — to depend upon the maintenance of civil peace, a peace all too often threatened by those who sought an elusive purity in the church and were willing to sacrifice the bonds of charity in order to achieve it. We may admire dissenters' courage, and sympathize with their opponents' fears for the fragile nature of social peace, without resorting to praise or blame. What is more, we can, indeed we must, look out upon the religious and political landscape of our own time and set to work at the difficult balancing act that has always characterized the interplay between liberty and authority in human affairs.

Notes

1   On earthly goods, see *City of God* 15.4; on friendship as an earthly good, *Confessions* 4.8-9; on earthly peace, *City of God* 19.12-13, 17, 26; on love of neighbor, *City of God* 19.14.

2   *City of God* 2.22; 19.21, 24; 19.10-11; *Confessions* 10.28; *On Psalm 48*, Sermon 2.

3   *City of God* 19.17, 26; on the command to respect temporal authority, see *On Catechizing the Uninstructed* 21.37.

4   *City of God* 19.13.

5   I eschew the details of the Donatist schism, instead referring the reader to W.H.C. Frend, *The Donatist Church: A Movement of Protest in North Africa* (Oxford: Clarendon Press, 1952); and Geoffrey Grimshaw Willis, *Saint Augustine and the Donatist Controversy* (Cambridge: Cambridge University Press, 1950).

6   Willis calls this "rigorism" as opposed to liberalism, and although the terminology is somewhat anachronistic and unfortunate, there is some merit to it. See *Saint Augustine*, 1-3.

7   Letter 44.7-11.

8   Letter 100.1-2; Letter 133.1-3.

9   Letter 93.33 (trans. J. G. Cunningham; Edinburgh: T. & T. Clark, 1872); all subsequent references to Letter 93 are to this translation. See also more generally, Letter 93.31-32, 34, 36. See also *City of God* 1.35; 18.49. For the parable of wheat and tares, see Matthew 13:24-30.

10   *On the Correction of the Donatists*, 4 (trans. J. G. Cunningham; Edinburgh: T. & T. Clark, 1872); all subsequent references to *Correction of the Donatists* are to this translation.

11   Letter 93.42.

12   For the Pauline calls for unity, see I Corinthians 1:10, 3:3, 12:25; II Corinthians 13:11; Phillipians 2:2, 3:15-16; Ephesians 4:3; and Galatians 5:20.

13   Letter 87.9.

14   *Correction of the Donatists*, 46.

15   Letter 93.5. See also Letter 93.16.

16   Letter 93.17-18. See also Letter 93.2, 10.

17   *Correction of the Donatists*, 22.

18   Letter 93.8, also 16. See also *Correction of the Donatists*, 9: "It is not, therefore, those who suffer persecution for their unrighteousness, and for the divisions which they impiously introduce into Christian unity, but those who suffer for righteousness' sake, that are truly martyrs." Regarding the roots of the Donatist schism, Augustine asserts that "we maintain that [Caecilianus] belonged to the true Church, not merely because he suffered persecution, but because he suffered it for righteousness' sake..." (*Correction of the Donatists*, 10). On the necessity of righteousness for claims of persecution, see *City of God* 18.50 for Augustine's description of the early Christians as "true martyrs."

19   *City of God* 18.51.

20   The famous use of "*compelle intrare*" appears in *Correction of the Donatists*, 24; Letter 93.5.

21   *Correction of the Donatists*, 25. See also *Correction of the Donatists*, 18: "[S]carcely
      any churches of our communion could be safe against their treachery and violence and
      most undisguised robberies; scarcely any road secure by which men could travel to
      preach the peace of the Catholic Church."

22   *Correction of the Donatists*, 15. See also Letter 93.2.

23   Insofar as these toleration debates might be viewed as debates between different sorts
      of Calvinists, the connection with Augustine becomes a bit more clear. For the Calvinist
      Augustinianism of Puritans, see Perry Miller, *The New England Mind: The Seventeenth
      Century* (Cambridge, Massachusetts: Harvard University Press, 1939); also Patrick
      Collinson, *The Elizabethan Puritan Movement* (New York: Oxford University Press,
      1989).

24   Newcomen, *The duty of such as would walk worthy of the gospel: to endeavour union,
      not division nor toleration* (London, 1646) 8ff.

25   Rutherford, *A free disputation concerning pretended liberty of conscience* (London,
      1649) 61.

26   *Mischief* (London, 1680) and *Unreasonableness* (London, 1682).

27   The debate over *adiaphora* quickly reached a standstill. One side claimed that the
      church could not require a practice not specifically outlined in the Bible; the other
      pointed out that with no Biblical injunction *against* a given practice, the call for
      obedience of Romans 13 and the Pauline commitment to unity required dissenters to set
      aside their schismatic behavior.

28   Stillingfleet, *Mischief, passim; Unreasonableness*, 112-13.

29   [Maurice], *The antithelemite* (London, 1685) 46-47.

30   *The danger and unreasonableness of a toleration* (London, 1685) 1.

31   This was, apparently, also the view of Vincentius, to whom Augustine responded in
      Letter 93; see above.

32   Musgrave, *The conscience pleading for its own liberty* (London, 1647) 4.

33   Taylor, *Theologike eklektike; or A discourse on the liberty of prophesying* (London,
      1647) chapter 13; Walwyn, *The compassionate samaritane* (London, 1644) "Reason 1";
      idem, *A prediction of Mr. Edwards his conversion and recantation* (London, 1646) 3-4;
      idem, *A whisper in the ear of Mr. Thomas Edwards, minister* (London, 1646) 5; Busher,
      Religion's peace, or a plea for liberty of conscience (London, 1614) 2, 5; Overton, *A
      remonstrance of many thousand citizens* (London, 1646) 12ff. See also *Twelve weighty
      queries of great concernment* (London, 1646) query 1-2; *Toleration justified* (London,
      1645) 5; *Divine observations upon the London ministers' letter against toleration*
      (London, 1645) 5; [Francis Rous], *The ancient bounds, or liberty of conscience* (London,
      1645) chapter 6.

34   *The great case of toleration stated* (London, 1688) 4.

35   *A discourse of toleration* (London, 1691) 6. See also William Penn's *The
      reasonableness of toleration* (London, 1687) 9-11.

36   Buckingham, *A short discourse on the reasonableness of men having a religion* (2nd ed.;
      London, 1685) Preface; 20.

37   Williams, *The bloudy tenent of persecution* (London, 1644), in *The Publications of the
      Narragansett Club, Volume III* (1867) 41, 63.

38   Walwyn, *The compassionate samaritane*, 43; see also [Overton], *A remonstrance of
      many thousand citizens*, 11. This emphasis on inner convincement is drawn, as noted
      above, from Romans 14:23. See also *Twelve weighty queries of great concernment*

(London, 1646) 3.

39   Saltmarsh, *A new quaere* (London, 1646) 1. See also Samuel Richardson, *The necessity of toleration in matters of religion* (London, 1647) 5; Saltmarsh, *The smoke in the temple* (London, 1646).

40   Gillespie, *Wholesome severity reconciled with Christian liberty* (London, 1644) 32.

41   Ashenden, *No penalty, no peace* (London, 1682) 22.

42   *The antithelemite*, 18.

43   *Anti-toleration, or a modest defense of the letter of the London ministers* (London, 1646) 5; Rutherford, *Free disputation*, 15.

44   [Maurice], *The antithelemite*, 9-10, 51.

45   Assheton, *A seasonable discourse against toleration* (London, 1685) 8.

46   *A seasonable discourse*, 9-10.

47   Rutherford, *Free disputation*, 20. This notion of "erring conscience" was often associated with the idea that "natural" conscience may carry the seed of morality (as did, in Christian views, the Old Testament Law and the Commandments), but was also prone to error due to fallen human nature, and needed the "enlightening" of Christian revelation. See *Free disputation*, 6-7; and Robert Hitchcock, *A sermon on law, nature, and conscience* (Huntington Library Manuscript EL 8389, n.d.). Hitchcock argues that even Gentiles, "though they had not the law written in tablets of stone as had the Jews, yet they had as law which was the ground of that, the Law of Nature written in their hearts...for there being but two guides to direct us how to frame our lives, the Law of God, and the Light of Nature" (8, 35).

48   *Joshua redivivus, or Mr. Rutherford's letters* (Rotterdam, 1664) 511.

49   Rutherford, *Free disputation*, 140. Of course, both tolerationists and antitolerationists agreed that persecuting someone for a *correctly* informed conscience was indeed sinful, as, for example, Paul's persecution of Christians before his conversion (Acts 8:1-3; 9:4).

50   "New Interpreter," Huntington Library Manuscript EL 7801.

51   Ashenden, *No penalty, no peace*, 9. Such claims to conscience, according to Ashenden, "[set] up a tribunal in every man's factious fancy" (*No penalty, no peace*, 19).

52   Prynne, *Twelve considerable and serious considerations touching church-government* (London, 1644) 7.

53   Church of Scotland, *A solemn testimony against toleration* (Edinburgh, 1649) 7.

54   Gillespie, *Wholesome severity*, 23.

55   *The danger and unreasonableness*, 3, 4.

56   [Maurice], *The antithelemite*, 3, 4.

57   Falkner, *Christian loyalty* (London, 1684) 357-358. The finest example of Restoration Anglican orthodoxy is Samuel Parker, *A discourse of ecclesiastical polity* (London, 1669).

58   *The danger and unreasonableness*, 1; Edward Wetenhall, *The Protestant peace-maker* (London, 1682) 40. See also Ashenden, *No penalty, no peace*, 1-2.

59   William Assheton, *A seasonable discourse*, 17.

60   *The danger and unreasonableness*, 3.

61   *No penalty, no peace*, 13; also 232ff. See also Wetenhall, *Protestant peace-maker*, 40-50.

62   *Christian loyalty*, 292, 364.

63   On these accounts virtually no differences existed between Catholic "popery" and Anglican or Presbyterian uniformity. See John Milton, *Of Reformation, and the causes which have hindered it* (London, 1641); [Robinson], *Liberty of conscience*, "To every Christian reader"; [Overton], *The arraignment of Mr. Persecution* (London, 1645) 34. For essentially the same points, see *Toleration justified* (London, 1645) 2; and John Goodwin, *Independency Gods verity* (London, 1647) 7-8. We should also remember, as constant backdrop to these disputes, the broader contours of English anti-Catholicism: see Caroline Hibbard, *Charles I and the Popish Plot* (Chapel Hill, North Carolina, 1983); and Robin Clifton, "The Popular Fear of Catholics during the English Revolution," *Past and Present* 52 (1971) 23-55.

64   For this project, see John R. Bowlin, "Augustine on Justifying Coercion,"*Annual of the Society of Christian Ethics* 17 (1997) 49-70, esp. 65-70. Bowlin concludes his essay by claiming that critics of Augustine's view "must concede that their differences with Augustine are more accidents of history and circumstance than inferences from fundamentally different moral principles" (70), a claim that seems radically to understate the ways in which "accidents of history and circumstance" are in themselves deeply bound up with the "fundamentally different moral principles" displayed by Augustine and modern Christians, even highly orthodox ones. See also Jean Bethke Elshtain, *Augustine and the Limits of Politics* (Notre Dame, Indiana: University of Notre Dame Press, 1995) 98-101.

65   For this project, see William Connolly, *The Augustinian Imperative: A Reflection on the Politics of Morality* (Newbury Park, California: Sage Publications, 1993); see also Frend, *Donatist Church*, chapter 15; and John Milbank, *Theology and Social Theory: Beyond Secular Reason* (Oxford: Blackwell, 1990) 419-22.

PART IV
LIBERAL EDUCATION
SINCE AUGUSTINE

Chapter Eleven

Reading without Moving Your Lips: The Role of the Solitary Reader in Liberal Education

Marylu Hill

Introduction

Every few years or so, it seems, there is a flurry of concern in local and national newspapers about the state of education, and invariably test scores and other evaluative tools are invoked with a sober pronouncement that (yet again) Johnny can't read (or can't read up to grade level) or Johnny won't read because he prefers computer games to printed media altogether. But whatever the conclusion, the central point remains the same: reading, or the lack thereof, is at the heart of our educational concerns, and as such is perennially the benchmark of all academic activity from primary school upwards.

As an educator and as a parent, I too worry about these findings, and I am troubled as to what ought to be done. But I cannot altogether agree with those voices in the field of higher education who demand to know 1) why their students are not already good readers (meaning sharp, analytical, precise, and critical readers), and 2) why are primary and secondary school teachers falling down on the job. Although I concur that teaching the rudiments of reading skills is indeed the domain of our elementary schools, it seems to me that our job in the realm of higher education, particularly in the liberal arts, is to continue the process of teaching our students *really to read* — deeply, thoughtfully, critically, and individually — meaning to read for *oneself* what other thinkers have written. If we teach primary texts of any sort, then we must of necessity teach the reading that such texts demand.

To hear many students and faculty speak of this process, one might assume that our job is to condense the facts and concepts into lecture notes or into lectures disguised as artfully constructed discussion, while students scribble furiously in notebooks or highlight wantonly their barely-cracked editions of the text at hand. Teaching the text is not necessarily the same thing as teaching how to read the text in a mature and thoughtful manner, yet I would argue that, of the two, the latter is more important. Only through confronting a text one on one, and testing one's mind against long dead but still potent authors, can students truly learn to read.

Augustine and Reading: a Vehicle for Conversion

The frustrating questions, however, are how do we teach this kind of reading, why we should teach it, and perhaps even to whom. For some answers, or at least some suggestions, I must go back to the 19th century, where the modern concept of the liberal arts education came into its own. But for a more complete answer, I must go even further back — to the "*Ur*-reader" himself, Augustine of Hippo. It may seem strange in this context to invoke a fourth-century author for whose culture reading was still a novelty or at least the domain of privileged men. The format of books was barely recognizable; the codex was still a relatively new innovation remarkable for what it could offer scholars of any sort, and the written page still appeared an amalgam of letters and words driven together to make expeditious use of all the precious paper.[1] What can an author from those early days know about reading as an art form, as a means of interpretation, and a forum for understanding? But it comes as no surprise in this collection of essays on Augustine and the liberal arts that Augustine was the first truly modern reader, sensitive to the special skill that is reading — a skill which weds physical process with mental change and introspection. As Brian Stock states in *Augustine the Reader*, for Augustine, "[a]n act of reading is... a critical step upwards in a mental ascent: it is both an awakening from sensory illusion and a rite of initiation, in which the reader crosses the threshold from the outside to the inside world."[2] Throughout the *Confessions*, Augustine offers potent images of reading as both a tool of power and a means of conversion. When he relates his experiences as a school boy, transfixed by the wonderful stories he must memorize, his younger self was almost unaware of the tremendous gift he had received: the gift of literacy. In a tone of quiet confidence, he states "by means [of those early lessons] in literacy I was gradually being given a power which became mine and still remains with me: the power to read any writing I come across and to write anything I have a mind to myself."[3] The scope of the power to read is both startling and sweeping; reading is defined for Augustine as a form of freedom, with reading and thinking as two sides of the same coin. This freedom will cause trouble for Augustine spiritually as he moves through the *Confessions*, but the equation remains, as the later Augustine, bishop and theologian, will use this combination of reading and thinking in the service of God.

But even more pertinent to my argument is a later passage in the *Confessions* in which Augustine observes Bishop Ambrose in a moment of silent reading, thus setting up a comparison between reading as either a private experience or a shared experience — silent reading versus reading aloud. The latter was of course the norm in Augustine's day, a habit made necessary by the ways words were written on the page, demanding they be sounded for sense, sentence structure, and emphasis. In this context, Ambrose is remarkable for his erudition as well as his meditative skills:

> When he read his eyes would travel across the pages and his mind would explore the sense, but his voice and tongue were silent. We would sometimes be present, for he did

not forbid anyone access, nor was it customary for anyone to be announced; and on these occasions we watched him reading silently. It was never otherwise, and so we too would sit for a long time in silence, for who would have the heart to interrupt a man so engrossed? Then we would steal away, guessing that in the brief time he had seized for the refreshment of his mind he was resting from the din of other people's affairs and reluctant to be called away to other business. We thought too that he might be apprehensive that if he read aloud, and any closely attentive listener were doubtful on any point, or the author he was reading used any obscure expressions, he would have to stop and explain various difficult problems that might arise, and after spending time on this be unable to read as much of the book as he wished. Another and perhaps more cogent reason for his habit of reading silently was his need to conserve his voice, which was very prone to hoarseness. But whatever his reason, that man undoubtedly had a good one. (*Conf.* 6.3.3)

Augustine's surprise at Ambrose's technique is almost palpable, and it is easy and even amusing to envision Augustine and his cohorts lingering about, shuffling their feet and coughing, while Ambrose determinedly fixes his gaze on his book, knowing that eye contact is the fatal slip that will invite questions and conversation. Augustine's list of reasons for Ambrose's actions attests to the singularity of private reading, especially in the depiction of the discussion that never happens, with Augustine stealing away in embarrassment — not the expected protocol of readers and listeners. But the passage also marks a watershed moment for Augustine as Brian Stock notes: "The scene contrasts Augustine's restlessness with Ambrose's tranquillity: it is also a reminder within the Pauline design of Books 5-7 that one's proper business lies not in the world but with oneself."[4] As Stock further comments, Ambrose's example offers reading as a "means of withdrawing from the world and of focusing attention on one's inner life."[5] The "psychological barrier" of silent reading sets the reader apart from a world contrary to his values and as such it becomes a signifier of difference and of deliberate withdrawal.[6] I am reminded of one of my favorite, if more bizarre, reading experiences — reading Proust in my first year of graduate school as I commuted on the busy subways of New York. Proust became my shield as I traveled the IRT, placing me both visibly and mentally on a higher plane of introspection — or at least so I thought, rather snobbishly, at the time (to this day my memories of Proust are punctuated by the clatter of trains and the sound of doors beeping open and shut).

The clear sense of demarcation between types of reading plays out for Augustine in a perceived tension between a community of readers/listeners and the individual advanced reader. The community is necessary and beneficial in that it permits teaching moments of interpretation directed at those who are not as skilled in reading. In this context, the role of the preacher/reader is crucial for teaching the faith and protecting the "simple" from pagan or potentially heretical mistakes like Monica's habit of placing food offerings on the tombs of saints. The shared experience is likewise in itself critical in encouraging a sense of church and community as opposed to the intellectual sterility of one who reads and even "knows" of God yet fails to profess the faith among one's brethren, as the story of Victorinus is clearly meant to demonstrate. Private reading and even intense study of Scripture may still be a blind behind which an intellectual like Victorinus might cower, fearful of exposing himself to ridicule (*Conf.* 8.2.4).

But, despite Augustine's embrace of the communal activity reading can represent, he saves his most powerful experiences of conversion and enlightenment for the moments of private reading, and thus moments which represent a clear movement into spiritual maturity. The obvious example is Augustine's garden epiphany. Overcome by a fit of ranting and sobbing, Augustine is first calmed by the child's voice chanting "Pick it up and read," and then, continuing the move inward into silence, from words to Word, he picks up the book, "opened it and read *in silence* the passage on which my eyes first lighted" (*Conf.* 8.12.29, emphasis added). Conversion here becomes a function of self-interpretation as Augustine meets the Word one on one, without the mediator of a teacher or guide, and discovers that enlightenment has always been within him, just as the true Kingdom and true text have been within him and waiting for him all along. The joy that Augustine shows throughout *The Confessions* in knowing scripture "by heart" is part of this moment of spiritual realization, when the text "becomes part of oneself" and "texts and self interpenetrate."[7] This is not to say that one cannot learn "by heart" through oral discourse or shared listening — indeed, these are perhaps the first occasions where such learning takes place, as Augustine himself suggests—but true enlightenment and spiritual maturity occur when one returns to the text to seek it out for oneself.

Liberal Education and Reading — 19th Century Models

Thus, Augustine offers some interesting answers to the questions I first posed. Why should we read? Because reading, done rightly, is a vehicle for conversion and a symbol for how the kingdom of God might stir us from within. How do we learn to read this way? By heart, says Augustine, by consuming a text and making it part of yourself. And who should read, and what should they read? Only those who are capable of introspection without falling into pride and avarice for knowledge — and the only reading we need is the "true" word, or the Word of God.

But how do we apply these concepts to current models of higher education? On their surface, Augustine's ideas seem both dated and restrictive in the modern realm of education, yet there is still much in his model of reading to take seriously. For Augustine is clearly prescribing a personal system of reading that is thoughtful and serious, leading to the highest levels of self-inquiry and transformation, both religious and secular. It is a way of knowing the world that is both engaged and private, in the best senses of both words, meaning perhaps in the old-fashioned phrase, to be "in the world but not of it." Finally, Augustine suggests that it matters what books we read, and in order to produce the kind of reading detailed above, our books must reflect the same sort of thoughtfulness and potential for self-transformation.

However, perhaps Augustine's greatest legacy concerning the primacy of reading is his assertion that both spiritual and intellectual maturity are necessary to develop the ability to interpret and truly understand a text for oneself. The connection of reading to thinking for oneself becomes the hallmark of liberal education, particularly in the 19th century, when the term "liberal" education took on the meaning by which we recognize it today. What is more, it returns us to the critical question, *how* should we teach this type of reading, and perhaps of even more consequence to us in the teaching profession today, how do we institutionalize what is by definition a private and of necessity self-initiated process? And where does a system of reading deeply fit into typical campus life here in America?

The nineteenth century offered a variety of answers to these questions, several of which remain current in educational theory today. Thinkers like John Henry Newman and John Ruskin, among others, examined to some degree the relationship between the communal experience of university life and the solitary experience of the auto-didactic reader, and both came up with suggestions that correspond in large part to Augustine's observations about the power of reading.

John Henry Newman's landmark work on education, *The Idea of a University* (1852), still stands today as a classic definition of liberal education, i.e. knowledge which enlarges the mind with "an excellence of its own" without an aim toward pure utility.[8] As Newman describes it, this knowledge goes beyond mere fact gathering and instead represents the capacity for understanding and interpreting, as well as the ability to take "a connected view of old and new, past and present, far and near, and which has an insight into the influence of all these one on another; without which there is no whole, and no centre. It possesses the knowledge, not only of things, but also of their mutual and true relations..."[9] Newman values this interconnected view of knowledge so highly that it becomes the cornerstone of his vision of a university and, in so doing, it is clear that he leans toward the side of communal experience as that which makes liberal education truly liberal. The very existence of a community of scholars within a university setting creates what Newman calls "an atmosphere of thought,"[10] which faculty and students alike breathe and from which all benefit, even if individual students might only pursue "a few sciences out of the multitude."[11] The profession of intellectual faith these scholars make to each other (reminiscent of Augustine's Victorinus again) saves each from concentrating too narrowly on his own speciality, and thus committing the sin, at least to Newman, of "contract[ing] his mind."[12] Instead, they "adjust together the claims and relations of their respective subjects of investigation. They learn to respect, to consult, to aid each other."[13] Newman goes on further to argue that even if there were no official classes, or professors to teach them, there would still be educational benefit from bringing together young men in one space:

> When a multitude of young men, keen, open-hearted, sympathetic, and observant, as young men are, come together and freely mix with each other, they are sure to learn one

from another, even if there be no one to teach them; the conversation of all is a series of lectures to each, and they gain for themselves new ideas and views, fresh matter of thought, and distinct principles for judging and acting, day by day.[14]

What kills education is the mode familiar to Newman, particularly in his anti-Utilitarian mood, and ridiculed in such contemporary sources as Charles Dickens' *Hard Times* — the fact-gathering, passive receptor model of early Victorian classrooms with its

> . . . set of teachers, with no mutual sympathies and no inter-communion, of a set of examiners with no opinions which they dare profess, and with no common principles, who are teaching or questioning a set of youths who do not know them, and do not know each other, on a large number of subjects, different in kind, and connected by no wide philosophy, three times a week, or three times a year, or once in three years, in chill lecture-rooms or on a pompous anniversary.[15]

(Need I comment that this sort of classroom is found even today.) In particular, Newman rails against the multiplicity of subjects, intended to give students a wide breadth of knowledge and instead giving them concepts "which they have never really mastered, and so shallow as not even to know their shallowness."[16] The saving grace in these scenarios is the university model itself, which inculcates at least a self-education in the residence halls brought on by forced exposure to other students and other values. The only preferable alternative is a solitary education of reading and "ranging through a library at random, taking down books as they meet him [the "independent mind"], and pursuing the trains of thought which his mother wit suggests."[17] This may be desirable, or at least achievable by the "independent mind," but Newman is suspicious of the solitary nature of this enterprise, asserting like a good college administrator (and like Augustine too with his vision of community), that

> Few. . . can dispense with the stimulus and support of instructors, or will do any thing at all, if left to themselves. And fewer still (though such great minds are to be found), who will not, from such unassisted attempts, contract a self-reliance and a self-esteem, which are not only moral evils, but serious hindrances to the attainment of truth. And next to none, perhaps, or none, who will not be reminded from time to time of the disadvantages under which they lie, by their imperfect grounding, by the breaks, deficiencies, and irregularities of their knowledge, by the eccentricity of opinion and the confusion of principle which they exhibit. They will be too often ignorant of what every one knows and takes for granted, of that multitude of small truths which fall upon the mind like dust, impalpable and ever accumulating; they may be unable to converse, they may argue perversely, they may pride themselves on their worst paradoxes or their grossest truisms, they may be full of their own mode of viewing things, unwilling to be put out of their way, slow to enter into the minds of others. . .[18]

Too much solitude, Newman asserts, is not good for liberal education; the voracious and voluminous reading necessary to speak knowledgeably about anything becomes liberal education only when we test it in discussion against the ideas of others. There must be a balance between reading and discussing, with one thumb weighted slightly on the side of the communal experience.

But, as the century wore on, other voices were offering powerful arguments for a more private program of reading as the heart of a true liberal education. One of the most significant voices in his own time was John Ruskin, and in his pair of essays "Of Kings' Treasuries" and "Of Queens' Gardens" in *Sesame and Lilies* (1864), he advances a system of education independent of the trappings of college life, particularly the social determinants inherent in the Victorian university structure. Ruskin asserts that most people seek out education for the sake of social advancement — "the education befitting *such and such* a station in life" rather than "an education good in itself,"[19] (thus concurring with Newman about the importance of the latter). But unlike Newman, who professes that one of the positive results of a liberal education is the creation of a "Christian gentleman," with most of the implicit class distinctions intact within that definition, Ruskin argues for education that will diminish economic class difference even while emphasizing intellectual or moral "class." True education, according to Ruskin, can only occur outside the usual social frameworks wherein we seek preferment or economic advancement by expanding our networks with the class above us through the social structure deemed education (private schools, an Oxbridge degree, etc.). Thus, Ruskin offers another sort of educational aristocracy, "of labour and. . . merit," that is both uninfluenced and unaffected by the demands of social mobility, and furthermore, is available to all who wish it. This education is, of course, one of pure reading, deep and open-minded reading undertaken with a desire to be transformed through an encounter with the best minds of past generations. Like Augustine, Ruskin believes wholeheartedly in the power of reading as a vehicle for conversion — in this case, conversion to a mind both learned and ethical. And, in tandem with Augustine and Newman, Ruskin avers that education is not passive reception or fact gathering; indeed, he reminds us that reading demands more of the reader than any lecturer might:

> If you will not rise to us [books by past greats], we cannot stoop to you. The living lord may assume courtesy, the living philosopher explain his thought to you with considerable pain; but here we neither feign nor interpret; you must rise to the level of our thoughts if you would be gladdened by them, and share our feelings, if you would recognize our presence.[20]

There has to be a modicum of maturity and self-transformation already present, as in Augustine's ten years of intellectual struggles before he can finally receive the Word of God maturely in the garden. An old adage serves well here: if an ass peers into a book, a saint will not peer out. And, furthermore, a teacher's kindly explanations of the text will not achieve the same purpose: only if the student/reader finally takes it upon him/herself to approach the text and do his/her own reading and interpreting will s/he be truly educated.

Ruskin also goes so far as to state how and what one should read, once again demonstrating an Augustinian connection. The question of what we should read is relatively easy for Ruskin. He offers two basic categories and the distinction between them: "books of the hour, and books of all time."[21] The former is perfectly acceptable reading as long as it is acknowledged as such: the "useful or pleasant talk of some person whom you cannot otherwise converse with, printed for you."[22] Ruskin goes on to describe this type of book as a "book of talk. . . printed only because its author cannot speak to thousands of people at once; if he could, he would — the volume is mere *multiplication* of his voice."[23] (This distinction takes on particular significance for us today in the midst of electronically reproduced "talk" via email, the Internet, television, etc.). But the books to which we should give our best attention are the "books of all time," written with an eye toward "permanence" and longevity and hence a true book in Ruskin's definition:

> . . . [A] book is written, not to multiply the voice merely, . . . but to perpetuate it. The author has something to say which he perceives to be true and useful, or helpfully beautiful. So far as he knows, no one has yet said it; so far as he knows, no one else can say it. He is bound to say it, clearly and melodiously if he may; clearly, at all events... He would fain set it down forever; engrave it on rock, if he could, saying, "This is the best of me; for the rest, I ate, and drank, and slept, loved, and hated, like another; my life was as the vapor and is not; but this I saw and knew: this if anything of mine, is worth your memory." That is his "writing"; it is, in his small human ways, and with whatever degree of true inspiration is in him, his inscription, or scripture. That is a "Book."[24]

The books we should read, then, are the ones that seek to convey some truth as best they can in human language, an idea with which Augustine would certainly agree.

But the question of how we should read is even more paramount to Ruskin, and, I suspect, to Augustine as well, and certainly still to us as educators today. Once again, Ruskin offers a relatively straight-forward pair of recommendations which, however, suggest all sorts of interesting connections back to Augustine and forward to us in the late twentieth century. First Ruskin says the reader must embrace "a true desire to be taught by them [the authors of great books] and to enter into their thoughts."[25] What he means, Ruskin hastens to add, is that we must truly "enter into theirs, observe; not to find your own thought expressed by them."[26] As he goes on to say, "Very ready we are to say of a book, 'How good this is — that's exactly what I think!' But the right feeling is, 'How strange that is! I never thought of that before, and yet I see it is true; or if I do not now, I hope I shall, some day.'"[27] A willingness for transformation is at the heart of this action; instead of seeking out the safety of opinions that match our own, we must be open to both challenge and conversion from thinkers unlike us. Newman sees this accomplished by the conversation of young men from different places and upbringings, but Ruskin places it firmly within the personal encounter with past thinkers. What is more, it is a process that demands courage, open-mindedness, critical interpretation skills, and finally a willingness to revisit the same text time and time again as necessary: ". . . be sure also, if the author is worth anything, that you will not get at his meaning all at once; — nay, that at his whole meaning you will not for a long time arrive in any wise."[28] The best books generally demand hard work on the part of the reader, as much as any miner seeking gold, to use Ruskin's metaphor,[29] a fact discovered by Augustine so many centuries earlier as he struggled to comprehend the Bible:

> What I see in them [the scriptures] is something not accessible to the scrutiny of the proud nor exposed to the gaze of the immature, something lowly as one enters but lofty as one advances further, something veiled in mystery. At that time, though, I was in no state to enter, nor prepared to bow my head and accommodate myself to its ways. My approach then was quite different from the one I am suggesting now: when I studied the Bible and compared it with Cicero's dignified prose, it seemed to me unworthy. My swollen pride recoiled from its style and my intelligence failed to penetrate to its inner meaning. Scripture is a reality that grows along with little children, but I disdained to be a little child and in my high and mighty arrogance regarded myself as grown up. (*Conf.* 3.5.9)

Thus, reading for both Ruskin and Augustine demands a maturity (and humility) of spirit and a commitment to the hard work of truth-finding.

The second part of how we should read for Ruskin involves the depth and accuracy of our reading. The primacy of words is central in Ruskin's definition, coupled with a concern for accuracy and careful comprehension in reading. Accordingly, only those who truly read the words are capable of being transformed by them: ". . . you might read all the books in the British Museum (if you could live long enough) and remain an utterly 'illiterate' uneducated person; but that if you read ten pages of a good book, letter by letter, — that is to say, with real accuracy, — you are forevermore in some measure an educated person."[30] Ruskin goes so far as to insist upon a system of close reading that starts with words and definitions:

> . . . many words have been. . . Greek first, Latin next, French and German next, and English last: undergoing a certain change of sense and use on the lips of each nation; but retaining a deep vital meaning, which all good scholars feel in employing them, even at this day. . . if you think of reading seriously (which, of course, implies that you have some leisure at command), learn your Greek alphabet; then get good dictionaries of all these languages, and whenever you are in doubt about a word, hunt it down patiently. . . . It is severe work; but you will find it, even at first, interesting, and at last, endlessly amusing. And the general gain to your character, in power and precision, will be quite incalculable.[31]

Ruskin's assumption that the serious reader is a mature person with leisure time at command will coincide with my later point about who else we should include in our classes of learners/readers. But right now, suffice it to say that knowing what the words mean, and subsequently understanding why we might choose one word over another establishes a nicety and precision of intellect that not only marks the educated person, but also marks the mature writer and/or thinker as well. Certainly we could do worse, as professors today, than to require our students to define their words first before they use them in a critical sentence, and recommend that they buy their own copy of the condensed OED (cheaper than a laptop computer, the last time I checked).

However, the question that I've begged up until now is how Ruskin suggests the neophyte reader *attain* the maturity of intellect in the first place, in order to undertake the serious task of right reading. For that answer, we must look at his essay, "Of Queens' Gardens," which treats of women's education and, more specifically, the proper reading material for young women. Ruskin's remarks about women's education are of great interest for several reasons, not least of which are the wholesale attacks he has undergone by early feminist critics of the 1970s.[32] Some of his statements are indeed questionable and within a modern context distasteful; comments like "women's intellect is not for invention or creation, but for sweet ordering, arrangement, and decision,"[33] are construable as condescending as best and offensive at the worst, although certainly understandable by the standards of the time. Yet the entirety of "Of Queens' Gardens" is most notable, I believe, for the sensible and respectful recommendations Ruskin makes about women's education in general, and, in particular, the "serious" reading he felt (contrary to many of his contemporaries) women should be introduced to at an early age on account of the depth of their natures compared to the shallowness of young men of the same age:

> . . . if there were to be any difference between a girl's education and a boy's, I should say that of the two the girl should be earlier led, as her intellect ripens faster, into deep and serious subjects: and that her range of literature should be, not more, but less frivolous; calculated to add the qualities of patience and seriousness to her natural poignancy of thought and quickness of wit; and also to keep her in a lofty and pure element of thought.[34]

Likewise, Ruskin says, the best way to encourage maturity in reading and thinking is to let the girl read what she wants, without interference or censorship, within the confines of a "good library of old and classical books":

> Keep the modern magazine and novel out of your girl's way; turn her loose into the old library every wet day, and let her alone. She will find what is good for her; you cannot. . . . Let her loose in the library, I say, as you do a fawn in a field. It knows the bad weeds twenty times better than you; and the good ones, too, and will eat some bitter and prickly ones, good for it, which you had not the slightest thought would have been so.[35]

And finally, Ruskin says, treat women's education (and by extension their teachers) seriously (particularly an issue in nineteenth-century England when governesses were just slightly above the household staff in rank). In a nutshell, then, respect and solitude are the ingredients for a mature female intellect, and not a bad prescription for young males as well. Indeed, some of the women's colleges, in their infancy or birth pangs as Ruskin wrote these words, took his suggestions to heart and made the "room of one's own," to use Virginia Woolf's phrase, a hallmark of their curriculum. Girton College, Cambridge, in particular, became renowned by the turn of the century for both its serious female scholars and the coveted "Girton study" complete with a scuttle of coal a day so that each student might read and study in her room, unencumbered by social duties or domestic concerns.[36] When Virginia Woolf gave her lecture *A Room of One's Own* to Girton students in 1927, one can imagine what sort of special resonance the term had for them.

For the women's colleges, and Ruskin as well, the issue is how to create an educational collective that avoids the inevitable frivolity and hi-jinks that occur when large groups of young people are brought together without the usual parental restrictions. The silliness of the herd can be counteracted with doses of solitude and uncensored access to good books — or at least so the early administrators of Girton, Newnham, Bryn Mawr Colleges and the like all believed.

Where Have All the Readers Gone? Reading on Modern College Campuses

No doubt then that this technique worked well enough for Girton students who, it should be added, were already bright and largely autodidactic young women to start, given the still limited curriculum at many nineteenth-century English private schools for girls. But what happens when we apply Augustine, Newman, and Ruskin to present-day universities and students? What is the balance between communal experience, whether in the classroom or in the residence halls, and the experience of solitary critical reading, and are we getting the results that Augustine, Newman, and Ruskin all concur we should be getting as educators and readers?

The model for shared reading — i.e., reading and discussing out loud — which was standard in Augustine's time clearly has left its imprint on classrooms of today. The students are led by the professor who is marked by his/her place in the classroom as the primary reader and interpreter of any given text while the students offer their cautious comments for discussion. Sometimes, the class proceeds in a lecture format, which is most clearly the paradigm of reading aloud for less learned listeners. Every teacher feels the impetus to impart knowledge (that is, we suppose, what we are trained to do, after all), and the reading-aloud format, with commentary, is the easiest way to achieve this goal. More difficult is the task of ascertaining how well the students have read the materials at hand; we gauge it by quizzes and leading questions and essays in which we ask for critical responses to the readings. All these tools are more or less effective in telling us basically what we need to know: that student A did not do the reading at all; student B seems to have a basic grasp on what happened; and student C actually seems to understand it fairly well.

But the worrisome element is when we realize that there are impediments to deep, critical, and solitary reading built into the academic process which are almost impossible to counteract. One is the discussion format of many classes — an indispensable tool and a wonderful forum for the exchange of ideas, but sometimes a misleading event for the novice reader. How many times have we as teachers heard "I didn't understand the reading until we discussed it, but now I'm okay"? And how many times have the results been conversation, tests, or essays in which it is clear that the student's entire understanding of the text derives solely and exclusively from the discussion, with all its own misinterpretations, red herrings, exaggerations, and omissions? Worse yet, how many times do we find our students quoting us (even so far as putting us in the footnotes)? The power of lecture and/or discussion orally to disseminate information (and often misinformation) is shocking, especially when we realize how few of our students return to the text to compare or challenge the oral data they have received.

The fact of the matter is that discussion and even lectures are just plain easier from the student's point of view, and often more entertaining as well. "Just tell us what it means," beg my students when we encounter a puzzling and intricate text: no miners for gold here, to use Ruskin's metaphor again. And we oblige, our egos stroked, and offer our personal fount of knowledge, because it's easier for us too.

But perhaps this is just fine, because, according to Newman, it is the exchange of ideas that happens between the students, and also the faculty, that is the knowledge that enlarges. Certainly our students believe this to be so; ask a random sampling of exiting seniors what changed them the most in their four years of college, and the majority will answer "the people they've met here," or "the diversity of opinions they've encountered." A few might say, "the books I read for the first time" (as one of my colleagues is wont to say, these few are, no doubt, the ones who will trickle back into academia after a few more years reading books in graduate school). But generally, reading does not come into the picture, and certainly not the kind of wide reading that even Newman, with his emphasis on the community of university life, felt was necessary to be truly educated.

In adopting the Newman model, something got left out along the way, which would have dismayed Newman in its omission, at many colleges and universities, especially here in America. Watch any movie made about college life in the past forty years or so, and it becomes clear that as a society we envision college as a place where exchanges of phone numbers at a fraternity party rather than exchanges of ideas about books are a primary part of the experience, and any reading or thinking is both coerced and incidental. One of the few exceptions to this view (in that it defends the serious college reader against the Philistines of the rest of the college community), and one of the wittiest college movies ever made, entitled *The Male Animal* (1942), grapples with the distinction between "real" college life (i.e. sports and parties) and the poor second of the academic end. In it, Henry Fonda plays a beleaguered English professor struggling against the sports mania of his Midwestern university (a mania which centers around a beefy and lovably stupid Jack Carson as an aging football hero). Yet even in this clever send-up of the passion for sports and parties on American campuses, despite the fact that the scholarly geeks and "unmanly" men of the serious faculty have the last laugh, they are still perceived as just slightly more fashionable geeks and unmanly men.

In this sort of campus climate (except at a handful of "serious" schools, duly noted with an air of polite surprise in popular guides to choosing a college), there is little time and less impetus to find the opportunities of private introspection that solitary and critical reading demands. In addition to this tradition of privileging social life over academic work (a tradition which is, I suspect, at least as old as the universities themselves), the chances for students to do serious reading are further narrowed by such influences as mass media, computers, email, telephones, videos and computer games. Unlike Ruskin's girl in the library, or the Girton student of the late nineteenth century, overjoyed at the academic privacy of her own room, today's students retire to their rooms to do so much more than study: they can surf the Net, read their email, play some games, listen to some tunes, all in the comfort of their dorm. Couple this with the general noise levels in the average residence hall, and one begins to understand why our students are not using residence hall time for a quiet and thoughtful reading session. Finally, complicate matters further by adding a youth culture, raised on television, music videos, and clicking a computer mouse for instantaneous results, which is uncomfortable at best with the lengthiness of the reading process, as well as a general material culture that promotes what another of my colleagues calls an attitude of "learn to earn," thus raising a persistent spectre of cynicism when students are asked to read "old" and therefore "irrelevant" books — and all in all, reading as a joy and worthwhile challenge ends up at the bottom of the entertainment and employment pile.

So what's a professor to do?

I do not know that I can add anything entirely new or remarkable to this conversation, but, in the light of Augustine, Newman, and Ruskin, I would like to highlight some old ideas as well as some new developments in order to answer the question of what we can do. First, I would suggest that we as educators lower the bar in terms of our expectations — *not* regarding the quality of what we teach and how we test, but regarding, perhaps, the enthusiasm with which reading as reading is received by our students. Even young Augustine preferred playing ball to reading (to the tune of innumerable beatings by his teachers), so how can we expect our students to be much different? Without washing our hands of them, we do well to remember that our students are young, and with that youth comes a resistance to any number of things — work, authority, advice from elders, and reading stuffy old books. Perhaps we even remember being this way ourselves (back in the dark ages before the Internet!). It is comforting to be reminded that young students have always been this way, to some extent, and, as Mortimer Adler stated so provocatively over a half century ago,

> [t]he young cannot be educated. Youth is the obstacle. . . It follows, then, that precisely because they are immature, properly irresponsible, not serious, and lacking a great deal of experience, children in school are not educable. I do not mean they are not trainable. . . . The child, in all matters of simple habit formation, is much more trainable that the

adult; but the adult is much more educable, because education is not primarily a matter of training or habit formation. Though these are preparations for it, education in its essence is the cultivation of the human mind. Education consists in the growth of understanding, insight, and ultimately some wisdom. These growths require mature soil. Only in mature soil, soil rich with experience, can ideas really take root.[37] (212-213)

After all, one of the greatest lessons in *The Confessions* is that conversion is a function of maturity, explaining why it took brilliant young Augustine over ten years, from the time he arrives in Carthage as a student to his conversion at age thirty-two, to figure out what really mattered to him. Augustine the student was not all that different from our students — given to seeking pleasure, hanging out with his friends, making his mother worry over his exploits, falling in love, falling in lust, and reading books without moral or spiritual value.

Thus, the onus should be off us as teachers to impart all the wisdom of the world, and, instead, we should do something at once simpler and more difficult: give them the tools to be good readers and hence good thinkers. Newman talks of disciplining the mind through the liberal arts, Ruskin hands out the OED and suggests we use it, and all these thinkers, including not a few in our own century (Mortimer Adler, Mark van Doren, and Robert Hutchins, among others), insist that the primary tools for learning to read are the "great books" of western civilization. As more and more colleges and universities re-institute core courses in the humanities based on primary texts, including the university where I teach, it is clear that significant texts of intellectual history have re-emerged as useful guides for training our students in the reading process. Robert M. Hutchins, former chancellor of the University of Chicago during the height of its "great books" era, calls this system of reading an introduction to the "Great Conversation" that these texts represent.

Another suggestion for teaching the process is directly from Newman and Ruskin: less books and more time spent on the ones we do read. It is the hardest thing for me to prune my syllabus each semester, because I am convinced that my students need exposure to everything on that list, and then some, but I do a disservice to my students when I permit them to be hasty, inaccurate readers for the sake of getting through the entire syllabus. Better to read one true thing and read it accurately, as Ruskin suggests, than to rush through in the name of efficiency.

The last important tool we can offer our young students is our enthusiasm — the joy we take in sharing the conversation and reading aloud in the Augustinian sense, for surely all teaching is to some extent reading aloud. The example to set lies not in our professing wisdom to be copied into notebooks and memorized for the test, but simply sharing the joy of language and the stories of the human race, for that is what sends the listeners back to the text to re-experience that joy for themselves.

A Plan for Lifelong Learning

Finally, my most innovative suggestion for teaching how to read for transformation is to return to a concept originally highlighted in the University of Chicago "Great Books" movement back in the 1950s. This concept involved "adult" education and specifically addressed a need to restructure how we see education and its ultimate endpoint. As both Adler and Hutchins argue, the "books for all time" make the most impact on those who are ready to receive them, because the readers are spiritually, emotionally, and intellectually mature, much like Augustine at the time of his conversion. Before that point, Augustine was not ready to let the Word of God convert him and transform him, and likewise, as Adler and Hutchins suggest, significant texts "do not yield up their secrets to the immature."[38] But even though Adler and Hutchins made these observations more than fifty years ago, I would suggest that colleges and universities have yet to address adequately the role of the adult learner within the college community. Indeed, as Charles Anderson states in *Prescribing the Life of the Mind*, it remains an extraordinary fact that

> . . . we have organized higher education on the apparent premise that the capacity for insight, for general, reflective thought, is best cultivated in a short, intense burst of time in late adolescence and early adulthood. We are bound to be disappointed. But a handful, we know, of all our students will actually grasp the pattern underlying the details of their studies. We often chalk this up to differences in intellectual ability. But much of it could be a matter of time.[39]

Even more disheartening, according to Anderson, is the fact that the educational process ends so abruptly and often fails to set up a pattern of "lifelong learning": "Do we really believe that at the end of four years we have set a trajectory which will lead, inevitably, to the continued unfolding of the powers of the mind?"[40] And the few who do choose to carry on their learning within the academic environment find themselves, on the whole, unwelcome. While most professors are grateful to have such learners in the classroom because of the experience and life wisdom these students bring to the texts at hand, few places of higher learning systematically go out of their way to attract these learners or treat them as full participants in the intellectual life of the community when they are there. A stigma remains on the idea of adult education; we call it "night school" or assume that it belongs to the domain of the community college.

Yet if we as educators and administrators look about us and observe popular culture even superficially, the signs are clearly visible that there are a multitude of people out in the work world who crave intellectual stimulation (no doubt these are the same students who as freshmen couldn't wait to escape their humanities readings, and, now that it is no longer required of them, they realize they miss it). The explosion in book clubs and reading groups, fueled by the popularity of talk show host Oprah Winfrey's book club, suggests that there is a sizable population of thoughtful readers who would like to share their experiences, but have not found a welcoming place in the academic community. Even the recent influx of titles in bookstores on the subject of reading, ranging from Alberto Manguel's *A History of Reading* to Phyllis Rose's *The Year of Reading Proust*, among many others, indicates that there is a mature audience out there, who used to be called "the common reader" with respect by Dr. Samuel Johnson and Virginia Woolf — not common in the sense of social class, but common in terms of breadth of interests, separate from narrow specialists. Those of us in the academic profession tend to scorn the common reader as one who knows little of post-modern theory and the latest academic jargon, yet these are the readers of whom Newman and Ruskin speak, the ones for whom liberal education is a gift and not, as for our eighteen-year-old freshmen, a requirement. Colleges and universities are missing a grand opportunity once again by neglecting this population when we should be enticing them to return.

So if I could be Newman for a day (perhaps an hour would be long enough), my idea of a university would be a two-part experience. The first would be a regular three to four year experience directly following high school (or perhaps after one to two years in the work force), in which the rudiments of liberal education are offered, including an introduction to primary texts in the humanities. But the keystone of the program would be the returning student ready for conversion and transfiguration, whether it is a year, ten years, or thirty years after the initial exposure to college. This program would offer the chance to re-read the books one mis-read as a callow first-year student — a humanities seminar for mature readers. This would be the heartbeat of the university, with classes that crackle with enthusiasm and active engagement, both in argument and in agreement. And, unlike our current graduate school experience, dedicated to ever-narrowing spheres of specialization, the classes for returning students would involve reading that is both deep and interdisciplinary, as mature students with a variety of life experiences take on texts that have been known to change people's lives. Ideally, this education time would involve a "learning leave" from work, perhaps around the age of forty when many people experience a period of mid-life reckoning. Nor would there be a formal grading system; students would grade themselves on the basis of inner transformation.

No doubt this is, to use William Blake's phrase, "a memorable fancy" indeed, yet haven't we all in academia yearned for something like this every now and then — students who want to be there, with texts that ache to be read and re-read? In this scenario, Newman and Ruskin are both satisfied, for, unlike current college experiences, private reading and shared discussion are on equal footing and equally achieved. Better yet, Augustine as a reader (if not as theologian) is also served, for readers who are themselves transformed can go on to transform the world around them for the better.

Now it may be that the adult learners among us do not need the crutch of a classroom as a younger student might, and perhaps we should continue to allow them to pursue their reading in their own solitary fashion, as Ruskin might argue. But it is worthwhile to remember that Augustine and Newman put special emphasis on the community connection within the realm of reading. Spiritual or intellectual transformation begins as an almost alchemical process between book and reader, but the transformation is only complete when the transformed reader shares his/her experience with the greater community. Thus it seems to me that there is an obligation on the part of these adult learners to propagate what they have learned even as there is surely an obligation on the part of the university to bring them into the larger conversation that is intellectual discourse. And once we, as educators and administrators, reach out to these learners, the liberal arts will move beyond mere lip service to the phrase "furthering the life of the mind" and instead embrace a true model for life-long learning.[41]

Notes

1. I am indebted to Fr. Thomas Martin, O.S.A., at Villanova University for alerting me to the shape of reading in Augustine's day in a series of graduate lectures he gave in a summer Augustinian seminar, 1997, at Villanova University. Any errors herein are of course exclusively mine. For other discussions of the codex and its role in the development of book culture, see Alberto Manguel's *A History of Reading* (New York: Viking, 1996).

2. Brian Stock, *Augustine the Reader: Meditation, Self-Knowledge, and the Ethics of Interpretation* (Cambridge, MA: The Belknap Press of Harvard University Press, 1996) 1. Stock's discussion of Augustine as a reader was of immense help to me in formulating my argument, and, as such, informs much of my reading of Augustine.

3. Augustine of Hippo, *The Confessions* (trans. Maria Boulding; New York: New City Press, 1996) 1.13.20. All subsequent references to the text refer to this translation.

4. Stock, *Augustine the Reader*, 62.

5. Stock, *Augustine the Reader*, 61-62.

6. Stock, *Augustine the Reader*, 62.

7. Stock, *Augustine the Reader*, 38, 54.

8. John Henry Newman, *The Idea of a University*, reprinted in *Prose of the Victorian Period* (ed. William E. Buckler; Boston: Houghton Mifflin, 1958) 195. All subsequent references to the text refer to this edition.

9. Newman, *The Idea of a University*, 200.

10. Newman, *The Idea of a University*, 180.

11. Newman, *The Idea of a University*, 180.

12. Newman, *The Idea of a University*, 180.

13. Newman, *The Idea of a University*, 180.

14. Newman, *The Idea of a University*, 207.

15. Newman, *The Idea of a University*, 208.

16. Newman, *The Idea of a University*, 209. For a recent discussion of the problematic nature of a multiplicity of subjects in the university curriculum, see Charles W. Anderson, *Prescribing the Life of the Mind* (Madison, WI: The University of Wisconsin Press, 1993). Anderson addresses the "pluralist theory of knowledge" which prevails at most American universities at the cost of any sense of the inter-related nature of the disciplines As Anderson states, "This seems to be the way the student experiences

liberal education. One moves from class to class. No connecting threads are made manifest. One learns to turn on and turn off a certain style of discourse at hourly intervals. Now I think mathematically. Now I demonstrate Poe's inadequacies. Now I defend the autonomy of the state against critics. Nothing closer to sophistry can be imagined. The student's preeminent concern is to give the professors 'what they want.' One learns that it is highly inappropriate to use a language, or analytical approach, outside its intended context" (Anderson, *Prescribing the Life of the Mind*, 75).

17   Newman, *The Idea of a University*, 209-10.

18   Newman, *The Idea of a University*, 209.

19   John Ruskin, *Sesame and Lilies*, reprinted in *Essays English and American* (ed. Charles W. Eliot; New York: Collier & Son, 1910) 96. All subsequent references to the text refer to this edition.

20   Ruskin, *Sesame and Lilies*, 103.

21   Ruskin, *Sesame and Lilies*, 100.

22   Ruskin, *Sesame and Lilies*, 100.

23   Ruskin, *Sesame and Lilies*, 101.

24   Ruskin, *Sesame and Lilies*, 101-02.

25   Ruskin, *Sesame and Lilies*, 103.

26   Ruskin, *Sesame and Lilies*, 103.

27   Ruskin, *Sesame and Lilies*, 103.

28   Ruskin, *Sesame and Lilies*, 103.

29   Ruskin, *Sesame and Lilies*, 104.

30   Ruskin, *Sesame and Lilies*, 105.

31   Ruskin, *Sesame and Lilies*, 108.

32   The most notable, yet perhaps unwarranted in some ways, is Kate Millett's discussion of Ruskin in *Sexual Politics* (New York: Ballantine, 1970).

33   Ruskin, *Sesame and Lilies*, 149.

34   Ruskin, *Sesame and Lilies*, 155.

35   Ruskin, *Sesame and Lilies*, 156-57.

36   Martha Vicinus, *Independent Women: Work and Community for Single Women 1850-1920* (Chicago: University of Chicago Press, 1985) 129. It is impossible to overestimate the impact of possessing the privilege of a private room for young women in the late Victorian era. In her memoir *I Have Been Young* (1935), recounting her college years, Helena Swanwick described it thus: "When the door of my study was opened and I saw my own fire, my own desk, my own easy chair and reading lamp — nay, even my own kettle — I was speechless with delight. . . To have a study of my own and to be told that, if I chose to put 'Engaged' on my door, no one would so much as knock was in itself so great a privilege as to hinder me from sleep. I did not know till then how much I had suffered from the incessant interruptions of my home life" (reprinted in *Strong-Minded Women and Other Lost Voices From Nineteenth-Century England* [ed. Janet Horowitz Murray; New York: Pantheon, 1982] 241-242).

37   Mortimer Adler, "Education Beyond Schooling — The Task of a Lifetime," original 1942; reprinted in *Reforming Education: The Opening of the American Mind* (ed. Geraldine Van Doren. New York: Macmillan Publishing Company, 1977) 210-224: 212-13.

38   Robert M. Hutchins, *Great Books: The Foundation of a Liberal Education* (New York: Simon and Schuster, 1954) 91.

39   Anderson, *Prescribing the Life of the Mind*, 93.
40   Anderson, *Prescribing the Life of the Mind*, 93.
41   I am grateful to all my colleagues in the Core Humanities Program at Villanova University for the daily conversations which provided the seed crystals for many of the ideas in this essay. I also wish to thank Dr. Jack Doody, Birmingham Chair in the Humanities and Director of Core Humanities, for creating a space at Villanova where ideas about Augustinian education and the liberal arts can be discussed and enacted in a lively atmosphere of intellectual rigor and generosity of spirit.

References

Adler, Mortimer. "Education Beyond Schooling — The Task of a Lifetime." Original 1942. Reprinted in *Reforming Education: The Opening of the American Mind*. Ed. Geraldine Van Doren. New York: Macmillan Publishing Company, 1977. Pp. 210-224.

Anderson, Charles W. *Prescribing the Life of the Mind*. Madison, WI: University of Wisconsin Press, 1993.

Augustine. *Confessions*. Trans. Maria Boulding. Hyde Park, New York: New City Press, 1997.

Hutchins, Robert M. *Great Books: The Foundation of a Liberal Education*. New York: Simon and Schuster, 1954.

Manguel, Alberto. *A History of Reading*. New York: Viking, 1996.

Murray, Janet Horowitz. Ed. *Strong-Minded Women and Other Lost Voices from Nineteenth-Century England*. New York: Pantheon, 1982.

Newman, John Henry. *The Idea of a University*. Original 1852. Reprinted in *Prose of the Victorian Period*. Ed. William E. Buckler. Boston: Houghton Mifflin Company, 1958. Pp. 179-224.

Ruskin, John. *Sesame and Lilies.* Original 1864. Reprinted in *Essays English and American*. Ed. Charles W. Eliot. New York: Collier & Son, 1910.

Stock, Brian. *Augustine the Reader: Meditation, Self-Knowledge, and the Ethics of Interpretation*. Cambridge, Mass.: The Belkhap Press of Harvard University Press, 1996.

Vicinus, Martha. *Independent Women: Work and Community for Single Women 1850-1920*. Chicago: University of Chicago Press, 1985.

Chapter Twelve

The Motives for Liberal Education

Thomas W. Smith

The Motive Problem

One can acquire a craft or be an apprentice to a trade, one can learn the art of business or management, or one can be trained as a psychologist or a teacher. All of these are indisputably good modes of learning because they can lift up the human person and dignify her or his life with profitable labor that sustains families and helps larger communities flourish. However, none of them is liberal education. Liberal education aims at nothing other than the liberation of the whole human person, and in order to liberate the human person liberal education must aim at nothing but itself.

First, it must be free from the cycles of work and rest. Human work can have great dignity, but it cannot be the sole guiding purpose in our lives without reducing us to slavish worshipers of production. Liberal education frees us precisely insofar as it elevates us above the frenzied cycles of work and rest, enabling us to cultivate flourishing activities done for their own sake.[1] Second, only in a liberal education do we confront the essential questions of human life: Who am I? Where do I come from and what is my path? Why am I sexed, and how do I manage my sexuality? What is mortality, and how does it affect my life? What is freedom and how do I use mine? What happens to me after I die? Liberal education cultivates habits of critical reflection on these most pressing human questions. It accomplishes this above all by teaching us how to re-collect previous inquiries into these questions through reflective reading:

> It is no accident that the word for reading is so suggestive in several languages. In Greek it is *anagignoskein*, to re-know; in English *to read* is to un-riddle. The Latin *legere* means to gather, (as also in *intellect*); in Greek this same word *legein* means to speak rationally (so also *logos*, reason). My point is only that reading is always a hermeneutical business: the recovery of meaning, the reappropriation of reflection, the interpretation of speech. Therefore, reading contains within itself what has already been thought and said... The daily life of even the best schools must be a mundane mastering of other people's reflection — thought itself can be facilitated but not scheduled.[2]

This process of gathering up and reflecting on inquiries liberates us by making us more thoughtful about the human questions we must face. At the same time, it liberates us from our enslavement to dominant opinions. In the course of making paradigmatic inquiries present through reflective inquiry, we realize how our own culture's answers to human questions are inevitably partial and incomplete. We realize that there are different, often more profound ways of thinking through the question of justice or the meaning of equality or compassion than our own. In the end, through the cultivation of the practices inherent in liberal education we realize that liberal education broadens our horizons. Moreover, the practice of liberal inquiry is counter-cultural because it is profitless, if we define "profit" using conventionally respectable standards. Liberal inquiry does not improve our financial status. It seldom yields acclaim. Indeed, when we pursue learning for money or power or status rather than for the sake of wisdom, we are not engaging in liberal education, but training for a career. Liberal education must be strictly pursued as useless or it is not liberal education.

This means that justifying liberal education in any regime presents serious problems. Apparently, civilization is created and sustained by human work. Why should anyone withdraw from the realm of useful work in order to pursue disinterested inquiry? How could this possibly contribute to our responsibility to build up our civilization? Is not a life of thought really just a timid withdrawal from the "real world"? Indeed, is not such inquiry dangerous, because it saps talent away from the serious, practical tasks of life? Finally, how could such inquiry even be possible in a world that seems penurious and often mute to human desires? The demands of human suffering and need are so great that a retreat to useless thought is a flight from moral responsibility. In the face of such pressing questions, some tangible motive must be articulated in order to make it reasonable for people to engage in liberal education.

My thesis is that Christianity can provide a compelling set of reasons why liberal education is both possible and attractive. Many in today's academy think that liberal education and Christianity are mutually exclusive. Liberal education is about freedom of inquiry; while Christianity — perhaps especially in its Catholic forms — stands for authority, tradition, and intolerance. On this account, the liberal tradition provides the conditions for genuine liberal education precisely because it emphasizes freedom from tradition and authority. Yet I will argue that as the tradition of liberalism advances, it undermines the possibility of liberal education.[3] This is because its guiding assumptions render liberal education unattractive and perhaps impossible. Further, I will argue that while Christian colleges and universities are often held to be adverse to intellectual freedom, their perspective actually fosters free inquiry.

Aristotle: Justifying Liberal Education Implies Cultural Criticism

In order to gain a broader perspective, it is helpful to remind ourselves of previous efforts to justify liberal education. In the classical world, the ancient Greek political philosophers understood that justifying liberal inquiry is a counter-cultural effort. Aristotle, for instance, argued persuasively against his own regime's prevailing standards in order to justify liberal education. Sketching the obstacles he had to confront and the way he confronted them sheds light on our own problems.

To provide a motive for liberal education is to criticize culture. Each culture valorizes its own priorities. Yet liberal education precisely withdraws from conventionally respectable priorities, partly to liberate the human person from the narrowness and partiality of the culture. Thus every culture has its own unique sources of resistance to liberal education. It resists "useless" activity in the name of the value of its own notion of "usefulness." Since each culture has different conceptions of "usefulness," the pedagogical strategies employed to give people a motive for liberal education would have to be different in each case. The pedagogical problems convincing people of the attractiveness of liberal education today differ from the problems Aristotle confronted.

Aristotle sought to provide his audience of virile young Greek citizens a motive to engage in the liberal education of philosophy. He begins with his audience's presuppositions about a successful human life.[4] In the opening chapters of the *Nicomachean Ethics* Aristotle seeks a common starting point with his audience in their attraction to a life of noble action.[5] Nietzsche, a great student of the classics, captured this sense of life in his description of early nobility: "The knightly-aristocratic value judgements presupposed a powerful physicality, a flourishing, abundant, even overflowing health, together with that which serves to preserve it: war, adventure, hunting, dancing, war games, and in general all that involves free, joyful activity."[6] Thus nobility does not connote what we take to mean by "moral virtue"; rather, it means a shining vitality that demands recognition by others. This drive for distinction can lead one to master others through self-assertive claims to superiority. For a classical audience, the commitment to noble action manifests itself in the ambition for political power, since this seems the best way to achieve the noble action desired.[7]

How did the life of the mind appear to Aristotle's audience? When people in the presence of the wise become conscious of their own ignorance, Aristotle says, they wonder at someone who says something that goes over their heads — something big and grand (*Nicomachean Ethics* 1095a25). However, they also seem to believe that while philosophers are wise (*sophos*), they are not practically wise (*phronimos*), because they appear to be ignorant of things that are advantageous to them. While philosophers may know many wonderful things, most people think that the things they know are useless, because they do not concern the humanly good things (*ta anthropina agatha*). Practical wisdom, on the other hand, is concerned not with such useless stuff, but with what is actually good for people in the real world (*Nicomachean Ethics* 1141b39ff).

This ethos can manifest itself in a bemused indifference to thought. Yet it can also result in a profound hostility. In the *Gorgias*, Plato gives us a picture of a man with this attitude. There Kallikles argues that philosophy has a limited place in a scheme of liberal education, but also insists that in the last analysis, it is useless, perhaps even dangerous, to the business of everyday living in the real world:

> Philosophy, you know, Socrates, is a charming thing, if a man does it moderately in younger days. But if he continues to spend his time on it too long, it will bring him ruin. However well-endowed he may be, if he continues to philosophize too far into life, he must necessarily find himself ignorant of everything that ought to be familiar to a gentleman and a real man (*andra*)... For when I see philosophy in a youngster, I approve it; I consider it to be suitable, and I regard him as a person of a liberal mind. But when I see an elderly man still going on with philosophy and not getting rid of it, that is the man, Socrates, whom I know is in need of a whipping. For just as I said now, this person, however well-endowed he may be, is bound to become unmanly (*anandro*) through shunning the centers and markets of the city.[8]

To make a case for the liberating power of thought to this audience of "real men," Aristotle undermines the equation of nobility with power and mastery in various ways. In one case, he argues that the drive for despotic power is a variant of contemptible cases of overgrasping for external goods like pimpery (*Nicomachean Ethics* 1122a1-12). In another, he argues that since we depend on various communities in order to actualize our human potentials, we must be responsible with them in order to flourish. Friendship, not honor, is the most important external good, since friends help us engage in the very activities that constitute the source of our deepest satisfaction.[9]

In another famous argument, Aristotle presents a case for thoughtful inquiry by mediating a dispute between proponents of political activism and proponents of withdrawal from politics. The proponents of withdrawal from public life think that the life of a free man is the best life, and believe that this life differs from a life devoted to political activity. By contrast, those who engage in politics insist that the political life is best, for they emphasize that the life of withdrawal is inactive, and that it is impossible to be happy unless one is active (*Politics* 1325a19-23). Aristotle says that both sides believe that politics is the same as mastery; however, the withdrawers dislike mastery while the activists celebrate it. Aristotle reminds his audience that this mistaken view is common — most people equate all politics with the exercise of mastery (*Politics* 1324b32-33). Thus, he concludes, both sides are right in a sense. The person who withdraws from politics to avoid mastery is right to insist that the life of a free man is better than the life of a master. Yet such a person is wrong to think that all politics is of necessity akin to the rule of masters over slaves. In a like way, the person who emphasizes that happiness is activity is correct, but is wrong to say that happiness is in reality the exercise of mastery.

Aristotle then identifies another source of the confusion in the debate between the advocates of withdrawal and the advocates of politicking. Both sides not only misunderstand the nature of politics, they also misunderstand the meaning of human activity, because they think that thought is somehow different than and opposed to activity. Aristotle insists that happiness consists in the practical life, but thought itself is a kind of practice. The practical life is not necessarily in relation to others, and cannot be evaluated merely by referring to what external good or action results, for human activity also includes thoughts (*Politics* 1325b14-21). The differentiation of thought as an activity allows Aristotle to argue that his audience can satisfy their desire for noble action better through philosophy than through honor and political power.

The Sources of Resistance to Liberal Education in Liberal Regimes

Our cultural assumptions differ markedly from those of classical Greece. Since our resistance to liberal education has different roots, we must employ a different argument to provide a motive for liberal education. But first we have to identify the sources of resistance to liberal education in a liberal regime.

One source of liberal resistance to the notion of liberal education lies in the assumption that the world is disordered, penurious and insecure. Liberal education is impractical because the world is not generous enough to provide the leisure for disinterested inquiry. If liberal theorists hesitate to provide an account of nature, they still assume that rationality is the same as risk-minimization, and so their accounts cannot encompass the audacity of a life devoted to thoughtful action done for its own sake.

The guiding assumption of liberal theory is that individual human beings are the best judge of their own good: only I can know what makes me happy. There are a variety of different ways of phrasing this perspective in liberal theory. Early modern liberal political philosophers, for example, argue that people have a natural liberty to dispose of their persons and possessions however they see fit.[10] This entails that all people have the right to define happiness for themselves, without interference from an overbearing majority or religious or secular elites, or any other form of external authority which sets itself up in opposition to natural freedom. From this perspective, the only law that is legitimate to obey is a law to which one had already given one's assent beforehand.

The image of contract is consistently used in liberal theory to represent this notion. The theoretical architects of liberalism know that an actual "signing" of the social contract can not be historically proven.[11] Yet the social contract is the guiding image in liberal theory, because it describes so well the process whereby a citizen submits to the rule of law only because it is in her interest, thus both obeying law and preserving her original freedom to define happiness autonomously.

This social contract means that people sign onto a society in order to secure their own interests, whatever those interests might be. According to much liberal political theory, therefore, the just political order aims not at a public conception of the good, but at neutrality which "does not favor any comprehensive doctrine."[12] As political scientist Theodore Lowi has argued, liberal politics must be an instrumental politics which does not foster morality. For this reason, he insists, liberalism is "individualist" and "against morality."[13] On this account, far from seeking the common good or the promotion of virtues among citizens to create a decent society, law becomes the neutral means that allows individuals to pursue any private end they choose. Justice, therefore, becomes identified with protecting prepolitical rights, which safeguard our own preferred projects.

Liberal theorists are like salesmen: they want us to sign their contract. And like any good salesmen, they play up the benefits of the contract and play down its costs. In turn, to play up the benefits of the contracts, they play up the danger of its alternative, the state of nature. The point of articulating the state of nature is not to provide a theoretically satisfying developmental account of the origin of societies. Rather, the point is to give a sketch of what the "real world" is like. Life in the state of nature is presented as the only alternative to a liberal society, and that life is solitary, poor, nasty, brutish, and short (Hobbes) — or at extraordinarily inconvenient (Locke). The earth is poor and inhospitable. Radical insecurity lies at the heart of every human undertaking. The world is not generous enough to allow for activities not subordinated to accumulating wealth and security. Indeed, for both Locke and Hobbes, the driving force even in family life is not disinterested love but narrow self-interest.[14] In short, early liberal theory rested its pitch for individual autonomy and comfortable self-preservation by emphasizing the terrifying insecurity all human beings face.[15]

Often related to this emphasis on insecurity is an argument about the unknowability of the universe. Hobbes argues that that no *summum bonum* exists which could provide a non-arbitrary, non-despotic foundation for a common good. This flows from his nominalism, which asserts that any order that is present in the cosmos is imposed on us by our speech patterns.[16] Similarly, Locke insists that science cannot reveal any uniquely human function that could provide a universally attractive image of human flourishing.[17] Since we cannot know comprehensively the meaning of life, we cannot be sure whether any particular meaning in life is right or wrong. People must be allowed to live as they please, for to make them submit to any one else's conception of the good is by definition to force them to live arbitrarily. Liberalism justifies itself by seeking to convince people of the insecurity of life, and by arguing that the most attractive alternative is a life of comfort and security in which mistrust of other people's motives and the harshness of the world is overcome by independent autonomy.

How does the harshness of the world and mistrust of others result in the demand for autonomy? In order to be safe we must be able to protect ourselves. In order to be able to protect ourselves, we must become our own masters. This means we must relentlessly disentangle ourselves from any natural or social structure that has us in its power. Our safety entails the maximization of our choices, for only in this way can we circumscribe around ourselves a protected sphere in which we alone are lords and masters. To maximize individual freedom, every constraint that could interfere with free choice must be eradicated. And the only things that of necessity constrain our choices are the things we must depend on. Dependency is apparently the ultimate source of unfreedom. Thus liberalism demands that we be liberated more and more from everything we depend on. To depend on another individual, institution, social structure, or natural reality is by definition to be in its power; to be influenced by it; to be circumscribed (and thus potentially threatened) by it. Liberalism proceeds from risk minimization in order to secure self-protection. Self-protection entails maximization of choice, which then entails independence.

Perhaps liberal theorists will object that they do not require a grand theory of the universe in order to justify autonomous choice. John Rawls has argued that his account is political, not metaphysical; that is, he insists it does not rely on any account of the nature of nature to spin out his account of autonomy. Yet his account itself is a brilliant illustration of how liberal rationality is the same as risk aversion. In *A Theory of Justice*, Rawls has us imagine a group of individuals trying to determine what social rules they will live by before knowing what position they will occupy in the society they are founding. In this "original position" they would agree that inequalities in wealth will be considered just only if they result in compensating benefits for everyone, and in particular for the least advantaged members of society.[18] They also choose equality in freedom and rights and responsibilities. This is the result of a risk-minimizing strategy that takes the worst possible case as its guiding scenario: I want equal freedom in case someone tries to hurt me or gain power over me. Everyone in Rawls' original position is averse to risk, and so each actor wants to make sure that if he winds up on the bottom of the heap, that place is as attractive as possible.[19] While Rawls will not say what the world is like, in his account we still see how the liberal justification for autonomy comes from fearful risk-aversion.

How Liberalism Undermines the Conditions for Liberal Education: The Paradoxical Fruits of Liberal Individualist Theory

We must emphasize the greatness of the liberal tradition. At its roots it seeks to defend the value of human life and to alleviate human degradation and suffering. And it has to be congratulated on its grand achievements, which include fighting vigorously against slavery and racism, demanding recognition for the talents and dignity of women, and improving the lives of the handicapped, to name but a few. Yet paradoxically, as liberal individualist society progresses, it undermines the psychological and intellectual conditions for liberal inquiry.

Liberalism insists on autonomy to limit human dependence. Therefore it demands liberation from traditional authority. Yet it ends in enslavement to a variety of impersonal forces. Why? Liberalism seeks peace, security, and material wealth. Politically, it argues that these goods require a strong nation state that employs its monopoly on the use of coercive force to secure peace and the political conditions for economic growth. But Tocqueville sees this leading to unforeseen and undesirable consequences for the citizens of a liberal society:

Above this race of men stands an immense and tutelary power, which takes upon itself alone to secure their gratifications and to watch over their fate. That power is absolute, provident and mild. It would be like the authority of a parent if, like that authority, its object was to prepare men for manhood; but it seeks, on the contrary, to keep them in perpetual childhood: it is well content that the people should rejoice, provided that they think of nothing but rejoicing. For their happiness such a government willingly labors, but it chooses to be the sole agent and the only arbiter of their happiness; it provides for their security, foresees and supplies their necessities, facilitates their pleasures, manages their principal concerns, directs their industry, regulates the descent of their property, and subdivides their inheritances: what remains, but to spare them all the care of thinking and all the trouble of living?[20]

People in such a society will degenerate into a group of individualistic, venal citizens overgrasping for "petty and paltry pleasures," while their minds and wills atrophy.

In a similar way, the drive for economic prosperity leads to increasing global interdependence. Whatever their economic benefits, treaties like NAFTA have the unfortunate side-effect of, for example, putting every textile worker in lower Manhattan in direct competition with each and every other textile worker in the Western Hemisphere. The intrusion of the global market may produce prosperity, but only at the price of the insecurity and anxiety that attend deracination. If modern nation states and global markets are the necessary condition for security and prosperity, this means that decisions fundamental to our lives and those of our family and local communities are increasingly made by unknowing, uncaring, impersonal institutions utterly beyond our control. At the very time the liberal citizen celebrates his cornucopia of choice, he will experience his life to be constricted by mysterious forces he can neither comprehend nor control.

Further, liberalism seeks to liberate people from traditional forms of authority in order to insure freedom. But the paradoxical result is a paralyzing abyss of anxious unfreedom. In order to liberate individuals from their dependence on traditions that constrict their freedom by determining their choices, those traditions are undermined in the name of equality. Yet Tocqueville understands that this only substitutes one kind of authority for another. The authority of mass public opinion becomes the standard for thought, rather than religious tradition. And as mass opinion increasingly spills over into mass culture we realize that our tastes and mores are informed by predatory money-grubbers who manipulate our desires for their own profit. Tocqueville argues that the fruit of liberalism is a mind-numbing conformity; the drive for in-dependence leads to lack of independence of mind.[21]

To be sure, as individuals are disentangled from their old communal ties of religion and localism, the sheer number of choices available to them increases. Yet a citizen of a liberal regime may find herself incapacitated by an abyss of freedom which opens at her feet whenever she tries to make "her own choice" unconstrained by traditions.[22] So while there are more and more choices, there is also less and less inherited wisdom showing us how to engage them. People may become terrified in the face of a plethora of choices that all seem equally good and equally bad. Such citizens become anxious and restless, because they are confused about what to do with their freedom.

Since no other measure of freedom is available, Tocqueville argues, such a citizen will seek money as a secure standard of value. Material goods become the only incontestable value amidst the uncertainty of choice. But since material goods remain as unsatisfying as ever, the liberal citizen is unhappy, despite having many reasons to celebrate. So Tocqueville says that Americans are sad and grave in their pleasures. Moreover, since a focus on material prosperity is essentially tedious, liberal citizens who abandon themselves to it become bored and apathetic.[23] Of course, this emphasis on money and productivity is bolstered by the notion that the world is penurious and must be mastered in order for human life to flourish. Thus citizens increasingly impose on themselves the work ethic of a totalitarian labor camp. Usefulness and productivity are exalted. Festivals and holidays decline, except insofar as they are occasions for more buying and selling.[24] And liberal education must increasingly justify itself before the bar of productivity and wealth. Yet the second it decides to enter that court it loses its soul, for by arguing for its usefulness it implicitly accepts standards that are inimical to its constitutive activity.

Liberal political theory has no answers to the problems it helps creates; it renders itself impotent before the abyss of freedom. It cannot help its citizens because it insists on neutrality; it refuses to offer advice on how to live a meaningful life. Liberal theorists seek to avoid coercion by insisting on neutrality among competing accounts of the best life. Yet this means that they will not argue that the liberal way of life itself is best. When this strategy is followed, however, the question of the best life is posed only rhetorically: Most typical people would rather have comfortable self-preservation than virtue, or righteousness, or holiness, right? Liberal theory succeeds only on the assumption that if given the choice, most people prefer comfortable self-preservation to any viable alternative.[25] In some cases, liberal theory rests on a brilliant, often convincing pitch: if you want the kind of life most typical people in liberal societies want, here are the institutions and practices that you need to get it. Yet this means that the moment the answer to its rhetorical question is no longer self-evident to most, liberal theory has a problem. Since its "neutrality" has been exposed as a partisan way of life which its defenders will not justify rationally, the liberal order will be criticized as partial and oppressive.[26]

But all this means that as bourgeois culture progresses, it will inexorably undermine the psychological conditions for liberal education. Liberal individualism tends to produce a mass of venal, small-souled, acquisitive, anxious, risk-minimizing, bored, disaffected, lonely, depressed spectators of their own lives who believe that the world is so harsh that their happiness depends on their reduction to consumers — alimentary canals fit only for sucking and voiding out. The world is not generous enough to provide for the possibility of learning for the sake of learning. Indeed, the world is not ordered enough to investigate disinterestedly as liberal education demands. Instead, one must focus on what Hobbes calls "small powers" — goods like money or influence that allow you to achieve whatever you might desire or need to protect yourself. To be possessed by this ethos is to be ineducable.

And this same ethos affects institutions of higher education, undermining the possibility of liberal learning. Focusing on worldly success to stave off insecurity, colleges and universities who buy into the liberal ethos will seek in a myriad of ways to enhance their reputations, defined conventionally using standards set by institutions like the mass media that have little stake in the life of the mind. It will produce educational institutions that share the dominant traits of their parent culture. Liberalism will transform liberal colleges and universities into utilitarian training grounds for careers. So instead of liberating students from the inevitable partiality and injustice of their culture, it will further enslave them to it. To increase student enrollment, it will transform its campus into an environment that resembles nothing so much as a retirement home for the very young, who have access to cable television, gyms, pools, planned social and recreational activities, and long vacations in the tropics. Perhaps it goes without saying that the drive to increase enrollment entails less and less rigorous academic standards. In the name of financial viability, bean-counters will demand "more faculty productivity," and "outcomes assessment," and "better numbers," variously defined. Yet all this means that the university will become bureaucratized and marketed. Inexorably it will cease to take its bearings from those who seek wisdom in the life of the mind. Rather, it will be run by people who live so much on the surface of things that they cannot conceive of any alternative to a vision emphasizing size over proportion, volume over value, prestige over excellence, praise over praiseworthiness. Since its educational mission will be driven by the goals of the market — which worships usefulness above all — the liberal ethos will inexorably undermine the very possibility of free inquiry.

And it is not just that this ethos undermines the psychological motive for liberal inquiry. In addition, it undermines the intellectual conditions for inquiry. I have argued that this tradition often assumes that the world is penurious and unknowable. And this skepticism about our ability to know the truth about the cosmos and the meaning of human life is often used to justify freedom and tolerance.

Yet how should we respond to the confusion engendered by our lack of certainty about the meaning of life? To be sure, we do not know what the world means. We are not sure about the source of human values. Yet sometimes in the face of our confusion we are tempted to allow our knowledge of ignorance to betray our love of wisdom. That is, in flight from our confusion about meaning, we may be tempted to proceed from our knowledge of ignorance to assert the impossibility of knowledge. Yet this may be presumptuous complacency masquerading as tolerant skepticism. How do we know that the cosmos is unintelligible? How can we determine that it is chaotic and penurious? How can we be sure that we can never be sure about any true human values? Even in order to justify its basic assumptions, the liberal tradition requires thoughtful inquiry. Asking a question demands that we make ourselves aware of our own ignorance (*Apology* 2023b-e, for example). The problem with the skepticism of the liberal tradition is that it is insufficiently skeptical. Often, it simply asserts the unknowability of meaning and values. Yet this precisely undermines the condition for inquiry, because it insists on the certainty of an answer rather than admitting its own ignorance. Since we cannot be certain of the answers the liberal tradition provides (or perhaps the answers that any tradition provides), we must acknowledge our ignorance and submit ourselves to inquiry. We must admit our need for the kind of wisdom liberal education cultivates.

How Christianity Provides Motives for Liberal Education

Christianity can provide both a psychological and an intellectual motivation for liberal education in a way that the liberal tradition cannot. Christianity is above all a way of seeing the world.[27] The guiding star of the intellectual life for the Christian is the opening of the Gospel of John: In the beginning was the Word and all things came into being through Him. Intelligibility is at once both present to us and absent in its fullness. Creation is intelligible because it is the creative thought of the Word Who orders it and lovingly holds each part in being.[28] The fullness of this intelligibility, however, is hidden, insofar as the presence of the Word is not yet fully manifest to us. Human beings are the place where creation becomes self-aware. In seeking truth, we are seeking the fullness of the presence of the Word Who is with us, yet absent in His fullness. In thinking and in knowing any truth — however seemingly small and insignificant — our minds participate mysteriously in the creative mind of God that permeates and governs our being.[29] Liberal education is not merely useless, self-worshiping intellectualism. At its heart, the intellectual life glorifies God. Thus Christian liberal education at once presupposes a theology, a cosmology, and an anthropology. Christ's self-revelation of God also reveals the truth about humankind and the cosmos.[30] And the truth is that these realities stand redeemed by a provident God Who cares for them as a father does for his children.

Christ's redemptive sacrifice frees us to live as very small children; as children of God. This divine childhood is tremendously liberating. Young children are not bothered by their mortality, inasmuch as it is beyond their horizons. If their basic needs are met, they have no anxieties about where their next meal is coming from or whether their possessions will be taken away. Their characteristic activities are playfulness and wonder. They take delight in the extraordinary character of ordinary objects. They ask simple questions with profound implications about every reality. They take each day as it comes and take joy in their growth and learning.

By contrast, the mistake of Adam and Eve is the mistake of the liberal tradition. They insist on in-dependence and self-reliance rather than reliance on God. The *only* prohibition God gives Adam and Eve in the garden — the *only* thing they are not allowed to do — is to eat of the tree of knowledge of Good and Evil. What does this mean? When we eat we assimilate what is eaten, literally turning it into ourselves. Thus the only forbidden act is to make ourselves the sole principles of right and wrong — to be in-dependent of the standards that God sets. Adam and Eve eat the fruit; in this they seek to make themselves independent of God. The punishment for their self-reliance is their choice for self-reliance. That is, the consequence of their self-reliance is nothing other than the pains and anxieties that flow from a reliance on unself-sufficient, limited, broken, fragile human powers. In turn, the "punishments" that God bestows banish them from their original childhood of receptive trust – they must face the adult realities of procreation, work, and death.[31]

Christ's sacrificial action restores our status as children of God. His redemptive defeat of death allows us the freedom to romp in the mind of God. In this sense, the Christian vision not only provides a psychological motive for liberal education by rendering the world investigatable, it also provides a motive for learning by illuminating its deeper meaning. Why do we enjoy this learning stuff so much? Because it is an intimation of that life we will enjoy in the Banquet of Heaven.

By contrast, a young person who has been successfully manipulated by the liberal individualist consumer culture has been habituated to overgrasp for external goods. The cultivation of this overgrasping makes the child jaded and closed to wonder. His world is constricted by the obsession with getting and having. It is not that every child in a liberal regime is a brat. Rather, the tragedy is that their capacity for wonder and delight in ordinary reality is muted. Popular culture extends and trivializes childhood, because infantalized consumers are more manipulable. Yet by making us childish, our culture paradoxically makes us old.

Objection

Yet how does Christianity answer the charge that liberal education prioritizes inactive thought over useful work? Within the Christian tradition, many criticize the intellectual life as a flight from the active charity that Christ urges.

The doctrine of creation emphasizes receptivity to what is given. One might say that it elevates receptivity to the most fundamental human task. This has a humbling effect on our view of human action. The person who is aware of his dependence cannot conceive of himself as a self-created demiurge whose choices are the most important reality. Indeed, even one's own freedom is the result of interdependence and difference. When reality is seen as the divinely created context within which one lives and acts, one's actions can be conceived as a transitive reception of gift and giving back of gift. Thus the human person is the transitive partner in a community of being wherein what is received is the condition for acting, and, in turn, the act that is done is a loving, self-emptying giving in return. From this perspective, any genuine exercise of practical wisdom is the fruit of contemplation.

Since human beings are developmental creatures that require the community of being to actualize our own potentials, it makes no sense to strive for independence in a self-protective effort to maximize choice. The price for this is that one cuts oneself off from the very conditions that allow for one's flourishing activity. The attitude of receptivity entails the recognition that one's own achievements are a result of one's prior reception from one's family and culture, and ultimately that all these goods are from God.

Receptivity to what is given can be achieved through liberal education. In this sense, liberal education informs one's sense of one's place in the universe. Through liberal education, one becomes more aware that one does not create oneself nor the conditions for one's own development. Liberal education cultivates the conditions for right action by disposing the whole person to be aware of one's utter dependence on receiving. This attitude helps foster right action by encouraging us to be responsible to the encompassing contexts on which we depend, including our family, local communities, religious organizations, larger state, global community, and the earth itself. By contrast, in its relentless drive for in-dependence, liberalism obscures the awareness that we are inevitably dependent on reception. It encourages irresponsibility towards the realities we depend on. Ironically, while many "practical" people worry that liberal education will undermine fruitful action in the world, it actually protects human action from the ill effects of thinking that our own choices are the most important reality. So ironically, while the life of thought is sometimes criticized as a danger to right action, it might be the very condition for right action.

Conclusion

Christians are called to live as children of God. This does not mean that we are supposed to be childish, however. Socrates lived as a young child — with no care to status or wealth or sense of shame at his constitutive activity. Yet Socrates' fate provides a sobering lesson to us Christians. There are few rewards for wisdom, Socrates' murder tells us. His culture called his wisdom foolishness. It called his child-like wonder childishness. It called his care corruption of the young. We can expect nothing else from our own culture. This is the inevitable cost of discipleship (cf. Mark 8:31-38, to name but one of many possible examples). When people try to live at the center of things their culture will generally try to push them to its periphery.

Christ calls us to be children, but also to be as cunning as serpents. Christian liberal universities have to have courage to articulate their own standards of excellence in the face of a countervailing culture. To be sure, we must expect that our independence of mind will be excoriated. And our task as wise serpents will be to remind the adherents of the liberal tradition with all due humility and charity that their pretense to independence blinds them to the many ways they themselves depend on communities that set conditions on their inquiries.[32] Christians self-consciously take a stand and thus inquire from a certain perspective. But everyone else inquires from a certain perspective as well. A secular university is no less sectarian than its religiously affiliated counterpart: it articulates standards for admittance, it allows specific kinds of evidence and disallows others, it has particular conceptions of what constitutes compelling reasons and arguments, and thus it assumes certain particular characteristics of rationality; and it banishes certain forms of inquiry and research as beyond its moral pale.[33] Yet while it is sectarian, the secular university is less self-consciously aware of its own commitments and blind spots than its religious counterparts. Thus one great virtue of Christian liberal education is its awareness of the inevitable problems and tensions created by the fact that inquiry always proceeds from a certain perspective. For example, as anyone knows who has been around Catholic higher education for the last decade or so, nothing characterizes it so much as a serious concern with the relationship between its Catholic perspective and its insistence on free inquiry. By contrast, the vice of the academy in the liberal tradition is an illusory assertion of neutrality that smugly denies it has any perspective at all, so it does not raise the necessary questions that Catholic universities ask as a matter of course.

Because it is self-conscious about its perspective, any Christian liberal education inevitably presupposes an ecclesiology. Human inquiry can only be performed within traditions that make particular claims and take particular stands. Thus Christian liberal education keeps its bearings in service to the truth as it becomes manifest in a community of faith that loves and nurtures each woman and man. Ultimately, perhaps, a motive for liberal education can be found when inquiry proceeds from the heart of a church.

Notes

1   Josef Pieper, *Leisure, the Basis of Culture* (Notre Dame, IN: St. Augustine's Press, 1998).

2   Eva Brann, *Paradoxes of Education in a Republic* (Chicago: University of Chicago Press, 1979), 16-17.

3   I should make it clear that I am not using the term "liberal" in its contemporary sense in American politics to refer to the left-wing of the Democratic party. Rather, I am employing it to describe the account informed by social contract thinkers like Hobbes, Locke, Rousseau, Kant, or Rawls. In this sense, both the left-wing of the Democratic Party and the right wing of the Republican party (at least its more libertarian and capitalist elements) are squarely in the liberal tradition.

4   I owe much of my account of Aristotle's treatment of his audience's perspective on action to David O'Connor, "Overrating the Polis: Politics and Philosophy in Leo Strauss' Aristotle," paper given at the American Political Science Association Convention, Boston, MA, September 5, 1998.

5   The argument proceeds in several stages that build on each other. First Aristotle criticizes the Platonic notion of the Form of the Good as useless for action (*Nicomachean Ethics* I.6). Second, he develops the function argument, which emphasizes specifically human forms of action as the way to happiness (*Nicomachean*

Ethics I.7). Third, he employs the language developed in these sections to articulate his audience's strong attraction to a life of action (*Nicomachean Ethics* I.8).

6   Friederich Nietzsche, *On the Genealogy of Morals* (trans. Walter Kaufmann; New York: Vintage Books, 1967) 33.

7   *Nicomachean Ethics* 1095b4-8; cf. *Politics* 1324a25-1325a23; 1325a32-b11; 1325b14-23.

8   *Gorgias* 485a-d. With slight changes, this translation is taken from W.R.M. Lamb, *Lysis, Symposium, Gorgias* (Cambridge: Harvard University Press, 1973) 391. Of course, this passage is delightfully ironic, since Socrates hung around the market all day and showed remarkable courage in battle at Potidea. For this, see *Symposium* 220b-221e. Compare with 223d.

9   See my "Aristotle on the Conditions for and Limits of the Common Good," *American Political Science Review* 93 (1999) 625-636.

10   As Locke says, "To understand Political Power right, and derive it from its Original, we must consider what State all Men are naturally in, and that is, a *State of perfect Freedom* to order their Actions, and dispose of their Possessions, and Persons as they think fit, within the bounds of the Law of Nature, without asking leave, or depending upon the Will of any other Man," John Locke, *Two Treatises of Government* (ed. Peter Laslett; Cambridge, UK: Cambridge University Press, 1988) II.4 (p. 269), emphasis in the original.

11   Locke argues that the state of nature was so backwards that writing and history had not been invented yet: "For 'tis with Common-wealths as with particular Persons, they are commonly ignorant of their own Births and Infancies...," Locke, *Two Treatises of Government*, section 101 (p. 334).

12   John Rawls, *Political Liberalism* (New York: Columbia University Press, 1993) 194. To be fair to Rawls, he is not completely comfortable with the term "neutrality" because "some of its connotations are highly misleading, others suggest altogether impractical principles," 191.

13   Theodore Lowi, *The End of the Republican Era* (Norman, OK: University of Oklahoma Press, 1995) 15; see also his chapter 6.

14   For example, Hobbes says that a child is obliged to obey its mother because at any time she can withhold sustenance. The motivation for filial love is fear (see *Leviathan*, Part II, chapter 20). For Locke, the family is driven by guilt and economic calculation. One does not have to honor one's father and mother, except insofar as they treated one honorably (*Second Treatise*, VI.65). Parents care for their children so that the children will feel obligated to care for their parents in their dotage. Children care for parents either from a sense of guilt, or because they expect inheritance (VI.72). Marriage is not a sacrament for mutual, sacrificial self-giving. Rather, it is a contract that consists primarily in sexual exclusivity (VII.78). Thus the spouse is reduced to a piece of property that must be protected so that it can be exploited. As Wendell Berry points out, the result of this emphasis on self-interest in family life is mutual enslavement: "Within the capsule of marriage, as in that of economics, one intends to exploit one's property and to protect it. Once the idea of property becomes abstract and economic, both these motives begin to rule over it. They are, of course, contradictory; all that one can really protect is one's 'right' to exploit. The proprieties and privacies used to encapsulate marriage may have come from the tacit recognition that exploitative sex, like exploitative economics, is a very dirty business. One makes a secret of the sexuality of one's marriage for the same reason that one posts 'Keep Out/Private Property' on one's

strip mine. The tragedy, often more felt than acknowledged, is that what is exploited becomes undesirable. The protective capsule becomes a prison. It becomes a household of the living dead, each body a piece of incriminating evidence. Or a greenhouse excluding neighbors and the weather for the sake of some alien and unnatural growth. The marriage shrinks to a dull vigil of legality and duty. Husband and wife become competitors necessarily, for their only freedom is to exploit each other or to escape," *The Unsettling of America: Culture and Agriculture* (San Francisco: Sierra Club Books, 1977) 119-120.

15   This strange duality of liberal societies — their material comfort and their anxiety over the harsh insecurity of chaotic existence — is nicely captured, for example, in a typical Steven King horror novel. The setting is usually a bucolic, prosperous, apparently contented small town in America. Yet lurking beneath this illusory peace lies an unspeakable horror that will break the thin veil of security and reveal the primal, chaotic terror underneath it all. The success of this fiction is only partly due to King's obvious storytelling skills. In addition, it is due to the fact that this is the way many seem to experience their own lives.

16   "... *truth* consists in the right ordering of names in our affirmations...," Thomas Hobbes, *Leviathan* (ed. C.B. Macpherson; New York: Penguin Books, 1986) 105.

17   John Locke, *An Essay Concerning Human Understanding* (ed. Alexander Fraser; New York: Dover Press, 1959) 350-51.

18   John Rawls, *A Theory of Justice* (Cambridge, MA: Harvard University Press, 1971) 14-5.

19   Rawls never considers the perspective of a risk taker who might revel in the opportunities such a high stakes proposal presents. Such a person might reply to the problem of the original position this way: "I will structure principles of justice to benefit the *most* advantaged. To be sure, in the society we are constructing I may wind up being one of the *least* advantaged. But if so, at least I risked all for power and status and have the comfort of knowing that I am not a coward. Yet if my gamble pays off, I will enjoy all the privileges my society offers, with no corresponding duty to take care of those who are beneath me." Even in liberal societies, there are people who value goods other than material comfort, security, and self-respect, which are the things Rawls insists that everyone values, regardless of whatever else they value. There are people who disdain these liberal risk-minimizing goods in favor of such things as an exuberant love of crime, political power, honor, lordship, holiness, moral virtue or philosophy. What can Rawls do with such people except ship them off to prison or call them insane? For example, Rawls implies that Aquinas is "mad" because he refuses to see the aims of the self as heterogenous. Aquinas is a "dominant end" thinker who subordinates all desire to God (*Theory of Justice*, 554). That is, any rationality that departs from Rawls' view is irrationality; madness. Rawls' reductionist account cannot comprehend the desires of the saint like Aquinas or the nihilist like Nietzsche.

20   Alexis de Tocqueville, *Democracy in America* (trans. Francis Bowen; New York: Alfred A. Knopf, 1994) 318.

21   *Democracy in America*, Book I, chapter 15; Book II, chapter 2.

22   "Uncertain of his place in society now that all ranks have been levelled, no longer finding a guide in tradition now that the links of time have broken, uncertain of his opinions to the extent that he doubts the value of opinion as such, democratic man does not know how to orient his life," Pierre Manent, *Tocqueville and the Nature of Democracy* (trans. John Waggoner; Lanham, MD: Rowman and Littlefield, 1996) 59.

23   In his *The End of History and the Last Man* (New York: Avon Books, 1992), Francis
     Fukuyama argues that apathy and boredom are inevitable consequences of the focus on
     material wealth. For a harrowing example, pp. 330-333.
24   For this point, see Josef Pieper, *Leisure, the Basis of Culture*, passim.
25   Stephen Salkever, "Lopp'd and Bound: How Liberal Theory Obscures the Goods of
     Liberal Practices," in *Liberalism and the Good* (eds. R. Bruce Douglas, Gerald, Mara,
     and Henry S. Richardson; New York: Routledge, 1990) 167-202.
26   For a useful survey of anti-liberal critics, see Stephen Holmes, *The Anatomy of Anti-
     Liberalism* (Cambridge, MA: Harvard University Press, 1993).
27   Seeing is a way of understanding. Understanding is making present to oneself what one
     stands upon, what is under where one stands. In the act of belief, the Christian makes
     a decision to stand on a certain kind of ground and only on that ground. This ground
     provides the vantage point from which she sees the world, the ground of her under-
     standing. See Joseph Cardinal Ratzinger, *Introduction to Christianity* (San Francisco:
     Ignatius Press, 1990) chapters 1 and 2.
28   "Being is thought and therefore thinkable, the object of thought and knowledge, which
     strives after truth. The work of man on the other hand is a mixture of logos and the a-
     logical, something moreover that with the passage of time sinks away into the past. It
     does not admit of full comprehension for it is lacking in presence, the prerequisite for
     being looked at, and it is lacking in logos, in thoroughgoing meaningfulness," Ratzinger,
     Introduction to Christianity, 32.
29   Ratzinger, *Introduction to Christianity*, 32.
30   Surely there are other possible ways of providing a motive for liberal education. In the
     west, philosophy is an obvious alternative. Philosophy frees us from fear of death,
     because it refuses to engage in speculation about what happens after death. To fear
     death would be to assume that human beings had enough evidence about it to warrant
     fear. Fear of death implies not Socratic ignorance, but false knowledge (see *Apology*
     40c-41c). Philosophic skepticism also renders inquiry into the order of the whole
     possible. The philosopher knows he cannot know the universe as a whole and therefore
     cannot say whether it is cosmos or chaos. He hypothesizes that it is rational in order to
     provide the necessary condition for inquiry as to whether it is rational. So the act of
     philosophy rests not on faith in an ultimate reality that grounds intelligibility, but in an
     unproven, unprovable hypothesis that the cosmos is intelligible. The question is whether
     most people can both sustain this hypothesis and suspend judgment about the afterlife
     without going mad. If not, then philosophy can provide a motive for liberal education,
     but only for a select few.
31   I put "punishments" in scare quotes because each punishment can be transformed from
     a curse into a blessing. The curse of childbearing is a blessing if our love for our
     children spurs us to become better people so that we can raise them right. Parenthood
     forces us to become more serious in pursuing the good, true and beautiful. The curse of
     work can be transformed into a blessing if we allow our work to dignify us. Ultimately,
     through our human work we can participate in God's providential work. Death, too, can
     be a source of blessing. Awareness of mortality renders human life at once more serious
     and compassionate. By contrast, the gods in Homer's *Iliad* are brutal precisely because
     their immortality means that their lives are not suffused with knowledge of finitude and
     fragility. Their lives are inhuman and unserious because they are not subject to death.
     (A great modern meditation on the relationship between mortality and humanity is
     J.R.R. Tolkien's *Lord of the Rings*.) From this perspective, God's action in response to

sin is always a redemptive love that turns even the consequences of our own bad choices into blessings.

32   For example, it is absurd for contemporary universities to claim that academic freedom demands an "independent" and "autonomous" vantage point, free from any authority outside of the governing structure of the university. Universities regularly defer to a variety of accrediting agencies, such as the American Psychological Association, the American Bar Association, the National Council for Accreditation of Teacher Education, the American Assembly of Collegiate Schools of Business, not to mention agencies like Middle States. Institutions of higher education also depend on the Federal Government, in all its various forms like the Department of Justice, Health and Human Services, Labor, Agriculture, Equal Employment Opportunity Commission, Environment Protection Agency, National Science Foundation, National Endowments for the Humanities and Arts. The Library of Congress certifies copyrights to faculty members and sets standards for book catalogs. The National Institutes of Mental Health provide obligatory ethical norms for human experimentation in scientific research. The condition for every college and university is splendid interdependence. For more examples, see Richard John Neuhaus, "The Public Square," *First Things* August/September 1999 (95), 84.

33   For an extended account see Alasdair MacIntyre, *Three Rival Versions of Moral Inquiry* (Notre Dame: University of Notre Dame Press, 1990).